TEXAS DOCUMENTATION HANDBOOK

Appraisal, Nonrenewal, Termination

SIXTH EDITION

Created by

Frank R. Kemerer and John A. Crain

By

Jennifer Childress

and

Richard A. James

TEXAS DOCUMENTATION HANDBOOK
Appraisal, Nonrenewal, Termination
SIXTH EDITION

First printing: June 2016
Nineteenth printing: October 2022 (includes updates through September 2022 since the first printing)
Twentieth printing: April 2023
Twenty-first printing: August 2023
Twenty-second printing: July 2024 (includes updates with new T-TESS Alternate Domain I)
Twenty-third printing: December 2024

Copyright © ED311
(ED311 is the new name of the *Texas School Administrators' Legal Digest*
that published earlier editions)

All rights reserved. No part of this handbook may be reproduced or transmitted in any form or by any means, electronic or mechanical, including photocopy, recording, or any information storage and retrieval systems, without permission in writing from the publisher.

This prohibition does not apply to digital access and duplication of the focused observation instruments in Appendix B and of the forms in Appendix D. To obtain digital access, go to www.ed311.com/docbookforms6th/.

To order additional copies of the Texas Documentation Handbook or to obtain more information about the handbook, go to www.ed311.com/txdocbook6th/ or contact

512 W Martin Luther King Jr Blvd, #300 Austin, TX 78701

Phone 512-478-2113
Fax 512-495-9955
www.ed311.com I info@ed311.com

NOTE: The information provided in this handbook is intended to be accurate and authoritative at the time of printing. The handbook is published and marketed with the understanding that neither the publisher nor the authors are rendering legal advice. If specific legal advice or assistance is required a competent professional should be sought. Readers should be aware that with the passage of time, some of the information contained in this handbook may become out of date.

ISBN 978-0-9852527-5-5

TABLE OF CONTENTS

Preface

Chapter One: The Legal Framework
- Why Document? 1-1
  - Legal Considerations 1-3
  - Ethical Considerations 1-3
  - Political Considerations 1-3
  - Other Benefits of a Documentation System 1-4
- Teacher Appraisal 1-4
  - Appraisal System Options 1-4
  - Conducting Appraisals 1-6
  - Grievances Over Appraisals 1-8
  - Does a Positive Appraisal Shield a Teacher from Contract 1-9
    Nonrenewal or Termination?
  - What About Using Teaching Deficiencies from Prior Years to Build 1-9
    Support for Contract Nonrenewal or Termination?
- Appraisal of Principals and Other Administrators 1-10
- Texas Employment Law 1-11
  - At-Will Arrangements 1-11
  - Contracts for Professional Employees 1-12
    - Probationary Contract 1-14
    - Term Contract 1-18
    - Continuing Contract 1-21
  - Furloughs 1-22
- Conferences, Grievances, and Recording 1-23
- Reassignment and Resignation 1-24
  - Reassignment 1-24
  - Resignation 1-26
- A Word About Employee References 1-29
- Avoiding Impermissible Reasons for Employment Decisions 1-29
  - Free Speech 1-30
  - Academic Freedom 1-30
  - Federal Civil Rights 1-31
  - Texas Law 1-31
- Summary 1-32
- References 1-33

Chapter Two: Principles of Documentation
- When to Document 2-1
- Types of Documentation 2-2
  - Notes to the File Accompanying Oral Directives 2-2
  - Performance Appraisal 2-3
  - Specific Incident Memorandum 2-4
  - Last Chance Memorandum 2-4

  Writing Specific Incident Memoranda..2-5
    Examples of Poorly Constructed Specific Incident Memoranda 2-5
    How to Conduct an Investigation 2-6
    Lessons to be Learned 2-10
    Follow These Essential Elements in Writing a.......................2-11
      Specific Incident Memorandum
    Examples of Well Written Specific Incident Memoranda..................2-12
  Writing Last Chance Memoranda 2-16
    The Scenario..2-16
    The Memorandum 2-16
  Summary..2-19
  References..2-20

Chapter Three: The Marginally Effective Teacher
  Identifying the Marginally Effective Teacher..............................3-2
    Level of Abstraction 3-2
      Lack Instructional Knowledge and Experience 3-2
      Problem Solving, Situational Awareness, and Reflection............3-3
      Personal Problems 3-4
    Level of Commitment..3-4
      Burnout..3-5
      Balance of Personal and Professional Life 3-5
      Risk Tolerance and Fear of Change.............................3-6
  The Issues Involved in Supervision.......................................3-6
    Diagnosis...3-6
    Prescription..3-6
    Time Lines 3-7
  Matching Supervision Style with Teacher Level of Development 3-7
    Who Controls the Above Three Issues?................................3-7
      Quadrant I 3-9
      Quadrant II..3-10
      Quadrant III 3-11
      Quadrant IV 3-12
    Goals of Supervision..3-14
  Option 1: Nondirective Strategies and Language 3-15
    Teacher Makes All the Decisions....................................3-15
  Option 2: Collaborative Strategies and Language 3-16
    Teacher and Supervisor Share All the Decisions 3-16
  Strategies for Directive Supervision 3-17
  Focusing on Instruction in the Classroom................................3-18
  Summary...3-19
  References...3-20

Chapter Four: Documenting Instruction
    Methods of Gathering Data in Classroom Observations........................4-2
        Scripting..4-2
        Anecdotal Record..4-3
        Electronic Recording...4-3
        Focused Observation Instruments....................................4-4
    Gathering Data in the Marginally Effective Teacher's Classroom................4-4
    T-TESS Domains With Subsets Common to Best Practice.......................4-5
    Four Domains of T-TESS Rubric..4-6
    Lesson Scenario..4-7
    Gathering and Transcribing Data: Focused Observation Instrument #1..........4-10
    Formal Documentation: Focused Observation Instrument #1....................4-15
    Gathering and Transcribing Data: Focused Observation Instrument #2..........4-19
    Formal Documentation: Focused Observation Instrument #2....................4-24
    Gathering and Transcribing Data: Focused Observation Instrument #3..........4-28
    Formal Documentation: Focused Observation Instrument #3....................4-33
    Adjusting Classroom Data Collection for Small Group and Individual Tasks......4-36
    A Word About Subject-Matter Knowledge and Communication Skills............4-38
    Summary..4-41
    Appendix: PDAS and T-TESS Correlation Chart.............................4-42
    Reference...4-44

Chapter Five: Professional Communication
    The Legal Framework..5-1
    Documenting Unprofessional Teacher Communication........................5-5
        Inappropriate Written and Verbal Communication with Colleagues.......5-5
        Social Networking with Students Through Digital Devices..............5-8
    Summary..5-12
    References..5-12

Chapter Six: Writing and Monitoring Professional Growth Plans
    The Legal Dimension..6-1
    Why Write an Intervention Plan If One Is Not Required?.....................6-4
        When Job Performance Does Not Meet Expectations and................6-5
        More Extrinsic Motivation May Be Needed
            When Job Expectations May Not Be Clear............................6-5
        When the Supervisor Needs to Begin Laying Groundwork for..............6-6
        Nonrenewal or Termination of Employment
    How to Write an Intervention Plan..6-6
        Step 1: Notice of Areas of Job Performance in Which....................6-6
        Improvement or Change is Needed
            Classroom Instructional Issues and Student Performance..............6-6
            Compliance with Laws / Policies / Procedures.......................6-7
            Other Job-Related Behaviors......................................6-8
            "Affective Issues"..6-8

    Step 2: Offer of (or Directive for) Assistance and Support
        Through Growth Activities... **6-9**

    Step 3: Time Lines and Evidence That Will Be Used to Determine **6-10**
        If Growth Activities Have Been Completed

    Step 4: Directives for Changes in Behavior Plus Time Lines and **6-10**
        Evidence That Will Be Used to Determine if Improvement
        Has Occurred or is Occurring

        Why Write in Terms of Teacher / Employee Behavior? **6-12**

        Benefits of Using Instructional Indicators **6-13**

        Why Include Student Behavior in the Directives? **6-13**

    Writing Directives Related to Student Performance..................... **6-14**

        Success of Students During an Observation **6-15**

        Success of Students Over Time **6-15**

        Success of Students on Criterion-Referenced Test................ **6-16**

    Writing Directives for Nonclassroom-Based Intervention Plans **6-17**

    Providing a Reasonable Time Line for Growth and Improvement **6-19**

    Sample Intervention Plan for Teachers................................ **6-20**

    Sample Intervention Plan for Non-Teaching Employees **6-23**

Role of the Employee in Developing an Intervention Plan..................... **6-26**

Monitoring Intervention Plan Achievement................................. **6-27**

    Writing Specific Incident Memoranda................................. **6-27**

    Writing a Last Chance Memorandum **6-29**

Summary.. **6-31**

References **6-32**

Appendix A: Code of Ethics and Standard Practices for Texas Educators

Appendix B: Classroom Focused Observation Instruments
    Focused Observation Instrument #1: *Planning and Instruction (First Dimension)*
    Focused Observation Instrument #2: *Planning and Instruction (Second Dimension)*
    Focused Observation Instrument #3: *Classroom Environment, Routines and Procedures, Culture*

Appendix C: A Generic List of Remediation Activities and Sample Directives for Changes in Teacher Behavior Linked to Student Outcomes

Appendix D: Sample Forms
    Complaint Form
    Witness Statement Form
    Template for a Specific Incident Memorandum
    Template for Specific Incident Memorandum Related to Instruction
    Template for an Intervention Plan

About the Authors

PREFACE

In this edition, we have made a number of changes in all chapters and appendices to reflect the focus of the current teacher appraisal system and growing emphasis on student performance. When this edition is reprinted, we provide updates to keep the book current as much as we can.

The first chapter discusses the legal framework for documentation of both auxiliary and professional employees beginning with a discussion of appraisal systems for the latter. Then we examine the key elements of Texas employment law. The second chapter focuses on basic principles of effective documentation and how they apply outside the classroom in the context of auxiliary and professional employees. Examples are provided of both good and bad documentation.

In the third chapter, we shift our focus to discuss how important the choice of supervisory style is to improving the marginally effective teacher's performance or for preparing for contract nonrenewal or termination.

The fourth chapter introduces three focused observation instruments that are designed to simplify gathering data during classroom observations. We provide illustrations of how to complete the instruments and then use the information to write follow-up memoranda anchored in district expectations for effective teaching and linked to desired changes in student performance. A long list of additional ways of linking teacher behavior to student performance is set forth in Appendix C. The documentation process discussed in this chapter complements T-TESS and locally developed teacher appraisal systems by providing an easy way of gathering cumulative data over time that can be incorporated into the overall teacher appraisal. The chapter addresses the four domains of the T-TESS appraisal process including the new Alternate Domain I.

The fifth chapter centers on professional communication including the use of digital devices. The final chapter describes how to write and monitor invention plans developed outside of the formal appraisal system for auxiliary and professional employees when serious deficiencies require doing so. Sample intervention plans are set forth illustrating how to state deficiencies and expectations for improved performance within a specific time frame. If correction does not occur, then the supervisor may have no choice but to recommend ending the employment relationship.

Appendices include the Code of Ethics and Standard Practices for Texas Educators, blank copies of the three focused observation instruments, a generic list of remediation activities for both auxiliary and professional employees, a long list of sample directives for changes in teacher behavior linked when possible to student performance, and sample forms and templates to be used in various stages of documentation. The observation instruments, forms, and templates may be copied by purchasers of the book and are available via the digital link.

We want to thank Jim Walsh of the Walsh, Gallegos, Trevino, Russo & Kyle, P.C. law firm for providing us his comments on the first chapter. We also want to thank Phaedra Strecher, who since the first edition has worked as our designer and formatter. Excellent work, Phaedra!

We hope that the Texas school community will find this sixth edition useful in fostering personnel decisions that both treat the employee fairly and are legally defensible. That ultimately is the purpose of the documentation process.

Jennifer Childress
Richard A. James

CHAPTER ONE: THE LEGAL FRAMEWORK

A carefully developed documentation system has become essential for conducting effective evaluations and making informed personnel decisions. The purpose of this chapter is first to examine why documentation is necessary and then to explain how significantly documentation is affected by the legal framework within which it occurs. As we will see, personnel documentation does not occur in a vacuum. Readers should be cautioned, however, that our discussion is not exhaustive. Rather, we seek to set forth the basics, referring periodically to more comprehensive sources.

WHY DOCUMENT?

In this section we describe three important reasons why effective documentation is essential for all employees.

Legal Considerations

Some years ago, the U.S. Court of Appeals for the Fifth Circuit, which has jurisdiction over Texas, disregarded the testimony offered by the employer to support the contract termination of a 56-year-old employee. While witnesses had testified at trial that the employee's performance was deficient, no written documentation existed to support the contention. The employee argued that he was the victim of illegal age discrimination. The appeals court concluded that "when an employer's stated motivation for an adverse employment decision involves the employee's performance, but there is no supporting documentation, a jury can reasonably infer pretext" [i.e., that the adverse decision actually was based on discrimination]. The court added, "This conclusion is reasonable in light of the complete lack of documentation to support [the employer's] assertion that [the employee's] performance was unsatisfactory."[1]

During the same year as the Fifth Circuit's decision, a federal appeals court in another part of the country agreed with the trial judge that administrator testimony about alleged complaints concerning a teacher was hearsay and should be excluded because there were no signed complaint forms and because those making the complaints were not present to testify at trial.[2] Permitting testimony about the complaints would deny the teacher the opportunity of cross-examination. The teacher was 65 years old and had been employed in the district for many years. Evaluations over the years showed the teacher's performance to be satisfactory. In an apparent effort to force the teacher to retire, school administrators suddenly began visiting his class repeatedly and pointing out numerous deficiencies. A few months later, the administrators recommended nonrenewal of the teacher's contract. At trial, the jury concluded that the teacher had been forced out because of his age.

How much documentation is necessary to defeat a hearsay claim depends upon who is conducting the hearing and what negative employment decision is at issue. Courts and hearing officers must follow rules of evidence that require a significant amount of evidence to overcome a hearsay claim. School governing boards conducting a nonrenewal hearing are not governed by Texas Rules of Evidence so the amount of evidence to overcome a hearsay claim is less.[3] As we will discuss later in this chapter, a mid-contract termination takes away a constitutionally protected property right in public employment, so the amount of documentation to justify the decision needs to be significant. This is less so when a nonrenewal hearing is involved because the employee's property right is over. However, from a practitioner standpoint, we believe it best serves the interests of both school employees and employers for the amount of documentation of job-related deficiencies to be substantial in all cases. Having one or more job-related reasons for contract nonrenewal or termination with little supporting documentation not only opens up hearsay claims but also lessens the chances that the employer will prevail. In effect, it is like clapping with one hand.

The absence of carefully prepared documentation also can jeopardize a district's case before the Texas Commissioner of Education, whose jurisdiction under Texas Education Code Section 7.057 encompasses appeals of actions or decisions of any school district governing board, but not an open-enrollment charter school board, that violate the school laws of the state or a provision of a written employment contract that causes or could cause financial harm to the employee. School laws of the state refer to the first two titles of the Education Code and the rules adopted under these titles (to locate them, see p. 4). Under Section 21.301 and related sections, the commissioner also has jurisdiction over the termination of a probationary contract during the term of the contract, the termination of a term or continuing contract, the nonrenewal of a contract, or the suspension of the contract. The claims must be filed within a specific time period as noted in commissioner administrative rules. In a 1996 case involving the nonrenewal of a teacher contract for alleged failure to maintain effective working relationships with parents, the commissioner rejected most of the district's documentation as hearsay. The district relied in part on a petition signed by community members demanding the dismissal of the teacher for inequitable grading, irregular and improper disciplinary actions, and repeated confrontations with parents and students. However, there was no documented evidence to support the claims. The only parent who testified said his experience with the teacher was "pleasant." Further, the teacher's overall appraisal rating was "clearly outstanding," and the principal had described the teacher positively. Since the evidence did not support the proffered reason for nonrenewal, the commissioner granted the teacher's appeal.[4]

Some years ago, the commissioner ruled that a chronology of events assembled by a teacher's supervisor should have been excluded at the nonrenewal hearing as hearsay. Chronologies are often assembled by administrators, and they serve a very important purpose in charting events that lead to a major personnel decision. However, the chronology itself should not be relied upon to establish the basis for the decision. Rather, the events or items listed in the chronology are what are important. For example, if one of the events in the chronology states that the employee threw spaghetti at food service workers in the cafeteria, written statements to this effect from the food service workers would not be hearsay. Preferably, the written complaints should have resulted in a specific incident memorandum sent to the teacher as discussed in some detail in the next chapter. In this case, the commissioner upheld the teacher's nonrenewal, because there was other evidence to support it and because the teacher had been given an opportunity to remediate her behavior.[5]

Documentation also can be important in protecting school administrators from personal liability in federal court. In recent years, school administrators have found themselves vulnerable to charges that they had been deliberately indifferent to students' constitutional rights to be free from sexual abuse and other bodily harm by failing to take seriously students' complaints that school employees or fellow students were engaging in inappropriate behavior. A good illustration is a federal appellate court ruling involving anti-gay harassment of five students over a number of years by classmates in a California school district who perceived them to be lesbian, gay, or bisexual. The harassment included pornography and notes such as "Die, dyke bitch" posted on one of the student's locker, a beating of a male student by six students who said "Faggot, you don't belong here;" and repeated name-calling, sexual gestures, and food-throwing. The evidence established that despite repeated complaints to school officials, the harassment continued. The question was whether the school officials could be assessed damages for violating the students' right to be free from peer sexual harassment under the equal protection clause of the Fourteenth Amendment to the U.S. Constitution by not effectively enforcing the district's anti-harassment policies. The absence of documentation to establish that the officials had thoroughly investigated the complaints and taken appropriate action to stop the harassment resulted in the appellate court's finding them liable. In legal terms, they were viewed as deliberately indifferent to the gay students' rights.[6] The point is that if administrators do a thorough job of investigating and documenting employee or student wrongdoing, those filing lawsuits (plaintiffs) will have difficulty in meeting the deliberately indifferent standard.

Ethical Considerations

In addition to legal considerations, there are also ethical reasons why good documentation is important. Consider the Golden Rule: "Do unto others as you would have them do unto you." This maxim yields several important principles for effective personnel administration:

- Alert employees to performance deficiencies.
- If the deficiencies are remediable, provide employees with written directives for improvement and provide a reasonable time frame for improvement to occur. Include directives for professional development if you think they are warranted.
- Provide feedback through periodic assessment.
- If a negative employment decision is contemplated, notify affected employees of their rights under district policy.
- Follow school policies and regulations scrupulously.

If employees facing contract nonrenewal or termination perceive that they have been treated unfairly, they may seek revenge by filing a lawsuit even if they realize that their chances of winning are slim. For this reason, treating employees fairly, even if they are hostile, can reap dividends later by lessening the chances that they will seek to "get even." The documentation process we recommend in this handbook serves first and foremost the goal of fair treatment of school employees. Secondarily, it is meant to provide the rationale and supportive evidence to withstand legal challenges.

Political Considerations

In addition to legal and ethical concerns, remember that you are operating within a political environment. The first, and sometimes most difficult, hurdle to be cleared if an employee challenges your negative employment decision often will be the governing board. It helps a board member who is concerned about political fallout from a tough personnel decision to know that you have treated the employee fairly and that your decision is based on poor job performance. Fair treatment also will diminish the employee's ability to undermine your credibility among staff members by alleging arbitrary administrative action.

Other Benefits of a Documentation System

A carefully developed documentation system can give you the opportunity to acknowledge those employees who have remedied deficiencies or have done outstanding work. A documentation system can aid your memory by providing you with information about past employee performance. It can minimize misunderstandings between you and the employee about performance problems and reveal to you patterns of deficiencies that emerge over time. A documentation system will stimulate you to think carefully about employment decisions. Finally, a documentation system will support your successor who inherits the personnel problems that you didn't have time to remedy. However, an administrator must be careful about carrying forward documentation from one year to the next as noted a bit later in this chapter.

The remainder of this chapter examines the legal framework within which documentation occurs.

TEACHER APPRAISAL

Appraisal System Options

With the focus more and more on school effectiveness, it is essential that schools be staffed by effective teachers. Procedures relating to teacher appraisal frequently change by virtue of new legislation set forth in the Texas Education Code (TEC) and revised Texas Commissioner of Education rules set forth in Title 19 of the Texas Administrative Code (TAC). Both the provisions of the Texas Education Code and the Texas Administrative Code can be easily accessed by going to the Texas Education Agency website at http://tea.texas.gov/, clicking on "About TEA," and going to "Laws and Rules." Commissioner rules for educator standards and appraisals will be found in Chapter 149 and 150 of Title 19 of the Texas Administrative Code, respectively. The discussion in this section reflects the state of appraisal law currently in effect. Under the provisions of Texas Education Code Sections 21.351-21.353, school districts may use either the state-recommended system (currently the Texas Teacher Evaluation and Support System (T-TESS)) or their own teacher appraisal system that is developed through the district's site-based decision-making process and approved by the board of trustees. No approval from the commissioner is required if districts choose the latter. Under commissioner rules, campuses within a school district also may choose a local appraisal option with approval of the school board following recommendations made by the district-level planning and decision-making committee and the superintendent (19 TAC § 150.1007(b)). District superintendents are required to inform the executive director of the local regional educational service center when using an alternative teacher appraisal system at the start of the school year when the system is used and must submit annually to the service center a summary of campus-level evaluation scores for T-TESS or the locally adopted appraisal system in a manner prescribed by the commissioner of education (19 TAC § 150.1008). Districts that have adopted high quality instructional materials (HQIM) are to use the new T-TESS Alternate Domain I that was developed to evaluate teachers whose instructional preparation focuses on lesson internalization instead of lesson planning (19 TAC SS 150.1002).

It is important to note that charter schools and districts of innovation have discretion as to how they will evaluate teachers. Likewise, they are exempt from employment law relating to probationary, term, and continuing contracts. The largest number of charter schools in this state are open-enrollment charters now granted by the commissioner of education. A much smaller number are campus charters operating within a school district. Many of these follow the appraisal process used by their authorizing school district.

In accord with Section 21.351 of the Education Code, both the commissioner's recommended appraisal system and a traditional school district (meaning not a district of innovation) alternative appraisal system must encompass observable job-related behavior including implementation of discipline management procedures and student performance. The latter is discussed in Chapter 6 in the context of writing directives related to student performance. For districts and charter schools using T-TESS, the commissioner of education has set forth performance standards to be used to inform the training, appraisal, and professional development of teachers. While these standards do not apply to alternative assessment systems chosen by districts and charter schools, they offer a goal-oriented alignment opportunity for all appraisal systems in the state so that that there is consistency in teacher assessment and professional development. The standards encompass the following:

Standard 1: *Instructional Planning and Delivery.* Teachers are to demonstrate understanding of instructional planning and delivery by providing standards-based, data-driven, differentiated instruction that engages students, makes appropriate use of technology, and makes learning relevant for today's learners.

Standard 2: *Knowledge of Students and Student Learning.* Teachers work to ensure high levels of learning, socio-emotional development, and achievement outcomes for all students, taking into consideration each student's educational and developmental backgrounds and focusing on each student's needs.

Standard 3: *Content Knowledge and Expertise.* Teachers exhibit a comprehensive understanding of their content, discipline, and related pedagogy as demonstrated through the quality of the design and execution of lessons and their ability to match objectives and activities to relevant state standards.

Standard 4: *Learning Environment.* Teachers interact with students in respectful ways at all times, maintaining a physically and emotionally safe, supportive learning environment that is characterized by efficient and effective routines, clear expectations for student behavior, and organization that maximizes student learning.

Standard 5: *Data-Driven Practice.* Teachers use formal and informal methods to assess student growth aligned to instructional goals and course objectives and regularly review and analyze multiple sources of data to measure student progress and adjust instructional strategies and content delivery as needed.

Standard 6: *Professional Practices and Responsibilities.* Teachers consistently hold themselves to a high standard for individual development, pursue leadership opportunities, collaborate with other professionals, communicate regularly with stakeholders, maintain professional relationships, comply with all campus and school district policies, and conduct themselves ethically and with integrity. The commissioner of education's rules setting forth each of these standards include detailed information on how the standards are to be carried out (19 TAC § 149.1001).

T-TESS has four domains: Planning or Lesson Internalization, Instruction, Learning Environment, Professional Practices and Responsibilities. Each of the four domains encompasses a list of dimensions that relate to the standards for all teacher appraisal systems discussed above. To assist appraisers in determining the appropriate rating for each T-TESS domain, a set of descriptors is set forth for each. Rating levels are Distinguished, Accomplished, Proficient, Developing, and Improvement Needed.

Conducting Appraisals

Texas Education Code Sections 21.351-21.353 set forth the requirements for conducting teacher appraisals in public schools other than open-enrollment charter schools and districts of innovation. For appraisals under these TEC sections, teachers must be given a complete appraisal at least once a year. However, any component of this appraisal such as STAAR or other test results that are not reported until the following year or beyond cannot be included. A teacher may be appraised less frequently if the teacher agrees in writing and the teacher's most recent evalua- tion rated the teacher at least proficient and did not indicate any area of deficiency. A teacher who is appraised less frequently must be appraised at least once every five years. Under current commissioner rules for T-TESS, a school district may choose annually to review the written agreement to have less frequent full appraisals with the teacher. The district may modify appraisal options through board policy and make changes in expectations for appraisals that apply to all teachers regardless of a teacher's participation in the appraisal process previously. For both T-TESS and a locally developed appraisal system, advance notice of the date or time of an appraisal may be given but is not required. Teachers are to be notified of the results of any appraisal in a timely manner so that the appraisal can be used as a developmental tool. A written copy of the appraisal is to be kept in the teacher's personnel file. Appraisals are to be focused on classroom teaching performance only. Extracurricular activities directed by the teacher are not to be included. Districts are to use a teacher's consecutive appraisals from more than one year, if available, in making an employment decision and/or developing career recommendations for the teacher.

Additional components of the appraisal process such as classroom observations and walk-throughs are required more frequently than the formal appraisal to ensure that teachers receive evaluation and guidance. This is especially true for inexperienced teachers and those with recognized deficiencies. In Chapter 4, we discuss and illustrate how to simplify the gathering of data during classroom observations and walk-throughs between formal appraisals using one of our specially designed focused observation instruments and linking the findings to T-TESS or a locally developed appraisal system.

Determining the weight to be accorded an unscheduled classroom observation in reconsidering a teacher's prior rating on a formal observation is a matter for the appraiser's professional judgment. In a 1991 appeal to the commissioner, a teacher contested the principal's refusal to change the credit for one indicator on her summative evaluation. The principal had conducted and documented numerous walk-throughs following the formal evaluation. The teacher alleged that during these walk-throughs, the principal must have noticed that the deficiency had been corrected but the principal refused to change the rating. The commissioner upheld the principal's decision, noting that "if [the principal] determined that [the teacher's] performance did not improve sufficiently to warrant credit for the indicator, then that was her assessment, and such exercise of judgment is not arbitrary and capricious."[7]

Under the commissioner-recommended appraisal process, the appraiser must be the teacher's supervisor or a person approved by the school board (TEC § 21.351). An individual other than the campus administrator may act as an appraiser if the person is certified and the district lacks a sufficient number of certified appraisers. A T-TESS appraiser who is a classroom teacher may conduct teacher appraisals on other campuses but not on the same school campus unless acting as a department or grade level chair with a job description that includes classroom observation responsibilities. T-TESS appraisals are to be detailed by category of professional skill and provide separate ratings for each category. The required conference between the teacher and appraiser is to be diagnostic and prescriptive regarding remediation needed in overall performance and by category. Qualification and training requirements for T-TESS appraisers are spelled out in commissioner rules (19 Texas Administrative Code § 150.1005). Whatever appraisal system used, teachers in traditional public school districts are entitled to receive promptly a copy of their completed evaluation (TEC § 21.352). After receiving a written copy of the observation or evaluation, a teacher may request a second appraisal by a different appraiser or may file a written rebuttal to the evaluation that is to be attached to the evaluation in the teacher's personnel file. For schools using T-TESS the request for a second appraisal or the response/rebuttal for Domain I or Alternate Domain I and Domains II-III must be filed within 10 working days after receiving a written observation summary or any other documentation associated with the appraisal unless the teacher has already received written documentation earlier in the appraisal year for which the teacher had the opportunity to respond. For Domain IV and for performance of the teacher's students, the second appraisal request or response/rebuttal only can be submitted after receiving a written summative annual appraisal report. T-TESS rules also note that the teacher may, but does not have to be, given notice of date and time of the second appraisal. Under commissioner rules, all appraisal processes used by traditional public school districts must guarantee a diagnostic and prescriptive conference between the teacher and the appraiser. Schools are authorized to send copies of a teacher's evaluations, along with any rebuttals, to a district, open enrollment charter school, or private school to which the teacher has applied for employment if the school requests such information.

The appraisal of a teacher or administrator at both a school district and open-enrollment charter school is considered confidential unless requested by TEA as part of an investigation (TEC §21.355). In 2006, a Texas court of appeals construed this provision to apply to a letter of reprimand concerning complaints about the teacher and directive corrective action.[8] The Texas Attorney General has construed Section 21.355 to apply to any document that evaluates the employee's performance. Further, the attorney general has construed the provision to apply only to certified teachers engaged in teaching and to certified administrators functioning in that capacity. Thus, teacher interns, teacher trainees, librarians, educational aides, and counselors are excluded (ORD-643, 1996). However, Section 21.355 has been amended to encompass both certified and non-certified persons employed in an open-enrollment charter school. And an open-enrollment charter school may provide a performance evaluation to a school district or open-enrollment charter school to which a teacher or administrator at the open-enrollment charter school has applied.

Section 150.1003 of Title 19 of the Texas Administrative Code sets forth detailed information on T-TESS appraisals, data sources, and conferences. There are several points made in them that are important to know. First, appraisals are to include a completed and appraiser-approved Goal-Setting and Professional Development (GSPD) plan. For teachers in their first year of T-TESS appraisal or new to the district, the plan is to be submitted to the appraiser within the first six weeks following completion of T-TESS orientation. A conference with the appraiser is required prior to the teacher's submitting the plan. For other teachers the plan is to be drafted in conjunction with the teachers' end-of-year conference the previous year, revised as necessary, and submitted to the appraiser within the first six weeks of instruction in the next school year. The plan is to be used by teachers to track progress in attainment of the goals and to participate in professional development activities as set forth in the plan. The plan is to be shared with the teacher's appraiser prior to the end-of-year conference and used after the conference in the determination of ratings for the goal-setting and professional development dimensions of the T-TESS rubric. After a teacher's first year of appraisal under T-TESS within the district, an observation pre-conference is to be conducted prior to announced observations.

Second, the T-TESS appraisal rules require that any documentation that will influence the teacher's summative appraisal must be shared in writing with the teacher within 10 working days of the appraiser's knowledge of the occurrence. If the appraiser is not the teacher's principal, then the principal is to be informed as well. In a 2015 decision involving the prior Professional Development and Appraisal System (PDAS), the commissioner of education noted that "if the certified appraiser decides to conduct additional walk-throughs or observations, he must disclose a written summary of each observation within 10 days of the observation, regardless of whether he ultimately uses the results of the observation in drafting the teacher's summative annual appraisal."[9] Routinely providing this information to the teacher preserves the ability of the appraiser to incorporate it in a summative appraisal should the appraiser later decide to do so.

Third, the rules require that any third-party information that the teacher's appraiser intends to use as part of cumulative data must be verified and documented. Questions have arisen in the past as to what this means. Does it mean, for instance, that the appraiser has to do more than just listen to what another teacher, parent, or student says? Does the appraiser have to share that information with the teacher? In an informative 2015 decision, the commissioner has provided some insight into these questions.[10] The commissioner pointed out that "An appraiser cannot just document that a parent, student, or staff member said that a teacher did something wrong, the appraiser is required to verify the claim is true. If an appraiser cannot verify that a claim is true, the appraiser cannot mark down a teacher based on a third-party claim." The commissioner added that "The original source of the information, be it a phone call or an email or letter, does not have to be shared with the teacher." One way to go about having verification of third-party information is to have the person complete either a witness statement form or a complaint form, neither of which needs to be given to the teacher after it is completed. We have provided templates for both in Appendix C. Then the administrator must decide whether what is written down is true and whether the person making the claim is worthy of belief. That will mean incorporating what is said into the administrator's own investigation into the matter.

Grievances Over Appraisals

All public employees have a right to present grievances to their employers under Ch. 617 of the Texas Government Code and under Article 1, Section 27 of the Texas Constitution. The commissioner of education has held that both the *process* by which an employment evaluation was conducted and the *content* of the evaluation are grievable.[11] Additionally, a school board can review the educational judgment of an appraiser but may reverse the appraiser's judgment only if the appraiser's educational judgment was "clearly erroneous or an abuse of discretion."[12] Administrators must be very careful not to retaliate against a teacher — or any employee, for that matter — who files a grievance. That point was illustrated in a decision from the commissioner in 1992 involving the Texas Teacher Appraisal System (TTAS), the commissioner's first recommended appraisal system. A principal commented negatively to the teacher's prospective employer about the teacher's filing grievances over her appraisals. The commissioner noted, "Under the Texas Teacher Appraisal System, teachers rest assured that no appraisal or evaluation of their work performance can affect their career without notice to them and an opportunity to respond." The

That said, we now turn our attention to those professional employees including teachers, administrators, supervisors, counselors, librarians, and nurses who are covered by Chapter 21 of the Texas Education Code. It will quickly become evident that the first step for an administrator considering recommending nonrenewal or termination of a contract is to know what the employment relationship of the employee is to the school district.

Probationary Contract

Except for superintendents and except for experienced principals and teachers who may be employed on term contracts when new to a traditional school district, professional employees are required to serve a one-year probationary contract if employed in the district for the first time or if not employed by the district for two consecutive school years after August 28, 1967 (see Figure 1-1). The latter provision means that a professional employee who resigns before serving two consecutive years of employment and then returns to the district must be re-employed on a one-year probationary contract. In the past, there has been some confusion as to when the probationary period is over for a teacher who is hired in mid-year. The Texas Commissioner of Education resolved the problem in 1996, deciding that the term "year" is to have the normal meaning it has in the school business, meaning a scholastic year.[21] Thus, the one-year probationary period for a teacher hired mid-year is not concluded until the end of the next school year. Persons who voluntarily accept assignments in a new professional capacity requiring a different class of certificate also may be employed on a probationary contract. Should the person be returned to the former position, the person is to be employed on the same contractual basis as before the new assignment.

Education Code Section 21.103 states that a probationary contract may be "terminated at the end of the contract year" if the district believes that it would be in the best interests of the district to do so. The term normally used in this situation is "nonrenewal." However, for some reason Education Code Section 21.103 uses the term "termination," and we will do so here as well.

Figure 1-1   THE ONE-YEAR PROBATIONARY CONTRACT

(All Employees Who Have Not Been Employed for Two Consecutive Years Except the Superintendent, Experienced Principals and Teachers at District Discretion. Also Employees Who Accept Reassignments Requiring a Different Class of Certificate)

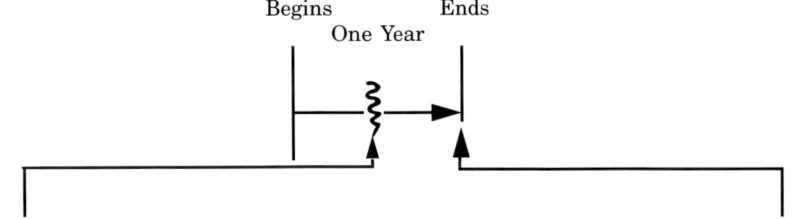

Discharge/Suspension Without Pay During Contract
- Property Right
- Good Cause
- Notice
- Hearing Before Hearing Examiner (board option for financial exigency)
- Oral Argument Before School Board
- Right to Appeal

TEC §§ 21.104 - 21.1041, 21.251 - 21.307

Termination At End Of Contract
- No Property Right
- 10-Day Notice
- Best Interest of School District
- Board Decision Final and Nonappealable (possible exception: use of force in student discipline)

TEC § 21.103

Due process is limited to providing notice of termination no later than the 10th day before the last day of instruction under the contract. The last day of instruction encompasses final exam and testing days.[22] The notice must be delivered personally by hand delivery to the teacher on the campus where the teacher is employed. If the teacher is not present when hand delivery is attempted, then the notice must be mailed by prepaid certified mail or delivered by express delivery service to the teacher's home address. The notice is considered timely if postmarked on or before the 10th day prior to the last day of instruction. If the board fails to give timely notice and the employee has served fewer than three years in the district, the person is to be given a probationary contract for another year in the same professional capacity.

From a documentation standpoint, an end-of-year termination of a probationary employee's contract is the easiest negative employment decision to make. During this "window of opportunity," the district only has to comply with the 10-day notice requirement. No other due process procedures are necessary. Further, the board's decision is final and nonappealable with one possible exception — use of force in student discipline because use of force is sometimes justified.[23] Still, the same concerns regarding at-will employees also pertain to probationary contract employees. While the Texas Commissioner of Education declines to hear appeals from probationary contract employees whose contracts are terminated at the end of the year, the employee can always file a grievance with the district or contact the EEOC or the TCHR to contest the action as illegally motivated based on such factors as race, color, religion, gender, age, and disability. In this sense, nothing is ever "final and nonappealable." Thus, if challenged, administrators should be prepared to defend their actions by having sufficient documentation to establish the legitimacy of the end-of-year termination. However, the burden is clearly on the employee to establish that the district had an impermissible motive for the action.

Terminating or suspending a probationary contract without pay during the contract is an entirely different matter. Doing so requires more administrative attention. Since the professional employee has a constitutionally protected property right to the salary (and to the position if the contract is worded to convey a specific job title), formal due process procedures must be followed. TEC Section 21.1041 provides that a mid-year termination of a probationary teacher's contract requires a hearing before a hearing examiner as set forth in TEC Sections 21.251-21.260 in the same manner as necessary for terminating term and continuing contracts, as well as suspending professional employees without pay. The one exception is personnel reduction caused by financial exigency declared under TEC Section 44.011. In this event, the school board has the option of conducting the hearing as it does with term contract nonrenewals. This in effect provides a somewhat less formal procedure than hearings before hearing examiners.

As outlined in Figure 1-1, hearings before hearing examiners assigned by the commissioner of education are formal affairs. The hearing must be closed unless the employee wants an open hearing, though the hearing officer may close the hearing "to preserve decorum." At the hearing the employee is entitled to have a representative of the person's choice, hear the evidence including a teacher's appraisal on which the charges are based, cross-examine adverse witnesses, and pres- ent evidence. The hearing is conducted like a trial without a jury in a state district court. Unless the employee and the district have agreed that the hearing examiner's decision will be final and nonappealable on all or some issues, the record of the hearing and the recommendation of the hearing examiner are forwarded to the school board or subcommittee of the board before principal had breached that assurance by providing negative employment references. The commissioner took the stringent action of revoking the principal's mid-management certification.[13]

Does a Positive Appraisal Shield a Teacher from Contract Nonrenewal or Termination?

The commissioner has ruled that satisfactory appraisal ratings do not insulate a teacher from having the teacher's contract nonrenewed based on deficient classroom performance, since the appraisal is not the only means of classroom evaluation. In a 2008 case, the teacher argued that because his most recent evaluation was very good, the board should not have nonrenewed his contract. But the commissioner noted that while the board must consider relevant recent evaluations before deciding not to renew, it is not limited to them and need not consider them as the most important evidence.[14]

There also are many reasons warranting contract nonrenewal or termination even though a teacher is effective in the classroom. For example, numerous grounds for a negative employment decision are set forth in a school district's contract nonrenewal policy including failure to comply with board policies, regulations, and administrative directives; failure to maintain effective working relationships with colleagues; assaulting an employee, student, or parent; illegal drug possession; conviction of a felony; and many more. What is important, of course, is to have effective documentation supporting any of these reasons to warrant a contract nonrenewal or termination. That is the focus of our discussion in the next chapter.

What About Using Teaching Deficiencies from Prior Years to Build Support for Contract Nonrenewal or Termination?

When classroom deficiencies are evident, it is important to make sure teachers are aware of them from one year to the next. This is especially true when one-year contracts are renewed. While TEC Section 21.352 requires traditional school districts to use consecutive appraisals for more than one year in making employment decisions, if no deficiencies are indicated on the appraisals, the teacher will be unaware of them and that could have significant consequences. As the commissioner has observed, "When a school district with full knowledge of a teacher's actions takes no action against the teacher and decides to offer the teacher a new contract, the district has waived any right it had to take action against the teacher's contract for the events in the prior school years."[15] Such is not the case for an employee on a multiple year contract when the deficiencies have been pointed out and the employee been given a remediation plan to correct them. In this event, it may take the duration of the contract or longer to determine whether the teacher has met the terms of the remediation plan. We will discuss remediation in the context of an intervention plan in Chapter 6.

For the one-year contract teacher when a remediation plan is not established, alerting the teacher on the school's appraisal form that despite an overall proficient or higher rating there are areas of teaching weakness that need to be addressed in future classes enables the administrator to rely on more than only deficiencies during the most recent contract to build the case for a negative employment recommendation. Still, an administrator can't expect to utilize past deficiencies to support a future contract nonrenewal of a teacher with high appraisal ratings when no remediation effort is ever extended to a teacher to remedy the areas of concern. Both a school board and the commissioner may find the nonrenewal unfair.

APPRAISAL OF PRINCIPALS AND OTHER ADMINISTRATORS

Education Code Section 21.3541 requires the commissioner of education to establish a comprehensive appraisal and professional development system for principals. In assessing principals, school districts are to use the commissioner's recommended system, currently the Texas Principal Evaluation and Support System (T-PESS), or a system developed locally. Principals are to be appraised annually. As with teachers, charter schools and districts of innovation have discretion on evaluating principals and other administrators.

For districts and charter schools using T-PESS to evaluate principals, the standards for appraisal encompass the following:

Standard 1: *Instructional Leadership.* The principal is responsible for ensuring every student receives high quality instruction.

Standard 2: *Human Capital.* The principal is responsible for ensuring there are high quality teachers and staff in every classroom and throughout the school.

Standard 3: *Executive Leadership.* The principal is responsible for modeling a consistent focus on and commitment to improving student learning.

Standard 4: *School Culture.* The principal is responsible for establishing and implementing a shared vision and culture of high expectations for all staff and students.

Standard 5: *Strategic Operations.* The principal is responsible for implementing systems that align with the school's vision and improve the quality of instruction.

The commissioner of education's rules setting forth each of these standards include detailed information on relevant knowledge and skills and on achievement indicators for each (19 TAC § 149.2001). Accessing them is the same as accessing teaching appraisal rules. As noted earlier with regard to T-TESS, while these standards apply only to T-PESS, they provide an alignment opportunity to all schools so that there is consistency in principal assessment and professional development.

The Texas Education Code also requires annual appraisals of other school administrators using either the commissioner's recommended appraisal process and criteria or one developed locally (TEC § 21.354). T-PESS can be modified to ensure that its rubric and components fit the administrator's job description. School administrators whose performance has not been appraised in the preceding 15 months may not be paid through school district funds.

Procedures for evaluating principals are set forth in commissioner rules (19 TAC § 150.1022 and following sections). For T-PESS, these include a pre-conference with the appraiser followed by a mid-year and end-of-year conference to discuss the goals and progress toward obtaining them in the context of the achievement indicators of the T-PESS standards. Starting in 2017-2018, each principal appraisal is to include campus-level student academic growth. The summative appraisal report is to be placed in the principal's personnel file by the end of the appraisal period. Any documentation collected after the summative appraisal that affects the evaluation triggers another summative report to inform the principal of the changes prior to the end of the contract term. For districts using an alternative to T-PESS, the superintendent is to submit details of the appraisal system at the start of the school year to the executive director of the local regional education service center. Each district is to submit annually to the education service center a summary of the evaluation scores from T-PESS or the district's locally adopted system in a manner prescribed by the commissioner.

In addition to appraising the performance of teachers, principals, and other administrators, many districts and charter schools have developed evaluation systems for staff members such as coaches, secretaries, and maintenance workers. It is important to follow the procedures for these systems because failure to do so will quickly undermine a negative employment recommendation, no matter how well intentioned.

While administrator appraisal is important, the discussion in Chapters 3-4 of this handbook focuses on teachers whose performance is marginally effective and where the supervisor's goal is either to improve the teacher's performance or have sufficient documentation to support a negative employment recommendation.

TEXAS EMPLOYMENT LAW

Understanding the basics of employment law is critical to successful documentation, because both the amount and types of documentation are heavily influenced by it. The purpose of this section is to provide an overview of the employment provisions of the Texas Education Code (TEC) as they apply to school districts and to discuss the implications for documentation. Since charter schools have the discretion to decide on what basis they will employ their staff, parts of this discussion may not be applicable to them. The same may be true of districts of innovation that are given more autonomy once a local innovation plan is established and approved by two-thirds of the governing board (TEC § 12A.001 and following sections). Quite obviously, employment law is comprehensive, complex, and frequently changing. For a detailed discussion, see Chapters 4 and 5 of *The Educator's Guide to Texas School Law*. Formerly written by Jim Walsh, Laurie Maniotis & Frank Kemerer, the 10th edition written by Jim Walsh and Sarah Orman was published by the University of Texas Press in August 2022.

At-Will Arrangements

At-will employment is most often used with auxiliary employees such as custodians, cafeteria workers, clerks, and secretaries. Some charter schools employ their teachers as well as other staff members on an at-will basis. School districts may also use the at-will option for non-certified teachers selected under the teaching permit option afforded by TEC Section 21.055, because certification is required for employment under the contractual options discussed below that afford procedural protection.

Frequently teachers are employed on an at-will basis to undertake supplemental duty assignments (e.g., serve as student council sponsor for a $500 stipend). "At-will" means that there is no expectation of continued employment. Either party may dissolve the employment relationship at any time. Because there is no expectation of continued employment, no constitutionally protected property right is at stake.[16] Furthermore, oral assurances of continued employment do not alter the status of an at-will arrangement.[17]

It would seem at first glance that neither due process nor documentation should be a concern for at-will arrangements. Such an assumption would be erroneous. Many schools employ auxiliary workers for some specific length of time (e.g., from one thirty-day pay period to the next). Charter schools may do the same for teachers. Thus, the employee may have an expectation of continued employment for the duration of the pay period. Termination during that period may require adherence to formal due process procedures and sufficient documentation to constitute good cause for discharge. This is so because school districts and charter schools are public entities that must follow the provisions of the U.S. Constitution. The due process clause is included in the Fourteenth Amendment and compliance with it is necessary when a property right is taken away by a public entity. A written employment agreement may fall into the property right category depending upon its wording. Based on federal court rulings over the years, "good cause" can be loosely defined to mean clear and convincing job-related reasons accompanied by sufficient supportive evidence to deprive a person of a constitutionally protected property right in employment.

If the district or charter school waits until the end of the pay period to sever the employment relationship, no due process would be required absent local district or charter school policy creating such a requirement. In the case of professional employees, one district ran into trouble when the commissioner of education construed conflicting terminology in a teacher's contract in favor of the teacher's argument that the supplemental duty assignment of assistant band director was part of the contract and could not be ended without following due process procedures associated with nonrenewal and termination.[18] Had the contract been confined to teaching responsibilities and the supplemental duty assignment been a separate at-will arrangement, the conflict would not have arisen. For this reason it is important to pay attention to the terms of any written agreement with the employee, to school policies, and to school past practice before terminating at-will employees from work.

Even when there is no contractual language or school policy that would require due process before discharging an at-will employee, documentation cannot be ignored. Consider, for example, the following scenario. A supervisor tells a female custodian late on a Friday afternoon not to report to work on Monday because her employment is no longer needed. Angered by this decision and concerned that she may not be able to find employment in a tight labor market, the custodian decides to contest the termination. She files a grievance under school district policy and contacts the Equal Employment Opportunity Commission (EEOC) or the Texas Commission on Human Rights (TCHR), asserting that the termination resulted from her refusal to grant sexual favors to the supervisor. In order to establish that sexual harassment was not a factor in the decision, the supervisor must have documentation relating to poor job performance or some other reason unrelated to the allegation.

This scenario demonstrates that documentation is important even when administrators have maximum discretion in terminating an at-will arrangement. How much documentation is needed? Enough to support a job-related reason for terminating the person's employment. In the next chapter, we will illustrate how a supervisor might go about preparing the necessary documentation for doing so.

Contracts for Professional Employees

The term "teacher" in Texas employment law is broadly defined to include principals, supervisors, classroom teachers, school counselors, or other full-time professional employees who are required to hold an educator certificate under Subchapter B of Chapter 21 of the Texas Education Code. A full-time school district classroom teacher is one who teaches an average of at least four hours per day in an academic or career and technology instructional setting. While non-instructional duties can't be counted toward the time requirement, functions related to teaching such as instructional planning and transition between instructional periods can be (19 TAC § 153.1022(a)). The Chapter 21 contract provisions setting forth the conditions under which probationary, term, and continuing contracts operate in Texas school districts also apply to school nurses and librarians who work full time. But they do not apply to teachers holding only a teaching permit.[19]* Superintendents are included within the definition of "teacher" under the term contract provisions only. Given the broad definition of "teacher," we will substitute the term "professional employee" in the following discussion. It is important to note at the onset that we are focusing our attention primarily on statutory provisions dealing with contract nonrenewal and termination. However, the actual wording of contracts cannot be ignored. In some cases, school districts and charter schools have approved contract provisions that are unique to the district or charter school and sometimes unique even to the employee.

What about employees who do not fall into the "professional employee" category as defined above? For example, surely a business manager and a director of maintenance are professional employees. Yes, they are. But the provisions of Chapter 21 dealing with probationary, term, and continuing contracts do not apply to them. We call these persons "non-Chapter 21 employees." They may have a contract of employment, but the contract is not governed by Chapter 21 unless the contract so provides. This means in effect that the conditions of their employment are defined by provisions set forth in the contract. Suppose a school district wants to nonrenew or terminate the contract of a non-Chapter 21 employee. Are there any procedures that must be followed? For nonrenewal of the contract when its term is up, the provisions of the contract will answer this question.** For termination of the contract during its term, the matter is more complex. Generally, unless the terms of the contract state otherwise, a public school employee including one employed in a charter school or district of innovation has an expectation of employment until the contract ends. This expectation is termed a property right. As noted above, under the Fourteenth Amendment to the U.S. Constitution, a political entity like a school district or charter school cannot take away life, liberty, or property without due process of law. In the context of a non-Chapter 21 contract, the basics of due process require that the employee:

- Be advised of the cause or causes of the termination in sufficient detail to fairly enable the employee to show any error that may exist.
- Be advised of the names and the nature of the testimony of witnesses against the employee.
- At a reasonable time after such advice, be given a meaningful opportunity to be heard in the employee's defense.
- Be given an opportunity for a hearing before an impartial tribunal.

This is the teaching of a venerable ruling of the U.S. Court of Appeals for the Fifth Circuit, which, as noted earlier, has jurisdiction for several states, including Texas.[20] The case involved the dismissal of a teacher during the teacher's contract. Today, the teacher would be entitled to more elaborate due process procedures that are part of Chapter 21. However, the four basic due process steps set forth above still apply to non-Chapter 21 employees.

---

* Non-certified teachers hired under the teaching permit option may be employed on contracts similar to those used with other employees whose position does not require certification. As noted a bit later, these are termed "Non-Chapter 21" employees.

** What if a non-Chapter 21 employee is reassigned during the contract to a school administrative position? Does the contract nonrenewal procedures set forth in TEC Chapter 21 now apply? The matter is complex because it relates to both contract wording and contract law. See the Texas Commissioner of Education's discussion in *Solis v. Mission C.I.S.D.*, Dkt. No. 056-R1-07-2013 (Comm'r Educ. 2021).

which the parties later have the right to make an oral argument. The hearing officer's conclusions of law including a determination regarding good cause for contract termination or suspension without pay may be adopted, rejected, or changed by the school board or board subcommittee. The same is true of a hearing officer's finding of fact if not supported by substantial evidence. The employee has a right to appeal the board's decision to the commissioner of education. Thereafter, either party may appeal the commissioner's decision to state district court.

Given the formality of the termination process and the high cost involved, administrators will want to prepare carefully. The central concern is documenting "good cause" to support the decision. Good cause for terminating professional employee contracts is defined in TEC Section 21.104 to mean "failure to meet the accepted standards of conduct for the profession as generally recognized and applied in similarly situated school districts in this state." This includes failure to comply with specific state or federal law such as student grading and testing. As we noted earlier, a practical definition of good cause from a documentation standpoint is *clear and convincing job-related reasons accompanied by sufficient evidence to justify taking away a constitutionally protected property right in employment.*

When the behavior is remediable, the administrator first must (1) give the employee an explicit directive to change or improve his or her conduct or to cease certain behaviors, and (2) provide the employee an opportunity to comply before mid-contract termination will be justified. Isolated instances of misconduct often can and should be handled by less drastic means than termination. The legislature has enacted a mentoring program for classroom teachers who have less than two years of teaching experience in the subject or grade level to which the teacher is assigned (TEC § 21.458). If a school district decides to assign mentors, the mentors to the extent possible must teach in the same schools as the novice teachers, preferably teach the same subject or grade level, and meet qualifications specified by the commissioner of education. The qualifications include completion of an approved research-based mentor and induction training program and at least three years of teaching experience with a superior record of improving student performance. Clearly, helping novice teachers improve via mentoring is preferable to either end-of-year contract termination or mid-year contract termination. In the next chapter, we will discuss how to prepare sufficient documentation to support a mid-year termination or suspension without pay and in Chapter 3 what the implications are for appropriate supervisory style. In Chapter 6, we will elaborate on remediation requirements and when they are required. Suffice it here to say that mid-contract actions are not to be taken lightly.

Once the professional employee has served the one-year probationary contract, the district has three options regarding future employment as outlined in Figure 1-2. School district policy will delineate which of the options is to be used for its professional employees.

> *Option 1.* The district can continue to employ the person who has served fewer than five of the previous eight years of employment in public education on a probationary contract for two additional one-year periods. A fourth year of probationary status is also permissible if the district is uncertain whether to give the employee a continuing or term contract. Following the fourth year, the district either must end the employment or give the employee a term or continuing contract as provided by district policy. TEC § 21.102(c).
>
> *Option 2.* The district can offer the employee a term contract.
>
> *Option 3.* The district can offer the employee a continuing contract.

Figure 1-2 THREE OPTIONS FOR DISTRICTS AFTER ONE-YEAR PROBATIONARY CONTRACT

Option 1: Probationary Contract Continuation

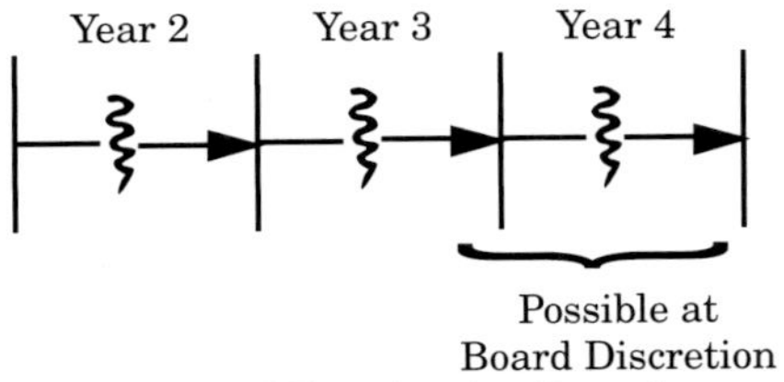

Year 2 — Year 3 — Year 4

Possible at Board Discretion

Discharge and Termination Procedures Same as for First Year Probationary Contract

Option 1 is not available for employees who have worked in a public school for at least 5 of the previous 8 years. TEC § 21.102

Option 2: Term Contract

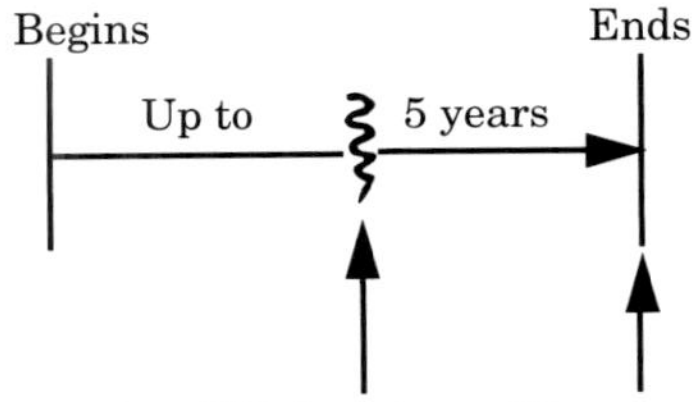

Begins — Up to 5 years — Ends

Termination/Suspension Without Pay During Contract*
- Property Right
- Good Cause
- Notice
- Hearing Before Hearing Examiner (board option for financial exigency)
- Oral Argument Before School Board
- Right to Appeal

TEC §§ 21.211, 21.251 - 21.307

Nonrenewal At End Of Contract*
- No Property Right
- 10-Day Notice
- Hearing Before School Board** (board may opt for commissioner-appointed hearing examiner)
- Right to Appeal

TEC §§ 21.206 - 21.209, 21.251 - 21.307

*In lieu of termination or nonrenewal, may return employee to a probationary contract with employee consent. TEC § 21.106

**In districts with at least 5,000 students the school board may select an outside attorney to conduct the hearing.

Option 3: Continuing Contract

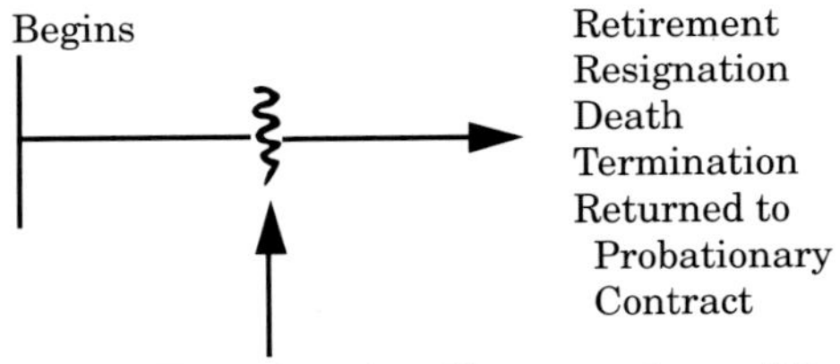

Begins → Retirement / Resignation / Death / Termination / Returned to Probationary Contract

Termination/Suspension without Pay During Contract*
- Property Right
- Good Cause***
- Notice of Reasons and Grounds
- Hearing Before Hearing Examiner (board option for financial exigency)
- Oral Argument Before School Board
- Right to Appeal

TEC §§ 21.156 - 21.159, 21.251 - 21.307

***At any time for good cause; at end of school year for reduction-in-force.

*NOTE: Open-enrollment charter schools and districts of innovation have considerable discretion to develop their own employment arrangements. In following TEC Chapter 21 employment requirements, traditional school districts often expand beyond them. Thus it is always important to check school employment policies and follow them consistently.

Under the first option, nonrenewal and termination procedures are the same as those previously discussed for first year probationary employees. However, the procedures are quite different for the term and continuing contract options. We will discuss each in turn.

Term Contract

If hired initially on a term contract (experienced principals and teachers only) or after completing a probationary period, a professional employee may be employed on a term contract for up to five years. Term contract employees are entitled to a copy of their contracts and a copy of the district's employment policies. The school board is required to consider the most recent evaluations before making a decision not to renew an employee's term contract, if the evaluations are relevant to the decision. If the evaluations for the current year have not been completed, there is no requirement that they be considered. The commissioner has ruled that a board's violation of its own policies that themselves go beyond Chapter 21 requirements in the context of contract nonrenewal is not grounds for overturning the decision. The case involved a Dallas I.S.D. school administrator who argued that her nonrenewal was invalid because the board did not consider her most recent evaluations prior to proposing nonrenewal as required by district policy. The commissioner noted that TEC Section 21.203 requires the board to consider the most recent evaluations prior to actually making a nonrenewal decision but not before proposing to do so. There was no evidence that the board failed to do so prior to making the nonrenewal decision.[24]

Current law requires school board policies to contain reasons for contract nonrenewal, and documentation for nonrenewal must support one or more of these reasons. If the reason for nonrenewal is not listed in board policies, the board's nonrenewal decision is not valid.[25] The law specifically states that the term contract does not convey property rights beyond the term of the contract. The same is true for "stopping the roll" of a multi-year term contract that is routinely extended one year every year. Stopping the routine extension does not interfere with a property right that exists during the term of the contract. However, as we will point out later, the employee can always challenge the action as legally impermissible. Thus, it is important to base such action on job-related deficiencies and, of course, follow local district policy in making such a decision.

Under TEC Sections 21.206-21.209, the key procedural requirements for nonrenewing term contracts include:

- Notice of the proposed nonrenewal by the school board at least 10 days before the last instructional day in the school year. The notice must be delivered in the same way as the notice of nonrenewal of probationary contracts described earlier. Failure to give timely notice will result in the employee's being employed in the same professional capacity for the following school year. The commissioner of education has advised in several decisions that the reasons for the proposed nonrenewal should be stated specifically in the notice so that the employee can prepare to defend against the allegations at the nonrenewal hearing.[26]

- Right to request a hearing not later than 15 days after the notification of the proposed nonrenewal. The board must actually receive the notice within this timeframe, and the notice may not be withdrawn and then later resubmitted. The hearing is to be closed unless the employee requests an open hearing. The hearing may be before the school board or, if the board chooses, before a hearing examiner appointed by the commissioner of education. In districts with at least 5,000 students, the board may designate an outside Texas licensed attorney to conduct the hearing on behalf of the school board as its designee. The attorney provides the school board with the record of the hearing and the attorney's recommendation not later than 15 days after the hearing. The board conducts a follow-up hearing at which each party is allowed to make oral arguments. The board may obtain legal advice from another attorney at the hearing and may accept, reject, or modify the hearing attorney's recommendation.

- Right to a representative of the employee's choice.

- Right to hear evidence supporting the reason for nonrenewal, to cross-examine witnesses, to present evidence, and to receive notification of the board's decision within 15 days of the hearing.

- Right to appeal to the commissioner of education. The commissioner will not substitute his judgment for the school board unless the decision was arbitrary, capricious, unlawful, or not supported by substantial evidence.

From a documentation standpoint, the task of nonrenewing a nonprobationary term contract requires careful preparation but is not as painstaking as necessary for a mid-contract termination where a constitutionally protected property right is at stake. If the school board opts to conduct the nonrenewal hearing rather than turn the matter over to a hearing examiner or, in the case of districts with more than 5,000 students, an outside attorney, political concerns may become prominent, because the board is a political body. Further, if the employee appeals a nonrenewal decision to the commissioner of education, it will be important for the school district to show that its decision was based on substantial evidence and was not arbitrary, capricious, or unlawful. In a number of decisions, the commissioner has ruled that so long as there is "some evidence" to support nonrenewal, the board's decision will not be disturbed. As the commissioner noted as far back as 1985, substantial evidence means "more than a mere scintilla" but less than the great weight and preponderance of the evidence.[27] This is true even if only one of the reasons for nonrenewal is supported by substantial evidence.[28] The preponderance of evidence standard, however, does apply to the nonrenewal hearing before the school board.[29] This is why, from a documentation standpoint, the school board hearing often represents a high hurdle for school administrators. Further, as a political body, the school board will be more comfortable with a nonrenewal decision that is backed by convincing documentation. Thus, sufficient documentation must be assembled to convince the school board and others in the community that the nonrenewal is based on one or more reasons listed in school board policies and that the employee has been treated fairly. In case of veteran teachers with a legacy of good performance, this may require several years of careful documentation to convince the board that contract nonrenewal is in the best interest of the district. As a practical matter, we advise administrators to assemble enough documentation to convince the board that substantial evidence — taken literally — does indeed exist to support the nonrenewal recommendation.

If the commissioner decides a teacher's contract has been improperly nonrenewed, the commissioner has the authority under TEC Section 21.304 to reinstate the teacher and order back pay and employment benefits. However, the district can avoid reinstatement by paying the teacher one year's salary.

Term contracts may be terminated at any time for good cause or for financial hard times that require a reduction in personnel. "Good cause" in this section of the Code is not defined but left to the discretion of the school board. The commissioner has provided some guidance by borrowing a definition used by a Texas court of appeal: "Good cause for discharging an employee is defined as the employee's failure to perform the duties in the scope of employment that a person of ordinary prudence would have done under the same or similar circumstances. An employee's act constitutes good cause for discharge if it is inconsistent with the continued existence of the employer-employee relationship."[30] Illustrations of reasons meeting the "good cause" standard from previous Texas Commissioner of Education decisions include, but are not limited to:

- Conduct potentially harmful to students such as inappropriate sexual contact and innuendo.[31]
- Assault or threats of assault.[32]
- Significant or repeated failure to follow board policy or administrative directives.*[33]
- Misappropriation of public funds.[34]
- Serious violation of the Code of Ethics and Standard Practices for Texas Educators.**[35]
- Violating the privacy rights of students under the federal Family Educational Rights and Privacy Act (FERPA).[36]
- Discovering confidential reprimands on a computer and giving students access to them.[37]

A school board may also suspend a professional employee without pay for a period not to extend beyond the school year pending discharge of the teacher or in lieu of termination. An employee whose contract is not terminated after being suspended without pay is entitled to back pay for the period of suspension. Both procedural due process and good cause are required under state law for suspensions without pay. As noted earlier, mid-contract terminations are not to be taken lightly. The procedures are the same as those discussed above for a mid-year contract termination or suspension without pay of a probationary contract employee. Note that in the case of terminations resulting from a reduction in force, the due process procedures are streamlined by allowing the school board to conduct the hearing rather than the hearing examiner. In lieu of these actions, the school district may return a term contract employee to a probationary contract with the employee's written consent (TEC § 21.106). The employee then must serve a new probationary period as though employed by the district for the first time. Note that the employee's consent must be obtained. In order for consent to be freely given, documentation of deficiencies should be thorough and fair, and should have been communicated to the employee.

---

* This reason is often known as "insubordination," an emotionally-laden term that should be avoided where only minor infractions are involved. "Repeated failure to comply with administrative directives" is preferable.

** Because of its importance in setting forth reasons for nonrenewals and terminations in combination with school board policy provisions pertaining to ethical behavior such as DH and DH (Exhibit), we have included the current *Code of Ethics and Standard Practices for Texas Educators* in Appendix A.

As noted in TEC Section 21.212, superintendents in Texas must be employed on term contracts but are not required to serve a probationary period. The term contract provisions provide that a majority of the school board may choose not to renew the term contract of a superintendent at the end of the contract period. The board must give the superintendent written notice of proposed nonrenewal and the reasons supporting it not later than 30 days before the last day of the contract term. The school board must have a policy that lists reasons for nonrenewal of the superintendent's contract. Failure to give timely notice results in the superintendent's being reemployed in the same capacity for the next school year. The superintendent has 15 days to request a nonrenewal hearing. Nonrenewal hearing procedures, as well as mid-contract termination procedures, are the same as those for other term contract employees. If financial exigency requires a reduction in personnel, the board may amend the terms of the superintendent's contract.

Continuing Contract

In the past, the continuing contract was the chosen option for employment of teachers past the probationary period by a number of Texas public school districts. But in recent years, most districts have shifted to term contracts. Still, there are a few districts that employ teachers on continuing contracts. And a number of others that have shifted to term contracts still have teachers grandfathered in on continuing contracts. While it remains uncertain whether administrators and others classified as "teachers" can be employed on continuing contracts, TEC Section 21.155 does provide that administrators who return to teaching can be so employed.

As noted in Figure 1-2, a professional employee who is given a continuing contract in effect has a property right until the employee retires, resigns, dies, is terminated, or is placed back on a probationary contract with the employee's written consent. The continuing contract provides the most job security of any of the employment arrangements used in Texas public schools. Accordingly, the documentation burden on the school administrator is heavy for preparing for a negative employment decision. The commissioner of education has overturned terminations of continuing contract teachers in the past because the documentation has been deficient. In one case, the commissioner cautioned administrators against "moving too fast to make a negative employment decision in the face of a *continuing* contract (emphasis in original)."[38] The teacher had been employed for 15 years in the district and had an unblemished record. Based on observations over a one-year period, a new principal sought to place the continuing contract teacher back on a probationary contract, which at the time required the same due process and documentation as terminating the teacher outright. The commissioner upheld the teacher's appeal.

Statutory provisions unique to the continuing contract include the following:

- Before the contract may be terminated or the employee suspended without pay not later than the end of the school year, the employee is entitled to written notice that includes the grounds for the action. The employee then has 10 days to request a due process hearing before a hearing examiner.

- An employee who is discharged or suspended without pay for actions relating to the inability or failure to perform assigned duties is entitled upon request to a copy of each evaluation or other written memorandum relating to the fitness or conduct of the employee.

- Contract termination for reduction of personnel may only be made at the end of the school year and must be based on teacher appraisals and other criteria determined by the board.

The procedures for terminating a continuing contract employee or suspending the employee without pay until the end of the school year are the same formal proceedings before a certified hearing examiner as described above for a mid-year termination of a probationary contract or a term contract. As with these contracts, if financial exigency triggers a reduction in personnel, the hearing can be conducted by the school board. Given the presence of a property right and the formality of the hearing examiner process for all but reduction in personnel actions, careful preparation once again is essential. In lieu of terminating a continuing contract, a school district may return the employee to a probationary contract with the employee's written consent. The employee then must serve a new probationary period as though employed by the district for the first time. The same documentation implications discussed above about returning the term contract employee to probationary contract status apply here as well.

While many districts no longer give continuing contracts, they may have a number of teachers who were given continuing contracts in the past. The district's decision to no longer give continuing contracts does not cancel previously issued continuing contracts. Thus, even though more recent employees are employed on term contracts, some veteran teachers will continue to be employed on continuing contracts. Therefore, as we noted at the beginning of this section, it is important for administrators to know the type of contract a particular teacher holds and the implications for both documentation and personnel decision making.

Furloughs

Normally, an educator is employed for a minimum of 10 months service constituting 187 days. A school district may institute a furlough program providing not more than six days reduction in service and commensurate reduction in salaries during the school year if the commissioner of education certifies that the district will receive less state and local funding than was provided in 2010-2011 (TEC § § 21.4021-21.4022). The professional staff must be involved in the development of the furlough program, and a public meeting must be held at which the school board and administration discuss the district's financial situation. The board must explain how the district intends through the furlough program to limit the number of employees to be discharged or whose contracts will not be renewed. The board's decision on implementing a furlough program is final and may not be appealed. Reduction in an employee's annual salary must be equally distributed over the course of the contract. Other provisions specify that all contract personnel are subject to the same number of furlough days and that educators may not be furloughed on instructional days (75,600 minutes of instruction with one day defined as 420 minutes is required under TEC Section 25.081 unless the commissioner approves otherwise because of some calamity). Educators may not use personal, sick, or any other paid leave while on furlough. Furloughs do not constitute either a break in service or a day of service under the Teacher Retirement System of Texas. It is also important to note that another law added in 2011 permits reduction in classroom teacher salaries as a result of financial shortfall (TEC § 21.4032). This law provides that if classroom teacher salaries are reduced from the year before, the salaries of school district administrators or other professional employees are to be reduced by an equal percentage. It is important to note that furloughs and finances can be significantly affected by unpredictable events such as the COVID-19 epidemic

CONFERENCES, GRIEVANCES, AND RECORDING

Sometimes administrators are startled to see an employee bring a lawyer or other representative to a conference. How should administrators respond? Employees are entitled to legal representation at any level when presenting a grievance.[39] Under TEC Section 11.171(c), this can be done via telephone conference call. However, in two decisions, the Texas Commissioner of Education has ruled that employees do not have a similar right during employer-employee conferences or during parent-teacher conferences. In the first decision, a school custodian requested that a representative from his professional association attend a meeting with his supervisor to discuss job complaints. The commissioner concluded that the right to representation does not extend to employer-employee conferences, including those that are investigatory.[40] The second decision involved a teacher who walked out of a parent-teacher conference, maintaining that she was entitled to legal representation because of possible disciplinary action against her. The commissioner concluded that "a teacher has no right to representation outside a formal grievance proceeding."[41] Similarly, the Texas Supreme Court has ruled that public employees do not have a right under the Texas Labor Code to have a union representative at an investigatory meeting that could result in disciplinary action.[42]

While an employee may not have a legal right to representation, would an administrator be better off allowing a representative to be present? We believe so for most conferences between an administrator and an employee, provided that the representative has been advised not to play an active role in the discussion other than to represent and advise the employee. Excluding a representative, particularly the employee's spouse, only polarizes the employer-employee relationship. Sometimes lawyers or association representatives schooled in confrontational tactics will seek to place the administrator on the defensive or to take over the meeting. If this happens, the representative should be first warned and then if the behavior continues, the meeting should be recessed or adjourned. In particularly sensitive situations, administrators may want to talk first with the school human resources director or school attorney before proceeding.

Public employees have a right to present grievances concerning wages, hours, and conditions of work to their employer. These generally are processed through a series of steps set forth in board policy beginning with informal discussion and ending with a hearing before the school board. Virtually anything is grievable, including evaluations, assignments and reassignments, and even the wording of a letter of reprimand. TEC Section 11.171 requires that the school district grievance policy must permit an employee who files a grievance the right to make an audio recording of any meeting or proceeding at which the substance of the grievance is investigated or discussed. This section also specifies that an employee cannot be required to present a grievance to the employee's supervisor if the grievant believes the supervisor has violated the law in the workplace or has unlawfully harassed the employee. Such a grievance is to be presented to another supervisor.

What about audio recording conferences that don't involve grievances? There are advantages and disadvantages to audio recording. The advantage is that an accurate record is made of the conversation. The disadvantage is that the presence of the recording device tends to inhibit a frank exchange of views. It also preserves slip-of-the-tongue remarks. Rather than make an issue of it, we advise administrators to let employees audio record the conference, provided that the administrator also audio records it. That way, the administrator will not have to rely upon the employee's audio recording for an accurate portrayal of what was said. The administrator's audio recording will be the official record of the proceeding.

Is it permissible to video record a teacher's performance in the classroom over the teacher's objection? Yes. A teacher in the Houston I.S.D. tried unsuccessfully to argue that her personal privacy was violated when the supervisor videotaped her class over her objection. The state appeals court observed that "Appellant has not cited any authority, and we have found none, relating to her claim of 'involuntary videotaping' of her performance as a teacher." The court went on to note that teaching in a public classroom does not fall within the zone of protected privacy, since public school teaching is by its nature open to public view.[43] While TEC Section 26.009(b) allows audio or video recording of students in the classroom without parent permission, this provision appears to apply only if the student is giving a presentation or otherwise engaged in learning. If the audio or video recording is being done as part of teacher assessment, then parent permission for each student in the class should be obtained before doing so. Video recording can be an excellent diagnostic tool for the supervisor. To use it effectively, the supervisor should endeavor to convince the teacher of its value and solicit the teacher's cooperation. And the supervisor should make sure that the video recording encompasses more than just what the teacher is doing, given the importance of student interaction. For this reason, parent permission for each student should be obtained before video recording is done.

Can an employee use a recorded conversation against a supervisor in a hearing before the school board if the supervisor was not aware that the recording was taking place? In Texas, there is no legal prohibition on a person's recording his own conversation. Of course, by implication, the person also records the remarks of parties to the conversation.

The admissibility of recordings into a court proceeding in this state is governed by certain standards.[44] Whether surreptitious recordings can be introduced into a school board hearing is another matter. While the rules of evidence used in a court of law do not apply to administrative hearings conducted by school officials, the hearing officer or school board president may well conclude that such recordings violate principles of fairness. On the other hand, there may be some situations where a recording may provide critical evidence necessary to establish truth. Thus, whether or not the recordings should be made a part of the record is a matter to be determined by the hearing officer.

REASSIGNMENT AND RESIGNATION
Reassignment

Does a reassignment require documentation? From a due process standpoint, the answer is usually no. Most Texas administrator and teacher contracts contain a clause indicating that the employee may be assigned and reassigned at the discretion of the superintendent or the superintendent's designee. Further, the position of employment in most contracts is now stated generically: One is employed as a "teacher" or "administrator." Much litigation has occurred in the past regarding whether or not the employee is entitled to notice and a hearing before being reassigned. Federal court decisions have put the matter to rest. No property right is implicated when an employee is reassigned from one position to another as long as the salary associated with the position is not diminished.[45] The one exception may be the superintendent, who occupies a unique position in the district.[46] While no constitutionally recognized property right usually exists in the position to which one is assigned, an individual does possess a property right to receive the designated salary during the life of the contract.

Having said that, we must once again note some caveats. First, if there is no reassignment clause in the contract and the employee is assigned a specific job title, then the employee has a strong claim to having a property right to the position. For example, if Ima Scholar is hired to teach sixth grade at Sterling Middle School and there is no reassignment clause in her contract, then Ms. Scholar likely has a property right in the named position for the duration of the contract. This being the case, her reassignment would be no different from a mid-contract termination — she would be entitled to notice and hearing. And, as noted above, documentation becomes important to establish good cause for the change in employment status. Thus, it is important to make sure that employment positions are listed in generic terms.

Second, the law requires that professional employees whose term contract is renewed must be employed "in the same professional capacity" in future years. The Texas Commissioner of Education has interpreted this clause to give considerable flexibility to administrators to reassign personnel to similar professional positions (hence the generic "administrator" and "teacher" employment categories spelled out in contracts). However, in a 1993 decision upholding the reassignment of a science supervisor to an assistant high school principalship, the commissioner cautioned that "if taken to extremes, this tactic would be against public policy as expressed in the Term Contract Nonrenewal Act [this provision is now found in TEC Section 21.206(b)]."[47] In 1985 the commissioner noted that it would not be appropriate to place an administrator in a teacher's position, a counselor in the position of nurse, or a nurse in the position of librarian. "In other instances, the validity of a particular placement might not be so clear. For example, a placement might be to another position within the same professional capacity (e.g., administrator), but nevertheless be invalid (e.g., from superintendent to assistant elementary principal). Factors to be considered in determining the validity of such a placement include, but are not necessarily limited to, differences in authority, duties, and salary."[48]

Third, employees may not be reassigned for impermissible reasons. As will be explained in the final section of this chapter, impermissible reasons include illegal discrimination and retaliation for the exercise of constitutional rights.

A Case-In-Point

In *Fife v. Curlee* a secretary who was employed on an at-will basis challenged her reassignment to a job duplicating and laminating documents after she removed her daughter from public school and enrolled the child in an all-white private school. Since the U.S. Supreme Court long ago recognized the constitutional right of all parents to choose a nonpublic school for their children, the U. S. Court of Appeals for the Fifth Circuit held that the reassignment amounted to retaliation for the exercise of a constitutional right. The appeals court sent the case back to the trial court for a determination of appropriate remedies.[49]

Employees always have a right to challenge the motives behind their reassignments by pursuing a grievance or by filing employment discrimination claims and lawsuits. Thus, it behooves administrators to have sufficient documentation of job-related deficiencies to provide an acceptable explanation for a reassignment.

Resignation

The answer to every school administrator's prayer in making difficult personnel decisions is a voluntary resignation. Resignations work to everyone's benefit. For the school district, they eliminate costly due process procedures. For the employee, they help pave the way to a new position. For both the administrator and the employee, they avoid the emotional toll of an adversary proceeding.

For each of the three employment options illustrated in Figure 1-2, Texas law provides that professional employees may resign without penalty at the end of the school year by filing a written resignation with the school board or its designee no later than 45 days before the first day of instruction of the following year or at any other time with the school district's permission (TEC § § 21.105, 21.160, and 21.210). It is not possible, however, to include a resignation requirement as part of these contracts.[50]

Under these provisions, a written resignation mailed by certified or registered mail to the school board president or the board's designee at the school district's post office address is considered filed at the time of mailing. This means that it is self-executing and no acceptance is required. As the commissioner has noted, "Because acceptance is automatic, once filed, a resignation cannot be withdrawn before acceptance."[51] Contract sanctions may be imposed by the State Board for Educator Certification for employees who do not comply with these statutory resignation provisions.

For resignations that do not fall within the 45-day self-executing period, problems can arise if not handled carefully. Here are some simple recommendations for making sure they are:

- Consider having a witness present when discussing the option of resigning. A witness will help curtail employee claims later on that you threatened recrimination if the employee did not resign.

- If the employee wants to bring an attorney or other representative to the meeting, consult with the human resources director or superintendent regarding district practice. Since you are interested in treating the employee fairly, having a representative present should not compromise the value of the meeting, provided that you make clear to the representative that he or she is there at your discretion and that his or her role is to advise and represent the employee. The representative should not be allowed to question you or attempt to take over the meeting. In particularly sensitive cases, the school attorney should be consulted.

- Advise the employee about applicable school district grievance and due process procedures. Full disclosure of the rights the employee will relinquish by resigning will help demonstrate your commitment to fair play.

- Avoid coercion in discussing resignation. In some cases, you may be acting more like a counselor than an administrator as you help the employee weigh the pros and cons of resigning. On the other hand, do not be afraid to tell the employee in a non-threatening manner that you are sincere about following through on your recommendation of contract nonrenewal or termination. If you have done a careful job of documentation, the employee will be well aware of the basis for your intentions and will know that you are serious. **NOTE:** If you are considering "sweetening the pot" by telling the employee you will not formalize your termination recommendation or will write a favorable recommendation if the employee resigns, we strongly advise that you consult the human resources director or school district attorney first for the reasons described below.

- Require that the employee submit a written resignation by a certain date. That way, you will keep your own options open. For example, if the 10-day notice of proposed nonrenewal for a term contract employee is near, you can avoid holding off past the date in hopes the employee might submit a resignation.

- Have the employee submit the resignation to the governing board or to a person authorized by the board to receive it and to acknowledge its receipt.[52] Doing so will avoid a time lag between the submission and its official acceptance, in case the employee has second thoughts and decides to withdraw the resignation.

In addition, State Board for Educator Certification (SBEC) rules in effect in 2020 require a school superintendent or director of an open enrollment charter school, private school, regional service center, or shared services arrangement to report within seven business days to TEA staff whenever a certified employee resigns or the employee's contract is terminated in the face of evidence of misconduct with students, illegal drug involvement, illegal use of school property or funds, alteration of a certificate, or commission of a crime on school property or at a school event (19 Tex. Admin. Code § 249.14(d)). Before accepting the employee's resignation, the school administrator must notify the employee of this requirement and of the possibility that sanctions may be taken against the employee's certificate. It should be noted that employees may be dismissed for failure to disclose to SBEC or the district, open-enrollment charter school, private school, regional education service center, or shared services arrangement their conviction of a felony or misdemeanor involving moral turpitude (TEC § 22.085).

Depending upon the situation, a resignation can be the least painful way to resolve a difficult employment situation. However bullying an employee into resigning or making the job so difficult that the employee gets disgruntled and quits could work against you. The employee may decide to file a grievance or a lawsuit claiming the resignation was forced. In 1995 the commissioner of education was faced with appeals by a teacher and by a counselor who contended that their resignations resulted from duress, undue influence, or misrepresentation by the principal.[53] *Duress* is evident when an administrator (1) threatens to do something he has no legal right to do and (2) engages in fraud or deception that undermines the free will of the employee. *Undue influence* occurs when the employee's free will is so compromised that the employee's decision reflects the choice of the administrator who is exerting the influence. *Misrepresentation* involves a material misstatement that (1) the administrator either knew to be false or made without knowledge of its truth and (2) served as the basis for the employee's decision. Because the facts in the cases established that both the teacher and counselor had resigned of their own free will in connection with the falsification of a leave form, the commissioner rejected their appeals. In the case involving the school counselor, the counselor contended that the principal had threatened to revoke her certificate, terminate her contract, or put unfavorable comments in her file if she did not resign. Based on the testimony at the hearing, however, the commissioner chose not to believe the counselor. Had a witness been present when resignation was discussed, the matter may never have come up.[54]

At the extreme, a forced resignation may constitute "constructive discharge," rendering the employer liable for the illegal conduct leading to the discharge. A constructive discharge occurs when administrators make the job so uncomfortable that the reasonable employee has no choice but to resign.[55] While the employee's burden to prove such a case is demanding, constructive discharge cases increasingly are being litigated in federal courts. The second federal appeals court decision discussed on p. 1-1 involving the 65-year-old teacher whose classroom was visited repeatedly by administrators is a good example of a constructive discharge case.

As we noted earlier, an offer of resignation other than a self-executing one discussed at the start of this section becomes official when it is submitted to the person or persons designated by the governing board to receive it and that person acknowledges its acceptance. Normally, this is the superintendent and/or the human resources director. Occasionally, an employee will have second thoughts after submitting a resignation and will attempt to rescind it. Such was the case with a special education teacher in the San Benito Consolidated Independent School District in 1994.[56] After her hand-delivered resignation was forwarded to the superintendent, the superintendent sent the teacher a letter accepting the resignation. The next day, the teacher hand-delivered a letter to the superintendent rescinding the resignation. But it was too late. The so-called "mailbox rule" had gone into effect. Under the "mailbox rule," the superintendent's acceptance of the teacher's resignation became effective as soon as he deposited the acceptance letter in the mailbox. When the superintendent accepted the resignation by sending his letter of acknowledgement, a new agreement between the teacher and the district to sever the employment relation came into existence. Until this time, the teacher was free to revoke her resignation decision. In Texas, the "mailbox rule" does not apply unless the party submitting the resignation expressly or impliedly authorizes the use of the postal system for its acceptance. The teacher had not used the mail system to send her letter of resignation or her subsequent revocation. However, she had acknowledged that the mail system was a proper form for communication, because in her resignation letter she had implicitly authorized the superintendent to communicate through the mails by requesting that he forward her final check to her home address.

In a later decision, the commissioner elaborated on the mailbox rule.[57] The school district argued that the commissioner didn't have jurisdiction over the case, because the teacher had not filed an appeal with the commissioner within the requisite 20 days after receiving notice of contract nonrenewal from the district. The district asserted that the time line began when the notification was mailed on May 5, 2005. However, the teacher didn't receive the notice until May 18. If the notice is considered given on May 5 when mailed, the teacher had exceeded the 20 days by not filing her appeal until June 2. The commissioner noted an exception to the mailbox rule in the Texas Rules of Civil Procedure. If notice is not received within three days of deposit in the mail, then a court may extend the time line. In this case, because the notification was not received within three days of mailing, the time line for the teacher to file her appeal should have been extended to June 7, 20 days after she actually received the notice on May 18. Because the teacher filed her appeal on June 2, the time line to appeal was met. In making this decision, the commissioner assumed that the Texas Rule of Civil Procedure mailbox rule applies to nonrenewal appeals filed before his office. This decision illustrates how tricky the procedures involving resignations are. For this reason, school administrators once again are advised to work closely with the school district's human resources office.

In another decision, the commissioner ruled in favor of a teacher who resigned, then withdrew the offer of resignation before receiving notice of its acceptance.[58] The superintendent's designee dated the acceptance letter several days after receiving the teacher's hand-delivered letter of resignation. However, the teacher didn't receive that letter until after she formally rescinded her resignation. The envelope containing the acceptance letter had a postage meter marking showing that it was mailed after the teacher had submitted her rescission. What mattered in this case was not the date on the acceptance letter but the postage meter date on the envelope containing it. The commissioner ordered the district to pay the teacher the compensation she should have received for the school year.

A WORD ABOUT EMPLOYEE REFERENCES

Administrators are often uncertain how to respond to inquiries about former employees. They are concerned that a frank reply in writing or over the telephone might subject them to a defamation lawsuit. The law conveys a qualified privilege to employers with respect to employee decision making. Article 5206 of Texas Civil Statutes states that "Any written statement of cause of discharge, if true, when made by such agent, company or corporation, shall never be used as the cause of an action for libel, either civil or criminal, against the agent, company or corporation furnishing same." TEC Section 22.0511(a) shields school professional employees from liability from damage suits in most situations. Section 101.051 of the Texas Civil Practices and Remedies Code does the same for school districts. In 1991 a Texas appeals court upheld the grant of immunity for a school administrator under TEC Section 22.0511(a) [then codified as TEC Section 21.912(b)], noting that "a letter of reference written by a professional supervisor of a public school merely expressing his professional *opinion* on an employee's work performance under his supervision is an act within the scope of the employee's duties with the school district and is, consequently, not subject to libel action by virtue of section 21.912(b) unless such statements are false statement of *fact* or are libelous *per se*."[59] In 1999, the Texas Legislature added a provision to the Labor Code shielding employers from civil liability or damages for providing job performance information to prospective employers about current or former employees, unless at the time of disclosure the employer knew the information to be false or made the disclosure with malice or with reckless disregard of its truth or falsity (Texas Labor Code § 103.004). Job performance information can encompass attendance, attitudes, effort, knowledge, behaviors, and skills.

Of course, a former employee can always file a defamation lawsuit against an administrator, in which case the latter will be able to assert the various immunity defenses in court. The best protection against defamation lawsuits in the context of employment references is (1) to stick to the truth and (2) to secure the employee's permission to release the information before the employee leaves the district by signing a reference release form. An employee who authorizes a former employer to release employment information to prospective employers is less likely to file a lawsuit later on.

AVOIDING IMPERMISSIBLE REASONS FOR EMPLOYMENT DECISIONS

On several occasions we have mentioned the importance of basing employment decisions on reasons that are legitimately related to the interests of the school district or charter school and to job-related behavior. For the most part, these reasons will be found in board policies. School administrators must avoid basing negative employment decisions on impermissible reasons. Impermissible reasons generally fall into two categories: (1) retaliation for the exercise of constitutional rights and (2) illegal discrimination. We briefly discuss both in turn. A detailed discussion can be found in Walsh, Maniotis, and Kemerer's *The Educator's Guide to Texas School Law.*

Constitutionally protected conduct encompasses a number of activities including, but not limited to:

- Speaking on matters of public concern[60]
- Sending a child to a private school[61]
- Participating in the activities of a political party[62]
- Participating in unions and professional associations[63]
- Having a child out of wedlock[64]

Employees often allege that one or more of these rights are implicated in negative employment decisions. Administrators should be careful that the documentation about the employee does not support such allegations.

Free Speech

The most prevalent constitutional challenge to a nonrenewal or termination is retaliation for the exercise of free speech. Public employees, including those who are employed at-will, enjoy broad protection for expression in their role as citizens on matters of public interest, so long as (1) the statements are not made recklessly or with knowledge of their falsity, and (2) the statements do not impede either the school's functioning or the employee's performance. Comments made in the employee's role as a citizen that concern the community interest are constitutionally protected under the First Amendment to the U.S. Constitution. These might include a speech made to the PTA about deficiencies in the bilingual education program, a presentation to the school board about alleged discriminatory hiring practices by principals, or statements on social media about a lack of student discipline at the high school. However, if the employee makes the same comments while on the job, there is no constitutional protection.[65] Thus, a school human resources director who speaks out to the superintendent's cabinet about discriminatory hiring practices of a school principal may not be entitled to constitutional protection. Employee expression that relates to the employee's own working conditions also may not be constitutionally protected.[66] We will explore communication issues in more detail in Chapter 5. Unfortunately, it is often difficult to distinguish an employee's expression as a citizen on matters of public concern from expression as an employee concerning working conditions. Most educators, school board members, and citizens do not understand the difference. Consequently, any employment decision even partially related to free speech is likely to trigger an outcry about censorship and curtailment of protected rights. For this reason, it is usually best to try to avoid First Amendment issues altogether in documentation.

If a disgruntled employee produces evidence that the negative employment decision was made at least partially in retaliation for the exercise of protected rights, will the school likely lose? Not necessarily. Under a 1977 U.S. Supreme Court decision, if the administration *can document other legitimate reasons justifying the employment decision that are unrelated to the employee's exercise of the constitutional right,* then the fact that a constitutional right was substantially implicated may not make any difference.[67]

Academic Freedom

A final consideration involving protected rights of expression concerns a teacher's right to academic freedom in the classroom. How much academic freedom does a public school teacher have in that setting? Despite frequent assertions to the contrary, the law protects that right only minimally. In 1980, the Fifth Circuit held that teachers do have a right to lead classroom discussion on controversial topics and cannot be penalized for doing so unless the teacher's effectiveness to teach has been undermined.[68] However, this precedent would not support a teacher who deviates from the established curriculum.[69] An example would be an algebra teacher leading an extending classroom discussion on political issues unrelated to algebra. Texas Education Code § 28.0022 imposes certain instructional requirements and prohibitions. For example, a teacher may not be compelled to discuss a widely debated and currently controversial issue of public policy or social affairs and, if they do, they must do so objectively and in a manner free from political bias. Teachers cannot require, as part of a course, that students engage in lobbying and advocacy activities. Among other things, teachers are also prohibited from certain discussions regarding individuals' race or sex.

The 88th Legislature provided immunity under Education Code § 22.05125 from disciplinary proceedings for an allegation that the teacher violated Section 28.0022, the Establishment Clause of the First Amendment of the United States Constitution, or a related state or federal law. Immunity applies if the teacher used only instructional material included on the list of approved instructional material maintained by the State Board of Education under Section 31.022 and adopted by the district; and the allegation does not dispute that the teacher delivered instruction from instructional material with fidelity.

While classroom discussion is protected under the rubric of academic freedom, other teacher activities are not. Included among them are the awarding of grades, the use of teaching techniques not approved by the school board, and the use of profanity for motivational purposes.[70]

Federal Civil Rights

Employment decisions that violate the nation's civil rights laws are also impermissible. Here in capsule form are the civil rights laws most prominently related to employment:

Race. 42 U.S.C. Section 1981 accords all persons the right to make and enforce contracts free from racial discrimination. The statute also prohibits discrimination occurring during the contract term. Penalties include both injunctive relief and compensatory damages.

Race, Religion, Sex. Title VII of the 1964 Civil Rights Act prohibits discrimination on the basis of race, color, religion, sex (sexual orientation is included) or national origin in all aspects of public and aprivate employment. In addition to equitable relief such as back pay and reinstatement, the law allows monetary damages for intentional discrimination.

Disabilities. The Americans with Disabilities Act of 1990 (ADA) accords persons with disabilities meaningful access to the programs of a public or private entity. In conjunction with Section 504 of the Rehabilitation Act of 1973, the ADA prohibits employment discrimination against persons with disabilities and requires employers to make reasonable accommodation for persons with disabilities, once it is determined the person can perform the job. Penalties are similar to those for Title VII.

Age. The Age Discrimination in Employment Act (ADEA) prohibits discrimination in employment against employees age 40 and over unless there is a bona fide occupational qualification reasonably necessary to carry out job responsibilities (e.g., airline pilots). Penalties are similar to those for Title VII.

Administrators need to be sensitive to the protections given employees under these and other federal statutes and should avoid inadvertently documenting behavior that is protected by statutory provisions. Thus, for example, it would not be appropriate to document that a teacher's age was a major reason for removing the teacher as the cheerleader sponsor. Employees who advocate on behalf of other employees whose rights have been violated under these laws also are likely to be protected from retaliation.[71]

Texas Law

Finally, some employee activities are protected under Texas law and cannot serve as the basis for a negative employment decision. As we discussed earlier, public employees have the right to file a grievance and to be free from retaliation for doing so. Three other important activities protected by state law are (1) refusal to undertake an illegal act, (2) the reporting of suspected wrongdoing ("whistle-blowing"), and (3) the filing of workers' compensation claims. The first situation might occur when an employee refuses to undertake repairs to the superintendent's house or refuses to bury toxic chemicals on the school premises. The Texas Supreme Court has ruled that such refusal cannot be the basis for a termination.[72]

The Texas Whistleblower Act protects an employee from adverse employment action for reporting in good faith a violation or suspected violation of law to appropriate law enforcement personnel or to someone within the school district that the employee believes is responsible for enforcing the law allegedly violated (Texas Government Code § 554.002). School administrators must avoid the temptation to label these employees "malcontents" or "disloyal team players" or to retaliate against them because of the report.

One important provision of the workers' compensation statute prohibits employers from retaliating against an employee who files a compensation claim. Thus, school administrators must exercise great caution in making negative employment decisions about employees who do so.

Finally, there are several important Texas laws that affect the classroom documentation process beyond those we have already reviewed. Among them is Section 28.0027 of the Texas Education Code that restricts a school district from penalizing a teacher who does not follow the pacing of recommended or designated instructional materials or the pacing of the recommended or designated scope and sequence for a curriculum subject based on the teacher's determination that more or less time is needed to achieve student proficiency. For the teacher to be rated deficient in this context there must be classroom observational data or substantial third-party documentation. Similarly, TEC Section 21.351 requires the commissioner of education to establish rules that ensure a teacher is not given a deficiency rating simply because of the number of student disciplinary referrals or reports by the teacher of student classroom misbehavior. Again, there must be documented evidence to show the teacher is deficient in classroom management based on classroom observation or a substantiated report.

The use of physical force in student discipline is also a matter of concern. Under Texas Penal Code Section 9.62, professional employees may use reasonable physical force to further the purposes for which a teacher is assigned. In a 2019 decision, the commissioner of education noted that "Under Texas Education Code Section 22.0512, when a professional employee uses reasonable force, a district cannot take disciplinary action against the employee because he was directed by an administrator not to use force."[73]

While TEC Section 37.0011 permits school districts to allow corporal punishment with parent permission, Section 37.0023 sets forth a long list of impermissible aversive techniques that intentionally inflict significant physical or emotional discomfort and pain on students. Included among them are use of electrical shock, use of pressure points or joint locks, denial of access to a restroom, impairment of breathing, tying a student to a stationary object while the student is sitting or standing, and excessive timeout that precludes the student from participation and progressing appropriately in the required curriculum or, if appropriate, the student's individualized education program (IEP).

SUMMARY

In this chapter, we have sketched the major features of the legal framework within which documentation takes place. It should be clear that documentation is significantly influenced by federal and state statutes, Texas Commissioner of Education decisions, and court rulings. When all is said and done, the best advice is to know employment law and to follow the Golden Rule. That advice, coupled with common sense, will go a long way to assure that your employment decisions are fair and will be upheld if challenged. Now we turn in the next chapter to examine the basic principles of documentation and how they apply in the context of both professional and auxiliary school personnel.

REFERENCES

1. *Lloyd v. Georgia Gulf Corp.*, 961 F.2d 1190, 1195 (5th Cir. 1992); *Dietz v. Zodiac Seats US LLC*, 2020 WL 867977 (E.D. Tex. 2020)..
2. *Lee v. Rapid City Area School District No. 51-4,* 981 F.2d 316 (8th Cir. 1992).
3. An interesting discussion about the hearsay matter arose in a 2015 decision involving a teacher in the Los Fresnos C.I.S.D. who maintained, among other things, that his contract nonrenewal was based on hearsay evidence. He made this claim because, while the district relied on a number of written and signed student statements that were submitted to the school board during the nonrenewal hearing, the students were not called to testify. The teacher did testify at the hearing but called no witnesses. The Texas court of appeals pointed out that while the Texas Rules of Evidence do not apply to a nonrenewal hearing conducted by a school board (they do if the hearing is conducted by a hearing examiner), the board was free to admit and consider the written student statements at the hearing. Here, the student statements were obtained pursuant to two independent investigations into complaints about the teacher's classroom conduct. While the students were not called to testify by school officials, the teacher could have done so, could have called upon other students to rebut the statements, or otherwise demonstrated that the statements were false. He did not do so. Thus the hearsay claim was rejected and the nonrenewal decision upheld. *Los Fresnos C.I.S.D. v. Vazquez,* 481 S.W.3d 742 (Tex. App.– Austin 2015 , no pet).
4. *Dunlap v. Breckenridge I.S.D.*, Dkt. No. 34-R1-692 (Comm'r Educ. 1996). In reaching the decision, the commissioner referenced a well-known prior decision in which he had noted that adverse community or parental "perceptions" is an illegal reason for contract nonrenewal when the employee has excellent evaluations. Noting that when the evidence at the local hearing does not support the specific reason given the teacher for the nonrenewal, the commissioner may substitute his judgment for that the school board and decide in favor of the teacher. *Seifert v. Lingleville I.S.D.*, Dkt. No. 174- R1a-782 (Comm'r Educ. 1983). Later, the Texas Supreme Court affirmed the commissioner's conclu- sion but on the grounds that "community feeling of incompetence" was not one of the reasons listed in the district's policies for contract nonrenewal. Since the law requires that districts must provide employees with the reasons for the proposed contract nonrenewal, Seifert had not received fair notice. The high court avoided considering whether "community feeling of incompetence" might be a valid reason to support contract nonrenewal. *Seifert v. Lingleville I.S.D.*, 692 S.W.2d 461 (Tex. 1985).
5. *Carnot v. North East I.S.D.*, Dkt. No. 066-R1-605 (Comm'r Educ. 2005).
6. *Flores v. Morgan Hill Unified School District*, 324 F.3d 1130 (9th Cir. 2011). A noteworthy decision involving deliberate indifference in the context of employee sexual abuse of a Texas public school student over several years is *Doe v. Taylor I.S.D.,* 15 F.3d 443 (5th Cir.) (en banc), cert. denied sub nom *Caplinger v. Doe,* 113 U.S. 980 (1994). In this decision, the student sued the superintendent and the principal for ineffective supervision that resulted in repeated and continuing violation of her bodily integrity that is protected by the due process clause of the 14th Amendment. The Fifth Circuit dismissed the case against the superintendent but sent the case against the principal back to the lower court for trial, because there was evidence to suggest that the principal might not have investigated the matter properly. The case against the principal was eventually settled.
7. *Webster v. Alief I.S.D.,* Dkt. No. 288-R3-789 (Comm'r Educ. 1991).

8. *Abbott v. North East I.S.D.*, 212 S.W.2d 364 (Tex. App. – Austin, 2006).
9. *Parker v. Dallas I.S.D.*, Dkt. No. 008-R10-10-2014 (Comm'r Educ. 2015).
10. *Madden v. Dallas I.S.D.*, Dkt. No. 002-R10-2012 (Comm'r Educ. 2015). See also *Camara v. Dallas I.S.D.*, Dkt. No. 003-R10-2012 (Comm'r Educ. 2015).
11. See, for example, *Etzel v. Galveston I.S.D.*, Dkt. No. 231-R9-885 (Comm'r Educ. 1987); *Falvey v. Alief I.S.D.*, Dkt. No. 113-R3-1185 (Comm'r Educ. 1987).
12. *Navarro v. Ysleta I.S.D.*, Dkt. No. 007-R8-988 (Comm'r Educ. 1994). In this case, the commissioner originally had issued a decision that a school board is not the appropriate body to second-guess the conclusions of a trained appraiser. The decision was appealed to a state district court judge in Austin who ruled that the school may do so if the appraiser's decision was "clearly erroneous or an abuse of discretion." The judge sent the case back to the commissioner for reconsideration. Using this standard, the commissioner ruled that the Ysleta school board had no basis for overruling the assistant principal's denial of credit to a teacher on an evaluation. The commissioner granted the assistant principal's appeal.
13. *Sitzler v. Babers*, Dkt. No. 092-PPC-1191 (Comm'r Educ. 1992). In 1996 the commissioner overturned the decision of a school board to nonrenew the contract of a probationary teacher who complained through memos and the school's grievance system about various working conditions. The school board president had sent a letter to the teacher in which he indicated that her filing a number of grievances was a factor in the nonrenewal decision. The commissioner concluded that the school board failed to produce evidence to rebut the teacher's claim of retaliation for filing grievances. *Ostroff v. Manor I.S.D.*, Dkt. No. 320-R2-694 (Comm'r Educ. 1996).
14. *Anderson v. Tyler I.S.D.*, Dkt. No. 048-R1-0508 (Comm'r Educ. 2008). The commissioner also has observed that while third-party documentation cannot be used in the appraisal process if it has not been shared with the teacher in a timely manner, the appraisal rules do not prohibit the use of such documentation for other purposes. *Taylor v. Wichita Falls I.S.D.*, Dkt. No. 069-R10-601 (Comm'r Educ. 2002).
15. *Goodfriend v. Houston I.S.D.*, Dkt. No. 079-R2-703 (Comm'r Educ. 2003).
16. *Federal Express v. Dutschmann*, 846 S.W.2d 282 (Tex. 1993); *Cook v. Dayton I.S.D.*, Dkt. No. 133-R8-189 (Comm'r Educ. 1993); *Strother v. Columbia-Brazoria I.S.D.*, 839 F.Supp. 459 (S.D. Tex. 1993), aff'd without opinion, 32 F.3d 565 (5th Cir. 1994).
17. *Montgomery County Hospital District v. Brown*, 965 S.W.2d 501 (Tex. 1998). In *Brown* the Texas Supreme Court ruled that at-will status cannot be altered by oral assurances of discharge for good cause only, absent a definite stated intent to be bound not to dismiss the employee except under specific circumstances and absent an agreement on what would encompass good reason or good cause for termination.
18. *Salinas v. Roma I.S.D.*, Dkt. No. 058-R3-1196 (Comm'r Educ. 1997).
19. *Houston v. Nelson*, 147 S.W.3d 589 (Tex. App. – Corpus Christi-Edinburg, 2004).
20. *Ferguson v. Thomas*, 430 F.2d 852 (5th Cir. 1970)1.); *Houston Federation of Teachers 2415 v. Houston Indep. Sch. Dist.*, 251 F.Supp.3d 1168 (S.D. Tex 2017).
21. *Young v. Lipan I.S.D.*, Dkt. No. 102-R1-496 (Comm'r Educ. 1996).
22. *Kenyon v. Round Rock I.S.D.*, Dkt. No. 040-R1-08-2019 (Comm'r Educ. 2019).
23. *Almeyda v. Alief I.S.D.*, Dkt. No. 086-R2-0810 (Comm'r Educ. 2012).
24. *Strickland v. Dallas I.S.D.*, Dkt. No. 075-R1-0808 (Comm'r Educ. 2008).
25. *King v. Big Sandy I.S.D.*, Dkt. No. 006-R1-501 (Comm'r Educ. 2001).
26. *Lowry v. Brooksmith I.S.D.*, Dkt. No. 054-R1-0509 (Comm'r Educ. 2009). In a 1998 decision the commissioner commented that a notice of proposed nonrenewal worded to say "Deficiencies as pointed out in observation reports, appraisals or evaluations, supplemental memoranda, or other communications" is too broad to be very meaningful. *Kopycinski v. Fort Bend I.S.D.*, Dkt. No. 111-R1-598 (Comm'r Educ. 1998).
27. *Heger v. Frisco I.S.D.*, Dkt. No. 120-R1a-584 (Comm'r Educ. 1985).
28. *Black v. Hart I.S.D.*, Dkt. No. 087-R1-0612 (Comm'r Educ. 2012). The commissioner also has ruled that completion of an intervention plan does not insulate a teacher from contract nonrenewal, especially when deficiencies continue as evidenced in subsequent walkthroughs. *Kellogg v. Sinton I.S.D.*, Dkt. No. 077-R1-07-2014 (Comm'r Educ. 2014).

29. *Rodgers v. Edinburg Consolidated I.S.D.*, Dkt. No. 171-R1-898 (Comm'r Educ. 1998). See also *Whitaker v. Moses*, 40 S.W.3d 176 (Tex. App. - Texarkana 2001).
30. *Tave v. Dallas I.S.D.*, Dkt. No. 067-R2-501 (Comm'r Educ. 2001).
31. *Taplin v. Fort Worth I.S.D.*, Dkt. No. 276-R2-887 (Comm'r Educ. 1989); *Brown v. Crosby I.S.D.*, Dkt. No. 181- R2-781 (Comm'r Educ. 1983).
32. *Martinez v. Crosbyton I.S.D.*, Dkt. No. 079-R2-284 (Comm'r Educ. 1985); *Mitchell v. Pewitt I.S.D.*, Dkt. No. 186-R2-785 (Comm'r Educ. 1987).
33. *Jones v. Northside I.S.D.*, Dkt. No. 015-R2-1084 (Comm'r Educ. 1987).
34. *Brosette v. Wilmer-Hutchins I.S.D.*, Dkt. No. 190-R2-782 (Comm'r Educ. 1984).
35. *Green v. Irving I.S.D.*, Dkt. No. 042-R2-1086 (Comm'r Educ. 1988).
36. *McGilvray v. Boyd I.S.D.*, Dkt. No. 185-R2-597 (Comm'r Educ. 1996).
37. *Tave v. Dallas I.S.D.*, Dkt. No. 067-R2-501 (Comm'r Educ. 2001).
38. *Tyler v. Galveston I.S.D.*, Dkt. No. 132-R1b-783 (Comm'r Educ. 1984). See also *Richter v. Northside I.S.D.*, Dkt. No. 215-R3-885 (Comm'r Educ. 1986) and *McRuiz v. Cleburne I.S.D.*, Dkt. No. 047-R2-1087 (Comm'r Educ. 1990).
39. *Lubbock Professional Firefighters v. City of Lubbock*, 742 S.W.2d 413 (Tex. App. - Amarillo 1987).
40. *Arce v. Ysleta I.S.D.*, Dkt. No. 317-R8-692 (Comm'r Educ. 1994).
41. *Thrower v. Arlington I.S.D.*, Dkt. No. 190-R10-790 (Comm'r Educ. 1991).
42. *City of Round Rock v. Rodriguez*, 399 S.W.3d 130 (Tex. 2013).
43. *Roberts v. Houston I.S.D.*, 788 S.W.2d 107 (Tex. App. – Houston [1st Dist.] 1990, writ denied).
44. *Seymour v. Gillespie,* 608 S.W.2d 897 (Tex. 1990).
45. A leading case is *Jett v. Dallas I.S.D.*, 798 F.2d 748 (5th Cir.), aff'd in part, 491 U.S. 701 (1989). Further, it is not necessary to advance reasons for the reassignment unless required by district policy or requested to do so during an appeal process. *Schneider et al. v. San Antonio I.S.D.*, Dkt. No. 356-R10-794 (Comm'r Educ. 1997).
46. *Board of Trustees of Crystal City I.S.D. v. Briggs,* 486 S.W.2d 829 (Tex. Civ. App. - Beaumont 1972, writ ref'd n.r.e.).
47. *Carpenter v. Wichita Falls I.S.D.*, Dtk. No. 247-R3-491 (Comm'r Educ. 1993).
48. *Barich v. San Felipe-Del Rio C.I.S.D.*, Dkt. No. 117-R1a-484 (Comm'r Educ. 1985). For a full discussion of reassignments along with references to numerous commissioner decisions following the seminal *Barich* decision, see *Gustafson v. Canutillo I.S.D.*, 113-R10-0812 (Comm'r Educ. 2014). In 2017, the Court of Appeals in Austin applied the commissioner's *Barich* rationale in that the assignment of a principal at an intermediate school to assistant principal at a high school to improve the performance of the latter falls within the same professional capacity. *Jenkins v. Crosby Independent School District,* 537 S.W.3d 142 (Tex. App. – Austin 2017). What is important about these decisions is for supervisors to have a job-related justification for a reassignment.
49. *Fyfe v. Curlee*, 902 F.2d 401 (5th Cir. 1990), cert. denied sub nom *Curlee v. Fyfe*, 498 U.S.940 (1990).
50. *Helkey v. Judson I.S.D.*, Dkt. No. 024-R10-1001 (Comm'r Educ. 2014).
51. *Fantroy v. Dallas I.S.D.*, Dkt. No. 034-R8-0206 (Comm'r Educ. 2009).
52. *Harris v. Fort Bend I.S.D.*, Dkt. No. 028-R10-1011 (Comm'r Educ. 2014). In this case a principal's resignation during the school year was accepted by the human resources director. But the school board had not designated the director to accept resignations. The board had only designated the superintendent with this authority, and the commissioner noted that the superintendent cannot subdelegate that authority to someone else in the district. Thus, when the principal withdrew her resignation, this could be done because, while it had been received, it had not been officially accepted.
53. *Lazenby v. Spring Branch I.S.D.*, Dkt. No. 144-R8-193 (Comm'r Educ. 1995); *Hysell v. Spring Branch I.S.D.*, Dkt. No. 113-R8-1292 (Comm'r Educ. 1995).
54. *Hysell v. Spring Branch I.S.D.*, Dkt. No. 113-R8-1292 (Comm'r Educ. 1995).
55. *Woods v. Sheldon I.S.D.*, 232 Fed.Appx. 385 (5th Cir. 2007). In this unreported ruling, the Fifth Circuit identified six possible bases for a constructive discharge claim related to forced resignation, retirement, or employment on less favorable terms: (1) a demotion; (2) a salary reduction; (3) a reduction in job responsibilities; (4) reassignment to menial work; (5) reassignment to work under a younger supervisor; or (6) badgering, harassment, or humiliation by the employer. An unreported ruling means that it has no value as judicial precedent but is instructive. In the documentation context, the lesson from this ruling is to have job-related deficiencies clearly documented and revealed to the employee so that any negative decision is based on them.

56. *Cantu v. Central Education Agency,* 884 S.W.2d 565 (Tex. App.- Austin 1994).
57. *Carnot v. North East I.S.D.,* Dkt. No. 066-R1-605 (Comm'r Educ. 2005).
58. *Chilton v. Alvin I.S.D.,* Dkt. No. 031-R10-0107 (Comm'r Educ. 2009).
59. *Hammond v. Katy I.S.D.,* 821 S.W.2d 174 (Tex. App. - Houston [14th Dist.] 1991).
60. *Pickering v. Board of Education,* 391 U.S. 563 (1968).
61. *Pierce v. Society of Sisters,* 268 U.S. 510 (1925).
62. *Alaniz v. San Isidro I.S.D.,* 742 F.2d 207 (5th Cir. 1984).
63. *Professional Association of College Administrators v. El Paso Community College.* 730 F.2d 258 (5th Cir. 1984).
64. *Avery v. Homewood City Board of Education,* 674 F.2d 337 (5th Cir. 1982). Living together out of wedlock known as cohabitation raises similar rights of privacy and should be avoided as grounds for a negative employment decision.
65. *Garcetti v. Ceballos,* 126 S.Ct. 1951 (2006). The U.S. Supreme Court did recognize in this 5-to-4 ruling that speech related to scholarship or teaching made on the job may be constitutionally protected. However, it is likely that the majority was referring to academic freedom at the postsecondary level, because academic freedom for public school teachers enjoys little constitutional protection. The majority also recognized that a public employer cannot make job descriptions so broad that everything employees say falls within official duties.
66. *Connick v. Myers,* 461 U.S. 138 (1983). It is important to note that under Article I, § 8 of the Texas Constitution, free speech rights appear to be broader than under the U. S. Constitution. The Texas Supreme Court ruled as much in *Davenport v. Garcia,* 834 S.W.2d 4 (Tex. 1992). That ruling convinced a state district court in an appeal from a decision by the Texas Commissioner of Education to conclude that under Article I, § 8, even if speech is not on a topic of public concern, such speech is protected if it was invited, solicited, or encouraged by a governmental employer. Upon rehearing, the commissioner applied this rule of law to the termination action involving an at-will employee and concluded that because the employee's speech was not solicited, his job was appropriately terminated. *Rymkus v. Spring Branch I.S.D.,* Dkt. No. 058-R8-1091 (Comm'r Educ. 1996).
67. *Mt. Healthy City School District v. Doyle,* 429 U.S. 274, (1977).
68. *Kingsville I.S.D. v. Cooper,* 611 F.2d 1109 (5th Cir. 1980). In *Whalen v. Rock Springs I.S.D.,* the Texas Commssioner of Education found that a teacher who had led a graphic and prolonged classroom discussion on sexual topics and techniques in a science class had abused the right and thus the teacher's contract was appropriately terminated. Dkt. No. 065-R1b-284 (Comm'r Educ. 1985).
69. In *Kirkland v. Northside I.S.D.,* 890 F.2d 794 (5th Cir. 1989), the Fifth Circuit refused to extend academic freedom to encompass a teacher's selection of an unapproved supplemental reading list. In several decisions, the Texas Commissioner of Education has ruled against teachers who cited academic freedom in deviating from the established curriculum. One decision involved the non-renewal of a teacher who used sexually explicit plays in her drama class and had students read portions of books dealing with sexually explicit language, despite directives to the contrary from the principal. The commissioner noted that when classroom expression is related to the school curriculum, "a district may impose restrictions on the expression so long as they are reasonably related to legitimate pedagogical concerns." The commissioner noted that instructing students "is part of the school's curriculum and therefore constitute matters of private concern." *Hammonds v. Mt. Pleasant P I.S.D.,* Dkt. No. 322-R1-793 (Comm'r Educ. 1995).
70. *Hillis v. Stephen F. Austin State University,* 665 F.2d 547 (5th Cir. 1982) (no academic freedom right to award a grade); *Kirkland v. Northside I.S.D.,* 890 F.2d 794 (5th Cir. 1989) (no academic freedom right to select an unapproved supplemental reading list); *Martin v. Parrish,* 805 F.2d 583 (5th Cir. 1986) (no academic freedom right to use profanity in the classroom as a motivational technique).
71. *Jackson v. Birmingham Board of Education,* 544 U.S. 167 (2005).
72. *Sabine Pilots Services, Inc. v. Hauck,* 687 S.W.2d 733 (Tex. 1985).
73. *Zarsky v. Southside I.S.D.,* Dkt. No. 037-R1-07-2019 (Comm'r Educ. 2019). In 2022 the commissioner added a footnote to a decision dismissing a probationary teacher's appeal that it remains unclear whether use of physical force by probationary teachers is justified under TEC Section 22.0512 since that law relates to termination or nonrenewal of those under term contracts. *Long v. Fort Worth I.S.D.,* Dkt. No. 033-R10-2022.

CHAPTER TWO: PRINCIPLES OF DOCUMENTATION

WHEN TO DOCUMENT

Surprising though it may seem, not every employee deficiency should be formally documented. Not only is documentation time-consuming, it also has a tendency to polarize the supervisor-employee relationship. Consider the teacher who learns for the first time from a written message placed in his mailbox that he has failed to follow the principal's directive regarding returning parent phone calls. The principal requests that the teacher follow administrative directives in the future or face a formal reprimand. No doubt the teacher will be angry and defensive. These feelings will affect his working relationship with the principal. For this reason, we advise administrators to use simple oral directives when relatively minor problems with an employee's performance first arise.

Example

One of your teachers is late to school one day for no apparent reason. The most appropriate strategy is to talk with the teacher informally about the tardiness and the inconvenience it caused. No doubt the teacher will offer an explanation for the incident and probably will try to assure you that it will never happen again. Later, you make a brief note to yourself about the incident. These are called notes to the file, and we will discuss them shortly.

A few weeks later, the teacher is late to school again. As before, talk informally with the teacher about the tardiness. This time, be a little more direct. Warn the teacher that if it happens a third time, you will issue a formal memorandum, with a copy to the personnel file. Again, you write a brief note to yourself about the matter.

When the tardiness occurs a third time, you should begin formal written documentation to the teacher, incorporating the two previous notes you made to yourself. We will describe how to do so in this chapter.

There is a downside to oral directives. Their informality limits their usefulness later in a contract nonrenewal or termination proceeding. The employee is likely to challenge your recollection of the conversation. At the extreme, your testimony may be dismissed as hearsay. Keeping a record of the dates, times, and what you talked with the employee about has two advantages: (1) It will help bolster your credibility on the witness stand and (2) it preserves details to include in a memorandum if the deficiency persists. Still, be aware that oral directives have limited value in defending a negative employment recommendation.

Despite these drawbacks, we believe that the necessity of maintaining a good working relationship with employees justifies relying on informal oral directives when relatively minor problems first surface. Sometimes formal documentation in this context can work to your disadvantage. A Dallas school attorney provides an illustration from one of his first teacher nonrenewal cases. The principal assured the attorney that he had built up a large folder of documentation that more than justified contract nonrenewal. When the attorney opened the folder, the first memorandum caught his attention. "You failed to greet me this morning when we passed in the hall," it read. As the attorney thumbed through the other memoranda, he discovered similar trivialities weakly linked to job performance such as needing to smile more, asking too many questions at faculty meetings, and wearing dresses that were out of style. Despite the attorney's best efforts at the nonrenewal hearing, the school board voted to reject the proposed nonrenewal. Afterward, several board members told the attorney that they could not go on record to end the teacher's employment in the district based on documentation that merely established the existence of a personality conflict between the principal and the teacher.

The lesson is clear. Employ formal documentation when:

- School policy requires it.
- A pattern of behavior needs to be changed.
- A serious incident has occurred.

Remember that the quality of what you write is more important than the quantity of accumulated paper.

TYPES OF DOCUMENTATION

Much has been written about the various types of written documentation. We have chosen to focus on four. Each is briefly described here.

Notes to the File Accompanying Oral Directives

Notes to the file are memory-joggers. Their purpose is to assist you in recalling specific dates and facts for use in later conversations with employees or in drafting formal memoranda. They also are useful in establishing a pattern of behavior that later can be formally documented in written memoranda. Once incorporated in the latter or following a lengthy period without further incident (e.g., the remainder of the year) they can be destroyed.

Notes to the file should be kept systematically. Many school administrators keep a file or loose-leaf notebook for this purpose with a sheet of paper for each employee. Other administrators maintain a spiral notebook and keep running records of conversations, conferences, and telephone calls. Spiral notebooks have the advantage of demonstrating that the notes to the file were sequential and contemporaneous with the event. This can be used to defend against the accusation that these notes were created after the fact. Some administrators keep a file for each employee on their computer. Wherever kept, employees or their representatives have access to most of this information under the Texas Public Information Act.[1] Thus, it is important to keep notes to the file factual and unemotional. Write notes to the file in such a way that you would not be embarrassed if they were circulated to the entire teaching staff, surfaced in a due process hearing, or were reported in the newspaper.

With regard to the tardy teacher described in the previous example, here is how a note to the file should and should not be written:

DON'T WRITE IT LIKE THIS!

9/23/21 Mrs. Jones was late to school again today. Her excuse this time was that her alarm clock did not go off. Likely story! She is getting to be a real pain in the ass. If she is late to school one more time, I am going to show her who is boss.

WRITE IT LIKE THIS!

9/23/21 Spoke with Mrs. Jones at noon in the cafeteria about her being fifteen minutes late to school today. She said her alarm clock did not go off and assured me she would not be late again. This is the second time within the past 10 days she has been tardy.

Would it be a good idea to send a copy to the teacher? Our answer is no, unless school policy is otherwise. If you send the note to the teacher, it no longer is a note to the file. It now is a specific incident memorandum, as discussed below. Notes to the file are for your use. They are not part of the formal written documentation process. However, the employee should be notified verbally of the deficiency that made the note to the file necessary. And, if the employee insists on seeing your note to the file, check with the human resources office first as to how this should be handled and what content may have to be deleted. As previously noted, under the Texas Public Information Act, any file or note that administrators make in their capacity as employee supervisors has to be made available to the employee or the employee's representative if requested. However, some information may not be released (e.g., student personally identifiable information, matters relating to child abuse or neglect, and matters involved in pending litigation).

Consistent with the law, we strongly endorse a very simple maxim in personnel decision-making involving both professional and auxiliary personnel:

NO SECRETS, NO SURPRISES

The purpose of documentation is not to entrap. The purpose is to assure that personnel decisions are fair. Thus employees always should be informed of their deficiencies, even if minor. In the case of the tardy teacher, first tell the teacher about the problem. Then make a note to the file about the time and content of the discussion. If the incident is not repeated, then you can discard the note at the end of the year and the matter will be closed.

Can a verbal warning or directive serve as cumulative data for purposes of complying with the 10-day teacher appraisal rule? No. So if an administrator wants to include the subject of the oral directive as cumulative data, the administrator must communicate with the teacher in writing and do so within the specified time period. We believe that formalizing the documentation process in this way defeats the purpose of using oral directives. Their informality preserves the employer-employee relationship.

However, if several oral directives are not effective in changing teacher behavior, then it is time to formalize the documentation process by communicating with the teacher in writing. Information preserved in the notes to the file can be incorporated in the written communication. The written communication signifies that the administrator has concluded that failure to correct the behavior may affect the teacher's employment status. We address writing this form of documentation in the section on writing a specific incident memorandum below.

Performance Appraisal

The second type of documentation we address relates to performance appraisal processes mandated by state law or school policy. These processes have their own documentation formats and procedures. In Chapter 4, we present options for easily gathering observation data in the classroom of the marginally effective teacher to either improve the teacher's performance or prepare for contract nonrenewal or termination and to do so in a way that is compatible with the district or charter school's formal appraisal system. As will be illustrated in that chapter, the data collected are then presented in a follow-up memorandum to the teacher.

Specific Incident Memorandum

A specific incident memorandum applies to a specific episode or pattern of employee wrongdoing sufficiently serious that a written record must be made. Sometimes the term "letter of reprimand" is used, but this carries a negative connotation and should be avoided. The specific incident memorandum usually will include directives for future on-the-job behavior and may include a remediation component. With the remediation component added, this type of written documentation is sometimes called a "corrective memorandum." Regardless of the label, these memoranda will have similar purposes and characteristics. We discuss them in this chapter. In Chapter 4, we present a version of this memorandum called a specific incident memorandum related to instruction that is sent to the teacher following the collection of classroom data between formal appraisals through use of one of our focused observation instruments.

Last Chance Memorandum

A last chance memorandum pulls together the record of previous deficiencies discussed with the employee as recorded in performance appraisals, notes to the file, and specific incident memoranda. Last chance memoranda can include data from prior years if relevant to establishing a continuing pattern of deficiency.[2] However, as noted in the previous chapter, administrators need to be very cautious in using data from prior years. While there is no provision in the Education Code that says that contract nonrenewal or termination can only be based on matters occurring during the present school year, the Texas Commissioner of Education has cautioned that a school district should issue a proposed termination or nonrenewal within a reasonable amount of time from when the district is fully aware of the teacher's actions. If this doesn't occur, then the district may have waived the right to take employment action.

Clearly, it is not appropriate to include previous incidents that have been corrected. Assume, for example, that a teacher had several instances of arriving late to school during the teacher's first year of employment and was issued a written directive to arrive on time or face possible nonrenewal of the teacher's probationary contract at the end of the year. For the next two years, the teacher never was late. Then the teacher failed to attend a scheduled in-service meeting without a valid excuse. Citing the prior lateness episode in documentation would not be appropriate, because it has no relationship to the current incident and, indeed, never recurred after the directive had been issued. In effect, the teacher complied with the lateness directive, and the matter should remain closed.

The last chance memorandum puts the employee on notice that you are prepared to recommend contract nonrenewal or termination unless significant improvement is forthcoming in complying with directives set forth in prior memoranda and repeated in this memorandum. An example of such a memorandum is given later in this chapter and, with regard to classroom teaching deficiencies, at the end of Chapter 6.

WRITING A SPECIFIC INCIDENT MEMORANDUM

Examples of Poorly Constructed Specific Incident Memoranda

Consider the following two written communications, the first to a classified employee and the second in the form of an email to a middle school English teacher.

COMPUTER PRINTOUT LEFT ON MABEL MARBLEHEAD'S DESK

```
TO:   Mabel Marblehead, Senior Assistant
FROM: Charlie Chassis, DOT Director

I just learned from Fred Fiscal that you refused to talk with him
when he came to see me this morning. He said you also ignored two
bus divers who were in the office. Fred is our district's business
manager! He said you placed your hand over the phone and told him
you were on your breek. I can't believe that you would do such a
thing. As one of the oldest members of our staff you should now
better. I know you are not happy with some of the changes I have
made as the new director and especially when I sent you to what
you called charm school last June to improve customer relations .
You must change your behavior or else . I am out of the office the
rest of today and tom0row morning but you can talk with me when I
am back in.
```

EMAIL TO BOB INSTRUCTOR

(dated November 10, 2023 and sent at 5:17 pm)

```
To:      Bob Instructor
Subject: Faculty Meeting

You seem incapable of understanding a very simpel directive: attend
faculty meetigs. As I told you before, claiming you have papers to
grade before a weekend trip and saying up didn't find t he discussion
relevant to your needs is hardly reasons not to be there. Today, you
simply didn't show up at all. I have one word for you: BE THERE OR FIND
ANOTHER JOB. I am forwarding this email to the superintedant. Angie
O'Plasty, Principal
```

In both of these instances, the supervising administrators are clearly upset. Both have a right to be if the alleged incidents occurred. Employees cannot be allowed to willfully disregard job requirements, including administrative directives. But both Mr. Chassis and Ms. O'Plasty have committed some major errors in writing these memoranda. First and most importantly, both have neglected to follow a cardinal rule in documentation:

INVESTIGATE FIRST!

An investigation encompasses speaking with the employee. Can Charlie be sure that Mabel did what Mr. Fiscal said? Can Angie be certain that Bob purposely played hooky from the faculty meeting? What is necessary in both instances is some spadework before reaching conclusions and writing memos. Before continuing, let us pause a moment to consider some suggestions about conducting investigations.

How to Conduct an Investigation

Conducting investigations often requires considerable time and effort. However, if your investigation is poorly done, the quality of your documentation may be seriously, if not fatally, compromised. Of course, the scope of your investigation will be determined by the seriousness and complexity of the alleged incident. Here are some pointers on conducting investigations.

- *Do not delay beginning an investigation into either alleged wrongdoing or ineffectiveness.* Decide whether an investigation is warranted after receiving a complaint. Generally, an investigation should be conducted when an allegation, if proven true, would violate school policy or regulations. As we noted in Chapter 1, matters involving employee free speech or private conduct off campus often are beyond the legitimate interests of the school. Some administrators assume that if persons who witness events are unwilling to prepare a statement or step forward to testify, nothing can be done. While it is true that employees have a right to confront witnesses against them at a due process hearing and therefore witness statements are essential, nothing precludes an administrator from beginning an investigation. Don't dismiss rumors or anonymous tips. Look for strong, independent corroborating evidence. In some instances such as allegations involving sexual harassment or abuse, administrators who fail to initiate an investigation risk exposing both the school district or charter school and themselves to liability.

- *Decide whether the matter is sufficiently serious that the human resources director, school attorney, or outside investigator should be involved.* In matters involving allegations of employee sexual harassment or abuse of students, alert the district's Title IX coordinator and, depending upon the circumstances, school security or law enforcement. When matters are potentially serious, the school attorney will need to be involved and actually may direct the investigation. This is most likely to be true when complaints also have been filed with law enforcement or outside administrative agencies such as Child Protective Services. In such cases, it will be necessary to contact them to coordinate efforts and to assert the school district's or charter school's obligations, such as maintaining confidentiality of records, safeguarding privacy rights of students, and protecting the professional reputation of employees. Together with the human resources director, superintendent, and/or school attorney consider whether the matter is sufficiently serious that suspending the employee with pay is warranted.

- *If students are victims of alleged employee wrongdoing, notify their parents at the earliest opportunity.* Under Texas law, parents are considered "full partners" in the education of their children. They have a right under Texas Education Code (TEC) Sections 26.004 and 26.008 to see all the documents relating to their children except those involving child abuse.[3] Include parents in interviews and allow them to bring legal counsel, if desired. Remember that you would rather have parents be partners with you in your investigation than for them to learn about allegations of employee wrongdoing involving their child later on. It is the latter situation that triggers lawsuits from angry parents. When the student reaches adulthood at the age of 18 and is no longer subject to the compulsory school law, the parents generally do not have to be informed or involved in the investigation. However, there may be situations where it would be prudent to involve the parents (e.g., the student is cognitively impaired or otherwise in need of legal assistance). For this reason, the school's human resources director, Title IX coordinator, or other appropriate official should be consulted before a decision is made not to involve the parents of older students in an investigation.

- *If a complaint has been registered against an employee, ask complainants separately to fill out and sign a complaint form, describing the nature of the wrongdoing and identifying other witnesses.*[4] (See Appendix D for a sample complaint form.) Follow up with an interview to ascertain the credibility of the allegation. Do not promise confidentiality, because the accused may have the right to confront accusers if formal action is taken.

- *Interview witnesses separately and have each complete and sign a witness statement form.* (See Appendix D for a sample witness statement form.) Follow a set of questions prepared in advance targeted toward what you want to learn. Do not reference witness comments in memoranda unless you have secured a completed witness statement form. And then it is best not to include the names of those signing the witness statement form in the memorandum with certain exceptions (e.g., those higher up in the employee's chain of command such as a department chair, campus principal, central office official). This avoids possible retaliation and violation of privacy rights. If the employee in- sists upon learning the identity of the witnesses, consult the human resources director or school attorney about disclosure. If students are witnesses, it would be wise to alert their parents ahead of time that you are going to ask them to complete a witness statement form and secure their consent. Again, do not promise confidentiality to persons completing witness statement forms because they may be required to testify in a due process hearing down the road. Make sure that your investigatory procedure is in accord with school policy and practice. Consult district or charter school officials if in doubt.

- *Interview the accused, following the same procedures used when interviewing witnesses.* Do not assume guilt. Treat the accused in the same manner you treat complainants and witnesses. Do not encourage resignations or make settlement offers unless the accused asks about them. Consult the human resources director or school attorney before taking any final action on either matter. Do not release complaint statements to the accused that contain personally identifiable information about students. However, the attorney general has advised that letters sent to a school board complaining about a teacher are to be made available to the teacher with this information redacted (ORD- 332, 1982). The commissioner of education issued a similar decision in 2014.[5]

- *With few exceptions, do not disclose personally identifiable information about students or families.* Because this information is protected from disclosure by the Family Educational Rights and Privacy Act (FERPA), obtain written authorization from parents before releasing a student's name and any written statement. In the absence of such authorization, remove personally identifiable student information from witness statements and other documentary evidence.

Statements from students in their own handwriting should not be disclosed because the handwriting may be personally identifiable. Note that under TEC Section 26.009 (a)(2), parent permission is necessary before audiotaping or videotaping a student. Further, Section 552.135 of the Texas Government Code includes students within the protection of the "informer's privilege." That provision excludes from public disclosure the name or statement of an informer who reports to the school district or regulatory agency an alleged violation of a law or regulation absent the informer's consent or complicity in the alleged wrongdoing. Sometimes, teachers ask to see a letter of complaint submitted by a parent. While the teacher has a broad right of access to information in the teacher's personnel file, FERPA gives parents the right to request that personally identifiable information (e.g., names, phone numbers, addresses) about themselves and their children not be released. While teachers do have access to personally identifiable information about students when there is a "legitimate educational interest,"* the teacher would not be authorized to see the letter under this provision. The attorney general has advised that letters sent to a school board complaining about a teacher are to be made available to the teacher, provided the names of the students and parents are deleted (ORD-332, 1982). Once again, we advise consulting the human resources office before releasing personally identifiable information to a teacher.

- Work closely with the school district's or charter school's human resources personnel or officer of public information when requests for information about an investigation arise from third parties under the Texas Public Information Act (TPIA). This law presumes that information must be disclosed unless it is specifically exempted from disclosure under either federal or state law. As already noted, personally identifiable information about students and families is exempted from disclosure. Under Section 552.101 of the Texas Government Code, information that is considered to be confidential by constitutional, statutory, or judicial law does not have to be disclosed. Section 552.102 provides that information in an employee's file does not need to be disclosed if it constitutes a clearly unwarranted invasion of personal privacy (however, with few exceptions, it does have to be disclosed to the employee or the employee's representative, if requested). Courts have interpreted these two provisions to mean that information does not have to be disclosed to third parties if it would be highly objectionable to a reasonable person and if there is no legitimate public interest in disclosure. Applying these principles, the Texas attorney general has advised that a school district had to release the documents in an investigatory file pertaining to sexual harassment in the absence of a summary report but must withhold the identities of the victims and witnesses. OR2000-1233 (2000). The attorney general has advised that records and documents resulting from the investigation of sexual harassment allegations against a principal must be released, with the deletion of identities of victims and witnesses but including references to the principal's name, because of the public's interest in sexual harassment in the workplace. OR2003-5194, OR2003-4773 (2003). In another decision, the attorney general

---

* You will note that the memoranda contained in Chapter 4 do contain the names of students. These memoranda reflect deficiencies in teacher classroom performance with regard to meeting the educational needs of students in the teacher's classroom. Because both the teacher and the principal need to know the identity of students who are not being taught effectively, student personally identifiable information is included, because it constitutes a legitimate educational interest under FERPA. Later, this student personally identifiable information will be redacted if the memoranda are used for other purposes (e.g., to support nonrenewal of a teacher contract in a hearing before the school board).

advised that information regarding the alleged improper conduct by a coach towards a student was not so embarrassing that it would be offensive to a reasonable person. Further, the public interest in knowing about the possible misconduct by the coach outweighed the coach's privacy interests. Therefore, the information had to be disclosed with some personally identifiable information redacted. OR2000-1319 (2000). Texas Government Code § 552.152 specifies that information relating to an employee or officer of a governmental entity is exempt from disclosure if disclosure would subject the employee or officer to substantial threat of physical harm. In sum, what must and must not be disclosed is complex and highly dependent upon the facts of a given situation. For these reasons, we advise you to seek assistance from human resources personnel or officer of public information before releasing information.

- *If complaints also have been filed with law enforcement or outside administrative agencies, contact them before beginning your investigation in order to coordinate efforts and to assert the school district's obligations.* Remember that the district has interests of its own such as maintaining confidentiality of records, safeguarding privacy rights of students, and protecting the professional reputation of employees.

- *Be cautious in communicating with the news media because student and family privacy rights and employee constitutional rights may be involved.* Use prepared statements, preferably handled by the school communications office. Remember that nothing is ever "off the record."

- *When the investigation is over, retain the investigatory file for possible use later on.* Where these files are stored varies. In some districts, they are kept by the school attorney. In others, they are kept in the human resources office or superintendent's office. In any case, they should not be inserted in the employee's file because of (1) the possibility of reprisal by the employee, (2) the difficulty of excising all personally identifiable information under FERPA, and (3) the potential damage that could accrue to the employee from portions of the investigatory file that are false or misleading. What should be kept in the employee's file is the specific incident memorandum that results from the investigation.

A careful investigation is essential to providing a firm foundation for effective documentation. What's more, it will demonstrate to all that you have not been careless, negligent, or callously indifferent to allegations of serious employee wrongdoing. As noted in Chapter 1, failure to take allegations seriously, especially in the context of student sexual harassment and abuse, can lead to potentially serious litigation involving both the school district and school administrators.

In the matter of Mabel Marblehead reflected in the computer printout above, if Mr. Chas- sis has talked to or received an email from the school business officer, he has evidence that Mabel ignored the school official when he entered the office. Same with the two bus drivers. But his investigation did not include talking with Mabel before he submitted the computer printout to her. Perhaps there is more to learn about this from her perspective. The same is true for Angie O'Plasty. She sent her email to Bob Instructor before talking with him. The point here is that prior to writing a specific incident memorandum, an investigation must be conducted encompassing all dimensions of the incident including talking with the employee.

Beyond the failure of the transportation director and the principal to investigate fully before they wrote, what else is wrong with the two memoranda as they are? Among other things, neither was written on official letterhead stationery, and both were poorly crafted. Both contain insensitive and inflammatory language that will make the employee angry (e.g., "You must change your behavior or else," "be there or find another job"). Both contain spelling and grammatical errors (e.g., "divers," "breek," "simpel," "meetigs," "superintedant," the verb "is" instead of "are"). And in both instances the administrators imply possible job action if matters don't improve. The problem is that administrators normally recommend termination or contract nonrenewal. The authority to take either action usually resides with the district or charter school board.

Not only will these two memoranda likely set up an adversarial relationship with the employees, they may prove embarrassing to the administrators who sent them. Mr. Chassis' computer printout left on Mabel's desk could easily be seen and read by others who come into the office. His reference to Mabel as "one of the oldest members of our staff" could prompt an allegation of age discrimination. Since Ms. O'Plasty has sent a copy of her memorandum to the superintendent, the superintendent may be as concerned with Ms. O'Pasty's actions as with those attributed to Bob Instructor!

There is another potential problem. Both Mabel and Bob may decide to share their communiques with colleagues — in the case of the email that Bob received, perhaps with the spelling, grammatical, and typing errors highlighted. The documents may well be circulated within the building and perhaps throughout the school district, especially if an aggressive employee association is present. What better way to recruit members than to produce written evidence of arbitrary and abusive administrative action! And the email to Bob may end up on the internet!

Lessons To Be Learned

What can we learn from these examples?

- **Investigate, confer, write — in that order.**

- **Avoid acting when angry. This is when mistakes are more likely to happen.**

- **Avoid sexist, racist, and inflammatory language that will provoke an employee to seek vengeance.**

- **Spell out acronyms (e.g., IEP, FAPE, DOT, TPRI) so that those who may review the memorandum in a grievance or nonrenewal hearing will understand the thrust of what is being said.**

- **Assume your memoranda and email messages will be widely distributed and read. Thus, craft them carefully.**

- **Avoid using email for formal documentation, given the ability of recipients both to change the content of emails and disseminate them widely.**

- **Have someone edit what you write if the matter is serious and could result in a negative employment decision down the road. This may be best handled in conjunction with the human resources office.**

In addition to these lessons, it is also important to treat all employees alike. Don't play favorites. Treat the employees you like in the same way that you treat those you don't like. And keep it simple!

Follow These Essential Elements in Writing a Specific Incident Memorandum

- *Letterhead Stationery*

    Use letterhead stationery to convey the importance of the memorandum. Letterhead stationery is preferable to electronic communication because it sets up the opportunity for a face-to-face meeting for delivery and because it is less likely to be forwarded to third parties in an altered form.

- *Date*

- *Subject*

    Keep it short and avoid conclusory subjects such as "Unprofessional Behavior." State the subject objectively. Examples: "Our November 14 Conference," "Meeting with Parents," "Faculty Meeting Attendance." Stating the subject neutrally will avoid a challenge that you were biased from the start.

- *Allegation and Investigation*

    Describe both the nature of the allegation and the investigation you conducted if one is necessary, the dates and times of specific incidents, and the dates when you spoke with the employee about the matter. Do this very briefly – one or two sentences. Example: "This memorandum concerns reports that you repeatedly have failed to attend scheduled parent meetings. To confirm these reports, I spoke with several parents and your instructional leader before talking with you on Tuesday, November 14." Note that you will want written, dated, and signed statements from those with whom you spoke (see Appendix D).

- *Findings of Fact*

    Set forth your findings of fact in objective terms resulting from your investigation, classroom visitations, conferences, etc. Use bulleted sentences if there are a number of them. Be sure to set forth all the findings of facts – even those that are contrary to the thrust of what you are learning. These likely will include what the employee says and even some witnesses.

- *Conclusions*

    State your conclusions regarding what happened and which laws, school policies, administrative directives, or ethical provisions were violated. Here is where you have to decide what happened. In effect, you are reviewing all the facts and, like a jury, reaching a conclusion: Is the employee guilty of the allegations or not?

- ***Directives***

    Issue specific directives regarding expected future conduct.* Include directives for professional development if you think they will help the employee improve performance. Remember that directives must be worded in such a way that the employee does not have discretion to avoid complying with them. Thus, stating "I suggest that you consider attending a workshop on incorporating digital devices in your teaching" is not really a directive; it is a suggestion. Thus the teacher is not required to attend the workshop. For it to be a directive, it needs to be worded like this: "I have made arrangements for you to attend the workshop on incorporating digital devices in your teaching."

- ***Opportunity to Respond***

    Offer the employee an opportunity to respond within a specified time period.

- ***Dated Employee Signature***

    Require the dated signature of the employee or if the employee refuses to sign, have a third party witness that the employee has received the memorandum.

To assist you in crafting a specific incident memorandum, we have provided a template in Appendix D. Note that the italicized information under each essential element in the template in Appendix D is for your benefit. Of course, these, along with the list of essential elements along the left side of the template, are to be deleted when the memorandum is completed. The value of the template is to give you a format that results in a standardized way of writing specific incident memoranda.

Examples of Well Written Specific Incident Memoranda

On the next two pages are much better written memoranda to Mabel Marblehead and Bob Instructor. Notice how the format of each reflects the essential elements of a specific incident memorandum (the essential elements are listed on the left side of the sample memoranda for illustrative purposes; you would not include them in the actual memorandum). We have provided brief commentary following both memoranda.

---

* It is important in giving directives to make sure that they can be linked to the terms of an existing employee contract. The commissioner has ruled that while the terms of employment contracts can be modified, the changes cannot apply to an existing contract unless the parties bound by the contract agree. *Uranga v. Culberson County-Allamore I.S.D.,* Dkt. No. 015-R10-11-2017 (Comm'r Educ. 2018). For example, suppose a contract for a custodian states that the employee is to work four days a week. Directing the employee to work a fifth day a week because of poor performance could be challenged as contrary to the terms of the existing contract. Of course, when the contract ends, then a change like this can be made.

Similarly, as discussed on p. 4 of Chapter 6, when a teacher whose performance is weak is directed to submit additional paperwork related to performance, the directive must be linked to the school's appraisal system embedded in the employment contract. This is because the Paperwork Reduction Act set forth in Education Code Section 11.164 limits the types of paperwork teachers must produce.

COYOTE INDEPENDENT SCHOOL DISTRICT
900 HIGH ROAD
COYOTE, TEXAS 70000

ESSENTIAL ELEMENTS

Letterhead Stationery

Date

September 15, 2023

TO: Mabel Marblehead, Senior Assistant
FROM: Charlie Chassis, Director of Transportation
RE: Customer Relations

Allegation and Investigation

Findings of Fact

This memorandum is a follow-up to our conference yesterday afternoon at which we discussed what Fred Fiscal, our school district business manager, told me occurred when he entered the office at 10:30 a.m. that morning. At the time two bus drivers also were in the office. He said that you were talking on the telephone about non-school business (you were speaking about your love of dogs). When Mr. Fiscal tried to speak with you, he said you responded, "I am now on break. You will just have to wait." He said he waited another 10 minutes for you to conclude your call. I spoke with one of the two drivers, who confirmed the report and said he and his fellow driver had been waiting for 15 minutes.

When I spoke with you about the matter at our conference, you admitted that this had occurred but pointed out that you had been working hard all morning and hadn't had your break. As I told you at our meeting, it is important that all of us serve the members of our school community in the best possible manner. This is the only way we can build positive support for our school district and for this office.

Conclusions

I find your actions yesterday to constitute a serious disregard of the needs of others and contrary to the expectations of the district as set forth in our staff handbook.

Directives

In the future, do not take your breaks when there are persons in the office waiting to be served. When the office is empty, you may take your 20 minute morning and 20 minute afternoon break by leaving the office as long as either I or the part-time filing clerk is present. It is important that there always be someone in the office during working hours.

Also, I expect you always to use the skills that you learned at the in-service presentation last June and that we reviewed yesterday in your interactions with other people while on the job. These include (1) promptly and positively greeting persons when they enter the office; (2) asking how you might assist them; (3) asking if they would like a cup of coffee or bottled water; (4) addressing their needs, or if not possible, making a note of the needs and indicating that we will get back to them as quickly as we can; (5) thanking them for coming by and indicating that they are always welcome. Please follow my directives so that I do not need to find a suitable replacement.

Opportunity to Respond

I have received a copy of this memorandum. I understand that my signature does not necessarily indicate that I agree with its contents. I further understand that I have a right to respond in writing within 10 working days.

Dated Employee Signature

/s/_____
        Mabel Marblehead   Date

ESSENTIAL ELEMENTS	**ALAMO MIDDLE SCHOOL**
	NORMAL CURVE INDEPENDENT SCHOOL DISTRICT
Letterhead Stationery	555 INTELLIGENCE STREET
	NORMAL CURVE, TEXAS 70000

Date	November 17, 2023
	TO: Bob Instructor FROM: Angie O'Plasty, Principal RE: November 16 Conference
Allegation and Investigation	During the past semester, you have failed to attend the regularly scheduled weekly faculty meetings in timely fashion. Specifically:
	• You were 25 minutes late to the faculty meeting on Friday, September 15. When I spoke with you about this after the meeting, you indicated that you had papers to grade in your room and had simply lost track of time.
Findings of Fact	• You left 15 minutes early at the Friday, October 13 faculty meeting. You responded to my email the following Monday indicating that you found the discussion not relevant to your grade level. I advised you that this is not a valid excuse to leave a faculty meeting and that you must make sure that any need to arrive late or leave early is approved by me ahead of time. You said you would follow this request. Copies of the emails are attached.
	• You did not attend the faculty meeting on Friday, November 10, nor did you explain the need for your absence before the meeting. At our conference on Tuesday, November 14, you explained that you thought the meeting had been cancelled, though you could point to no communication from my office to this effect.
Conclusions	Your failure to attend the weekly faculty meetings in timely fashion is a violation of the job expectations for Alamo Middle School. This is clearly indicated both in the faculty information packet that I distributed at our first meeting on Friday, August 25, and in my oral and email comments to you on September 15 and October 18. Further, your noncompliance does not meet the professional standards of our district in compliance with Dimension IV of our district's appraisal system.
Directives	In the future, I expect you to attend all scheduled faculty meetings. If you find that you will be late, leave early, or not be in attendance at all, you must convey the reasons to me in writing prior to the meeting. I reserve the right to approve or disapprove them.
	Att. Copy: Personnel File
Opportunity to Respond	I have received a copy of this memorandum. I understand that my signature does not necessarily indicate that I agree with its contents. I further understand that I have a right to respond in writing within 10 working days.
Dated Employee Signature	/s/_____ Bob Instructor Date

Certainly the memorandum from Charlie Chassis to Mabel Marblehead is much better crafted than the computer printout left on her desk. Notice how he directs her to change her behavior when persons enter the office but does not stop there. He goes on to lay out the skills she learned at the professional development workshop and that they discussed at their conference. Doing so not only helps Mabel understand what her supervisor expects her to do, it also shows that he is treating her fairly. Later if her at-will employment is terminated and she files a grievance, it will be difficult for her to establish that he was out to get her from the start.

Notice that while Angie O'Plasty used emails to follow up her informal discussions with Bob, she uses letterhead stationery for the formal specific incident memorandum. Notice as well how the communication corresponds to the characteristics of an effective specific incident memorandum. Here, an investigation was not necessary, because Angie directly observed Bob's attendance problems at faculty meetings. However, she did fail to confer with Bob before she sent the last email. When the facts are in dispute, it will be necessary to state the nature of the investigation that the administrator conducted (who was interviewed, what documents were examined, etc.) and the findings from it. The findings of fact must always be stated in objective terms. The same is true for writing the subject of the memorandum. It is critically important to avoid subjective wording that may be used to accuse the administrator of bias. Follow the Sgt. Joe Friday Rule based on the 1950s TV series "Dragnet": "Just the facts, ma'am, just the facts." And remember to include all the facts resulting from your investigation, even those that conflict with each other (e.g., one witness says one thing, another witness says something different, and the employee disagrees with both).

Notice how both Charlie and Angie anchor their conclusions based on the findings of fact in the published expectations of employment at their respective schools. This is the "law of the district" and avoids accusations that the supervisors are merely substituting their way of doing things for that of their employees. Sometimes it is difficult to arrive at a conclusion, because the facts might conflict. However, as the "trier of fact," the administrator will have to decide whether district or charter school policy and/or administrative directives have been violated. As noted earlier, this is what a jury does once a case has been submitted to it.

The importance of the opportunity to respond cannot be overemphasized. Given the detail in the memorandum to Mabel, it is doubtful that she will respond one way or the other. If Bob were to write a response with new information that Angie did not consider, then she will have the opportunity to reopen the investigation. Based on the new information, she may decide that she should be more accommodating. For example, suppose Bob sends Angie a response email that he must meet with her as soon as possible after he received her memorandum. At the meeting, Bob breaks down in her office, telling her that he is under treatment for leukemia and doesn't want anyone to know about it. His treatments are on Friday, and this is accounts for his behavior. He gives the name of his doctor to verify that this is the case. On the other hand, if Bob's response offers nothing new, then Angie should acknowledge this fact in a brief reply email or memo and place both Bob's response and her reply in his personnel file. There is no need for her to become Bob's permanent adversary pen pal.

If neither Mabel nor Bob replies within the specified time frame, it can be assumed each accepts the contents of the memorandum. It will not be very convincing for an employee to claim months later should a recommendation be made to terminate his or her employment that the contents of the specific incident memorandum amounted to a tissue of lies. If so, why hadn't the employee taken advantage of the opportunity to respond?

Finally, always check to make sure that your personnel decisions are in accord with district policy. In relatively serious matters, it is wise to have a representative from human resources participate in the investigation and memo writing. If litigation is possible, the school attorney also may become involved.

WRITING LAST CHANCE MEMORANDA

The Scenario

Melba Toast is serving her eighth year on an annual term contract in Piney Woods Independent School District. She is a sixth grade teacher. During a staff development program on August 25, she expressed great resentment toward a new discipline plan the principal proposed for the middle school.

She asserted that the plan is far too punitive and is unworkable. She took particular offense at a provision that provides for all-day in-school suspension for troublesome students, contending that the suspension period is too long. She stated that any teacher who complies with the plan is no better than a child abuser. "I will not carry out the plan," she said defiantly.

The next day, the principal, Ima Leader, held a conference with Melba to talk over the discipline plan and to explain her disapproval of the outburst at the faculty meeting. The principal told Melba that she, Ima, is the disciplinary leader for the school and that Melba must follow the plan as a condition of employment. The teacher listened but said she has no intention to do so. Ima followed up the conference with a specific incident memorandum in which she reviewed the substance of their discussion and directed Melba to follow the discipline plan despite her reservations.

The principal implemented the plan when school began. Melba grudgingly followed the plan but promptly filed a grievance against the principal contending that the plan interfered with her rights as a teacher. Then on October 11, Melba confronted Ima in the hallway. Visibly upset, the teacher told the principal that she does not want her to discipline her homeroom students when they are sent to the office by other teachers. Melba was upset because the principal disciplined one of her students for fighting on the playground. The principal explained again that she has the final authority regarding disciplinary matters at the school. Melba responded angrily, "You are incredibly ignorant about child development. Don't expect me to comply with your stupid militaristic discipline ideas." Melba's comments were overheard by several other teachers and students.

The Memorandum

Here is the last chance memorandum that Ima sent to Melba in October. The numbers in parentheses correspond with the observations in the commentary section following the memorandum. We have not included the essential elements template along the left side of the memo.

HIDDEN TRAIL MIDDLE SCHOOL
PINEY WOODS INDEPENDENT SCHOOL DISTRICT
123 WOODS PATH
PINEY WOOD, TEXAS 71234

October 20, 2023

TO: Melba Toast
FROM: Ima Leader
RE: Follow-up To Our October 12 Conference

This memorandum is a follow-up to our October 12 conference during which I expressed my concerns regarding your continuing antagonism toward me and toward my disciplinary policies.

As you know, we first talked on the afternoon of August 25, following the morning staff development program the day before on the new student discipline plan. You criticized the plan at the meeting, labeling teachers who comply "no better than child abusers." A number of teachers at the meeting were offended by this remark, as was I. You also stated "I will not carry out the plan." **(1)**

During our conference, I expressed concern over the unprofessional nature of your outburst and reminded you that I am responsible for student discipline in this building. Both at the meeting and in my August 30 follow-up memorandum, I directed you to follow the discipline plan whether you agree with it or not. **(2)**

Our October 12 conference resulted from the hallway encounter the previous day when you stopped me to say that you did not want me to discipline any of your homeroom students when they are sent to the office by other teachers. Your comment apparently was triggered by my disciplining one of the students from your classroom for fighting on the playground during lunch. I reminded you that as set forth in our campus discipline plan I have the final authority for discipline in this building. You responded by labeling me in front of other teachers and students as "ignorant" and my discipline approach as "stupid." **(3)**

As I explained, you have a right to express your views about school-wide matters such as the student discipline plan. At the same time, you have a responsibility to do so in a professional manner. Such was not the case at the August faculty meeting, nor during our hallway encounter on October 11.

Your criticizing me in offensive terms before other teachers and students is contrary to District Policy DOAD, which lists as one of the reasons for contract nonrenewal "Failure to meet the District's standards of professional conduct." **(4)**

I direct you to express your opposition to school programs and activities in more moderate terms that do not undermine your ability to work collaboratively and constructively with your colleagues and with me. If you have a personal concern you wish to address to me, please make an appointment to talk with me in my office and not in the hallways or other public areas of the school. I also remind you of my policy that any teacher may send a discipline problem to the office for appropriate action regardless of whether that student is assigned to that teacher. If you fail to comply with these directives and all the terms of our campus discipline policy, I will have no choice but to recommend nonrenewal or termination of your contract. **(5)**

I hope that we can put these unpleasant episodes behind us and work together for the mutual benefit of our students even when we disagree. I welcome your comments and criticisms so long as they are voiced in a professional manner. I will be pleased to talk with you further about this matter if you wish. **(6)**

Copy: Personnel File, Dr. Paul Peopleprocessor, Director of Human Relations

I have received a copy of this memorandum. I understand that my signature does not necessarily indicate that I agree with its contents. I further understand that I have a right to respond in writing within 10 working days. **(7)**

/s/_____
        Melba Toast   Date

Commentary

(1) Notice how promptly Ima acted on these incidents. Following each incident she met with Melba a short time thereafter. She wrote the memorandum within five days of her second conference with Melba. It is clear that Ima considers this a serious matter. The principal carefully spells out exactly what happened at the August 25 faculty meeting, during the October 11 confrontation in the hallway, and during her conferences with the teacher. She relies on information contained in her notes to the file, from her conferences, and from her first memorandum. She presents this information in a very objective and non-judgmental manner. Her doing so will go a long way to convince a school board member, hearing officer, or media reporter that she acted professionally. If these statements go unchallenged by Melba, they will convey an appearance of accuracy, thus easing the burden on the school lawyer to establish facts by calling forth witnesses at a hearing.

(2) Notes to the file are useful as memory-joggers and later may be incorporated in a specific incident memorandum.

(3) Note that Ima leaves mention of Melba's filing a grievance out of the memo. Doing so helps avoid a challenge later on from the teacher's attorney that Ima retaliated against Melba over the grievance filing.

(4) Ima is specific regarding the board policy implicated by the name-calling. As we noted in Chapter 1, the U. S. Supreme Court has ruled that complaints over working conditions are not constitutionally protected. Certainly name- calling of the type Melba employed in the hallway within earshot of others is unprofessional. If it is clear that Ima remained calm in the face of the epithets and did not encourage them, Melba will be on the defensive in challenging the appropriateness of Ima's directive.

(5) Ima is quite specific in her directives. Melba is clearly on notice of what the principal's expectations are for future employment behavior.

(6) Note how Ima closes out her memo on a positive note. The impartial reader likely will conclude that the principal is acting professionally and has no personal animosity toward the teacher.

(7) Ima has given Melba 10 working days to respond. If the teacher does respond, the two have another opportunity to meet again, particularly if Melba brings new information to light. Another meeting is preferable to an exchange of claims and counter-claims. If no reconciliation is possible, then the two memos will appear together in the personnel file along with a brief recognition memo from Ima indicating that Melba's communique was received and noted. As we pointed out with the specific incident memorandum, if new information is received that requires a change in Ima's conclusions and directives, better to make the changes now than to dig in her heels and lose later either at the grievance or contract nonrenewal hearing stage. If Melba does not respond, then the facts set forth in Ima's memo will convey an appearance of accuracy.

It is important to recognize that contract termination requires considerable supporting evidence. It is early in the school year, and Ima does not yet have sufficient evidence to support outright termination. In addition, remediation usually is required before terminating an employee's contract. Here, Ima has given Melba the opportunity to improve. If Melba does not, Ima will be in a strong position to justify contract nonrenewal and, depending upon the circumstances, even outright termination of Melba's contract.

Suppose Melba follows the directives explicitly and no further incidents occur during the school year. The next year, she asks Ima to remove the memorandum from the personnel file, asserting that the incident is closed and should not taint her employment relationship with the district. Should Ima do so? Many school lawyers believe it is better to leave the memorandum in the folder for possible use later on should the employee repeat the misbehavior. In such a case, the memorandum may become necessary to establish a pattern of failing to follow directives by the employee. Rather than remove the memorandum, administrators are better advised to place a second memorandum in the folder indicating that the directives outlined in the first memorandum have been followed.

SUMMARY

Here is a summary of the main points discussed in this chapter.

- Use oral directives to deal with minor employment problems, confining written documentation to more serious matters.
- Notes to the file are useful as memory-joggers and later may be incorporated in a specific incident memorandum.
- Keep employees informed of job-related deficiencies. Follow the maxim "No secrets, no surprises."
- Follow the essential elements of a specific incident memorandum to enhance your chances of changing employee behavior, having your employment recommendations upheld if challenged, and being consistent with all employees. Note the template for doing so in Appendix D.
- Whenever possible, employ remediation efforts before planning a negative employment action.
- Use a last chance memorandum to put the employee on notice that unless substantial improvement in performance occurs, you will recommend contract nonrenewal or termination. By its nature, a last chance memorandum must be carefully developed, usually in consultation with the human resources director or school attorney. Last chance memoranda should be used only when circumstances warrant.

In short, effective documentation takes time. Do not be in a rush!

REFERENCES

1. Texas Attorney General Opinion ORD-327, 1983. The thrust of this opinion is that employees have the right of access to notes to the file made by their superiors if the latter make such notes for use in the evaluation process.
2. *Dominguez v. United I.S.D.*, Dkt. No. 169-R1-690 (Comm'r Educ. 1991). In 2001 the commissioner of education upheld the contract termination of a teacher who was given a directive in 1991 not to be alone with students following an unconfirmed allegation from a second grader that the teacher had sexually assaulted her. Nearly 10 years later, a parent complained that the teacher had driven her son home after school without parental permission. Further, the teacher was alone with students in an unused classroom during the summer school. The commissioner observed that despite the passage of time, the teacher's actions constituted repeated failure to follow directives. *Allen v. Houston I.S.D.*, Dkt. No. 014-R2-1001 (Comm'r Educ. 2001).
3. *Lett v. Klein I.S.D.*, 917 S. W.2d 455 (Tex. App. -Houston [14th Dist.] 1996) (parent has access under the Texas Public Information Act to documents, memoranda, investigative notes, and statements prepared by school personnel relating to his child in connection with a low conduct grade in choir class). School counselors can withhold records only if the counselor is a licensed professional under Health and Safety Code § 611.001(2) and determines that release "would be harmful to the patient's physical, mental, or emotional health." Otherwise, all records must be released to the parent with few exceptions. Atty. Gen. Op. JC-0538 (2002).
4. Some years ago, the commissioner of education issued an instructive decision with regard to obtaining statements from non-English speaking complainants. The case involved the employment termination of an at-will bus driver, a member of the Texas State Teachers Association (TSTA), over her criticism of a directive that bus drivers work an additional fifteen minutes before and after bus runs without pay. The commissioner concluded that the bus driver had abused her rights of free speech and upheld the termination. However, he found the case a "close call," in part because of the manner in which complaint statements had been obtained. The statements presented to support the supervisor's termination decision were all written by someone other than the person testifying. This was apparently done because the complainants were Spanish-speaking employees.The commissioner advised that "a better practice would be for employees to first write their complaints in their native language and then have a disinterested person translate the complaint into English. This would obviate confusion as to the true meaning of the complainant and would provide evidentiary assurance in the record that the allegations were of that person's own doing – not someone else whose motives might be suspect." *Huerta v. Rio Hondo I.S.D.*, Dkt. No. 253-R8-593 (Comm'r Educ. 1995).
5. The decision involved a petition signed by some of an elementary teacher's students asking for a new teacher because their teacher yelled and screamed a lot in class. After talking with the students to verify the concern, the principal released the petition to the teacher within 10 days for cumulative data purposes but redacted the student names. The teacher challenged the principal's Teacher in Need of Assistance Plan (TINA) based on the student petition. Because the plan had been developed in consultation with the teacher and was based on the petition that had been timely shared with her, the commissioner rejected the teacher's appeal. *Meyer v. Brenham I.S.D.*, Dkt. No. 064-R10-07-2013 (Comm'r. Educ. 2014).

CHAPTER THREE:
THE MARGINALLY EFFECTIVE TEACHER

In a time of increased accountability for student achievement, many educators are concerned about the teacher who is marginally effective. The marginally effective teacher may be the teacher who is effective in some ways, but ineffective in others. This may also be the teacher who performs well when being observed by a supervisor, but chooses not to be effective the rest of the time. The supervisory strategies used with this teacher are often different from those used with the teacher who is consistently ineffective or willfully fails to follow recommendations or directives for improvement. With the marginally effective teacher, your main goal as instructional leader is to assist the teacher to improve. Failing that, your goal is to use the accumulated documentation to support a recommendation of contract nonrenewal or termination.

> **Know What You Are Trying To DO!**
>
> ▶ **Goal of Growth and Improvement:** Some language and strategies are counterproductive if your *real goal is nonrenewal or termination.*
>
> ▶ **Goal of Nonrenewal or Termination:** Some language and strategies are counterproductive if your *real goal is to help the teacher get better.*

You may be wondering why a handbook on documentation includes the topic of supervision. First, when you are working with a marginally effective teacher, it is extremely important to know which goal you wish to attain: helping the teacher improve or preparing for contract nonrenewal or termination. Language and strategies aimed at the goal of nonrenewal or termination (frequent written documentation or an intervention plan, for instance) are counterproductive when your goal is growth and improvement. Conversely, most of the coaching language and strategies aimed at the goal of growth and improvement (teacher choices and negotiating, for instance) can be counterproductive when your goal is contract nonrenewal or termination.

Supervision practices have evolved significantly, with a focus on helping teachers to improve their practice. For at least the last two decades, the literature in instructional leadership has emphasized various forms of coaching teachers (Schon, 1983; Costa & Garmston, 2002; Taggart, 2005; Marzano, 2012; Kee, 2012). Although there are a variety of approaches to coaching, one of the most widely accepted is coaching thinking, not necessarily coaching practice. The assumption is that if the supervisor/coach is skillful in getting teachers to think and reflect on their practice, over time they will make different decisions about the design of teaching and learning. That approach is addressed later in this chapter when we discuss nondirective and collaborative leadership styles.

There is a second reason we address supervision here. When your goal is nonrenewal or termination, you must use a directive style of supervision. Although many educators prefer to see themselves in a "helping" role and want to be collaborative or nondirective in all their professional relationships, a strong message of this chapter is: "Know what goal you are trying to accomplish and make sure you use the correct supervision style in accomplishing that goal!" Regardless of the desired outcome — teacher growth and improvement, contract nonrenewal, or contract termination — the principles of good supervision generally apply. Good supervision tools are essential to effective classroom observation and documentation.

IDENTIFYING THE MARGINALLY EFFECTIVE TEACHER

The *ineffective* teacher attracts a great deal of attention and is the target of intense supervision, while the *marginally effective* teacher typically is ignored as not "bad enough" to warrant much time and effort either for improvement or for termination. However, when you as a supervisor inevitably ask, "Would I choose to put my child in this teacher's class?" the honest answer must be no. Once a supervisor identifies the marginally effective teacher, the next step is to determine why the teacher's effectiveness is marginal. The 2002 Association for Supervision and Curriculum Development (ASCD) handbook entitled *Leadership for Learning* provides some useful insight into some of the reasons for weak teacher performance. According to its author, Carl Glickman, two factors lie at the heart of poor classroom performance. One factor concerns the level teacher's level of abstraction — the ability to identify classroom problems and generate solutions. The other factor is related to the teacher's level of commitment — the willingness to accept responsibility for student learning and to place students, not adults, first in decision-making. These two factors are discussed in the following sections.

Level of Abstraction

In an effective classroom a teacher must identify problems, generate solutions, act on those solutions, and monitor and adjust to the ever-changing classroom environment. A marginally effective teacher is one who may not even recognize a problem when it arises. Once the teacher knows about it, he* may have no idea how to solve it. There are too few teaching tools in his tool kit.

Sometimes it is hard for him to imagine making changes. He may be unaware of the relationship between his actions in the classroom and the success of his students. When students fail to learn, he is likely to believe that they are at fault. This teacher is often involved in many projects and activities, but rarely completes one before moving on to the next. Glickman describes a teacher with these characteristics as having a "low level of abstraction." A high abstractor, on the other hand, typically can diagnose problems and can generate alternatives for solving them. He understands the relationship between his actions and his students' success. If one strategy does not work, he looks in his "tool kit" and chooses another strategy. He takes responsibility for instruction and its impact on his students.

If one of the teachers you supervise is performing poorly because of a low level of abstraction, you first must address the *cause* for the low level. Below are three possible causes and some strategies for supervision.

Lack of Instructional Knowledge and Experience

Beginning teachers, in particular, often expend all of their physical and emotional energy just to get through each lesson. Each lesson is planned and taught for the first time – a frustration that veteran educators may well have

> **Lack of Instructional Knowledge and Experience**
>
> ▶ Every lesson is a first-time experience
> ▶ Small tool kit of instructional options
> ▶ Lack of understanding and/or appreciation of students from different cultural, social, ethnic and/or economic backgrounds
> ▶ More effective strategies outside their comfort zone

---

* We interchange "he" and "she" when referencing teachers in this chapter

forgotten! While a new teacher may be aware of instructional or management problems, he lacks sufficient experience from which to draw possible solutions— his tool kit is still relatively small. At other times he may not even be aware that problems exist; to him, everything is operating just as it should.

Many districts have found it desirable to orient the new teacher to the school and district and to follow up with a high-quality first year induction program with a good mentor teacher. This is true also of charter schools.

For this discussion, we'll assume that the teacher is knowledgeable about the subject he is teaching. Chapter 4 addresses supervision and documentation strategies to use when he is not. Our concern here is focused on instructional strategies.

Most marginally effective teachers plan their daily lessons within an instructional comfort zone that is defined by what they know how to do and what they are comfortable doing—their tool kit of instructional strategies is small. They may not teach well because they simply do not know or understand instructional strategies that lie beyond their current practices.

This lack of knowledge may increase when teachers are faced with students from different cultural, social, ethnic and/or economic backgrounds than students they have taught in the past. While effective in one teaching context, past teaching practices may not work with the current student population. Rather than admit that their reliance on traditional teaching practices is at fault, these teachers may blame students (or their parents, or society, etc.) for their ineffectiveness. Many teachers respond predictably to problems that arise in the classroom. For example, a beginning teacher may have a limited repertoire of skills for classroom management or for delivery of instruction. A more experienced teacher who finds the students in his classroom culturally, economically, or ethnically different from those he used to teach may become frustrated when the strategies he considers "tried-and-true" no longer work. The teacher in need of assistance is often a teacher who has failed to learn and/or implement new instructional strategies, as in the case of the ten-year veteran who has had the same year of teaching experience ten times. This teacher may face mounting classroom problems when his limited teaching practices prove ineffective.

Problem Solving, Situational Awareness, and Reflection

Teachers are sometimes so caught up in their own performance that they are unaware of the relationships between their own behavior and the behavior of their students. Much has been written about the concept of metacognition: "Thinking about thinking and conducting internal dialogue before, during and after an event" (York-Bar, xvii). Even when problems and solutions are identified, he may adopt a "just show me what you want me to do" attitude rather than taking the initiative to transform possible solutions into concrete action. When this teacher says, "I'm doing everything I know how to do," he is probably telling the truth!

An effective teacher with a high level of abstraction is able to analyze instructional decisions that are made before and during a lesson and routinely questions his instructional

> *"Clearly, teaching is a skill, and like any skill, it must be practiced. ... [T]eachers must ... examine their practices, set goals, and use focused practice and feedback to achieve those goals. These reflective practices are essential to the development of expertise in teaching."*
> —Robert Marzano

> **Problem Solving, Situational Awareness, and Reflection**
>
> ▶ What am I doing?
> ▶ Why am I doing it?
> ▶ How effective is it?
> ▶ How are my students responding?
> ▶ How can I do this better?

choices. Low abstractors typically do not ask themselves questions and reflect on their own practices either during or after a lesson.

Then, too, the teacher who is in need of assistance because of a low level of abstraction may be operating more from habit or from intuition than from conscious decision-making. Teaching is serendipitous rather than intentional. He may be unaware that few students are participating, that many students do not understand the instruction, or that several students have disengaged from the lesson. Teachers with low levels of abstraction may fail to recognize that the true measure of good teaching is the level of student engagement and success it evokes. As one teacher told co-author John Crain, "I think you should really observe me teach without any students in the room. Then you could see what my teaching is really like." This is a truly low abstractor!

Personal Problems

A teacher experiencing a serious crisis in his life outside the classroom may find himself emotionally and psychologically drained. If his problems diminish his classroom performance, his students may suffer. Marital difficulties or problems with family members, illness or injury, or financial woes may so occupy his attention that he is unable to devote much time and energy to the task of teaching, leaving him little to give once he arrives at school. If you believe that the teacher's personal problems are the source of his low abstraction, you must determine to what extent you can reasonably accommodate his problem. For example, you may have a teacher whose spouse has been diagnosed with cancer or who is the primary caregiver for a parent suffering from dementia.

While there is little that the supervisor can do, you must be sensitive to the teacher's problems while remaining attentive to the needs of his students. If his problems persist, it may become necessary to consider whether his problems are impairing his long-term classroom effectiveness and whether the problems are temporary or even remediable.

Your failure to attempt some reasonable, short term accommodation for these personal problems could jeopardize an eventual recommendation for contract nonrenewal. A school board may be reluctant to support a negative employment recommendation in these circumstances.

Level of Commitment

Suppose one of the teachers you supervise can think abstractly and has no difficulty solving classroom problems, and yet she is still only marginally effective. In this case, you will need to consider her general attitude toward the teaching profession and toward her specific instructional responsibilities – in other words, how high is her level of commitment?

> ▶ "Why bother? The students just don't care."
> ▶ Talks the talk, but rarely follows through
> ▶ Egocentrism: "What's in it for me?"
> ▶ Frustration with students and the system

A low level of commitment may be caused by a deliberate "why bother" attitude or it may be a result of circumstances beyond the teacher's immediate control. A teacher whose level of commitment is low may see no need to change, claiming that everything is "just fine." On the other hand, she may be the teacher who talks positively about changes but fails to follow through with effective action. Another manifestation of low commitment is the egocentric "what's in it for me?" attitude. The self-centered teacher fails to take action or make changes unless she can see some benefit for herself. Commitment is sometimes negatively impacted by the teacher's perception that the system has treated her unfairly, that trust has been violated, or that she has worked hard and received no recognition for her hard work.

Contrast this type of teacher with the highly motivated and committed teacher who is concerned about her students, her school, and the profession in general; who sees problems, chooses among alternative solutions, and follows through with decisions; or who continually seeks improvement and strives to make teaching and learning more interesting and exciting for her students.

In the preceding section, we noted that supervision of the teacher in need of assistance because of a low level of abstraction requires assistance that extends beyond identifying classroom problems and their symptoms. The same is true when you supervise a teacher who lacks commit- ment. In order to make informed decisions regarding remediation, the supervisor must identify and address the causes of low levels of commitment. As with the abstraction issue, the following is not an exhaustive list of causes, but it does provide a beginning point for supervision.

Burnout

The education literature is full of reports about teacher burnout. Some teachers have become frustrated because students today are very different from students they taught in the past. These teachers are often less effective in working with increasingly diverse student populations. While once quite effective, these teachers may simply have stopped trying. Others are disillusioned by what they perceive as administrative and bureaucratic structures that limit or interfere with their classroom autonomy. They may also have had one or more experiences in which they perceive that trust within the organization has been violated. In addition, misunderstandings and misinterpretations of the district's new teacher evaluation system or the State of Texas Assessment of Academic Readiness (STAAR) may contribute to teacher frustration and burnout.

- ▶ Burnout: frustration with students and the educational system
- ▶ Perceived violations of trust
- ▶ Overwhelmed: Cannot balance professional and personal obligations
- ▶ Fear or discomfort with change

Balance of Personal and Professional Life

Beginning teachers, in particular, may lack sufficient commitment because they are struggling to establish themselves professionally and to balance the demands of their personal and professional lives. It is difficult to make a commitment to be innovative and creative when just attending to the basics is overwhelming.

An experienced but ineffective teacher may be quite satisfied with the status quo and see little reason to change. Perhaps the teacher has good ideas but is unwilling to commit the necessary time and energy to carry them out. Her "What's in it for me? Why should I work harder and change what I do?" attitude may suggest that she is more concerned with her own interests than with the needs of her students.

Risk Tolerance and Fear of Change

Closely related to self-centeredness is the issue of change. Some teachers may simply be unwilling to change. They may realize that their old ways of teaching are not effective, but they are unwilling to commit the time and energy needed to learn and apply new pedagogy. Their old methodologies may not be very good, but they are very good at them! Change sometimes involves learning about and acting on new insights into the teaching-and-learning process: new curriculum and assessment standards, learning styles, differentiated instruction, brain research, inductive/inquiry lessons, integration of technology and electronic communication devices, and learning characteristics of children living in a culture of generational poverty. Some teachers may want society and students to change so that the old ways of doing business in the classroom can be perpetuated. They complain that poor parenting and social problems are the cause of low student achievement and resist pressure to adapt their teaching practices to include methods that are more effective for contemporary student populations. Other teachers may, understandably, simply fear change. Changing approaches to the design and delivery of instruction requires more risk than many are willing to accept, and there is comfort and safety in the old ways of doing things.

THE ISSUES INVOLVED IN SUPERVISION

In instructional supervision, there are at least three issues that will form the essential elements for a productive conference with the teacher: diagnosis, prescription, and time lines.

Diagnosis

The diagnosis responds to the question "What is effective and what is ineffective—what is working and what is not working?" The diagnosis may address issues related to the level of student participation and success, depth and complexity of the learning, connectivity of the learning to other disciplines and/or the world beyond the classroom, or the degree to which the classroom environment was supportive of student learning.

Prescription

Depending on the diagnosis, the prescription sets a direction for improving or maintaining teaching behavior. The prescription responds to the question "What must (or could) change?" Teachers with high levels of abstraction and commitment may generate their own prescription, but teachers with low abstraction and/or low commitment will need help in identifying areas for change and the direction in which changes must take place.

The following examples illustrate the language and the relationship between the diagnosis and the prescription:

DIAGNOSIS	PRESCRIPTION
The level of active, successful student participation does not meet the expectation of the district or charter school.	Plan and implement instruction in such a way that most students are actively, successfully participating in the teaching/learning process.

DIAGNOSIS
Monitoring and managing student behavior does not meet the expectation of the the district or charter school.

PRESCRIPTION
Monitor all students and intervene to stop or redirect behavior that is inappropriate or disruptive in such a way that this behavior stops.

Time Lines

Time lines establish checkpoints at which teaching behaviors will change and/or at which professional growth activities will be completed. When considering improvements in instructional behaviors, a common question is, "How much time is reasonable for change/improvement to occur?" The answer may be somewhat ambiguous because the length of time that is reasonable depends on a number of variables, including the teacher's contract, length of service, previous evaluations, seriousness of the behavior, and the complexity of the needed changes in the teacher's behavior, as well as district or charter school policies.

Longer Time to Improve		**Shorter Time to Improve**
• Term or continuing contract	vs.	Probationary contract
• Multiple years of experience	vs.	New to teaching
• History of good evaluations	vs.	No evaluations or consistently weak evaluations
• Minor/remediable problem	vs.	Serious/irremediable problem
• Complex changes in teacher behavior	vs.	Simple changes in teacher behavior
• Employee politically connected/popular	vs.	Employee not politically connected/popular

When the desired changes in behavior are complex (e.g., designing student-centered, inductive/inquiry lessons instead of teacher-centered, deductive lessons), it is reasonable to expect an extended period of time for those changes to occur. However, if the desired changes in behavior are rather simple (e.g., post rules for student behavior in the classroom), it is reasonable to expect changes within a much shorter time frame.

There may be some behaviors that are not remediable and will require no time for improvement. Assaulting a student would probably be considered irremediable behavior. The issue of remediation is addressed in more detail in Chapter 6.

MATCHING SUPERVISORY STYLE WITH TEACHER LEVEL OF DEVELOPMENT

Who Controls These Three Issues?

In the supervisor/teacher relationship, it is critical that you consciously understand who the decision-maker will be: Who will decide what is effective/ineffective (the Diagnosis), who will decide what (if anything) will change (the Prescription), and by when will changes occur (the Time Lines)? Will you be the decision-maker? Will the teacher be the decision-maker? Will you and the teacher share decision-making?

Supervisory goals are generally focused on assisting teachers in improving their instructional practices and professional habits, and a central concern of administrators is how to match their supervisory style to individual needs of the teachers they support. In this handbook we consider three supervisory styles: nondirective, collaborative, directive. These three styles move on a continuum of less supervisor control to more supervisor control.

| **Low Supervisor Control** | | **High Supervisor Control** |
High Teacher Control		**Low Teacher Control**
Nondirective	**Collaborative**	**Directive**

Each of these styles requires a different level of supervisory control of the three decisions. When the collaborative style is employed, the supervisor and teacher share control of diagnosis, prescription, and time lines. A nondirective approach places the teacher in control of these three issues. And a supervisor implementing the directive supervisory style retains control over all three supervisory issues. Each of these supervisory styles supports improved instructional practice when properly implemented and appropriately applied.

The modified version of Carl Glickman's paradigm shown in the figure below and the discussion which follows suggest ways that you may achieve this match by using what you know about the teacher's level of abstraction and level of commitment. (**Note:** While the paradigm is Professor Glickman's, the interpretations and applications are those of the authors.)

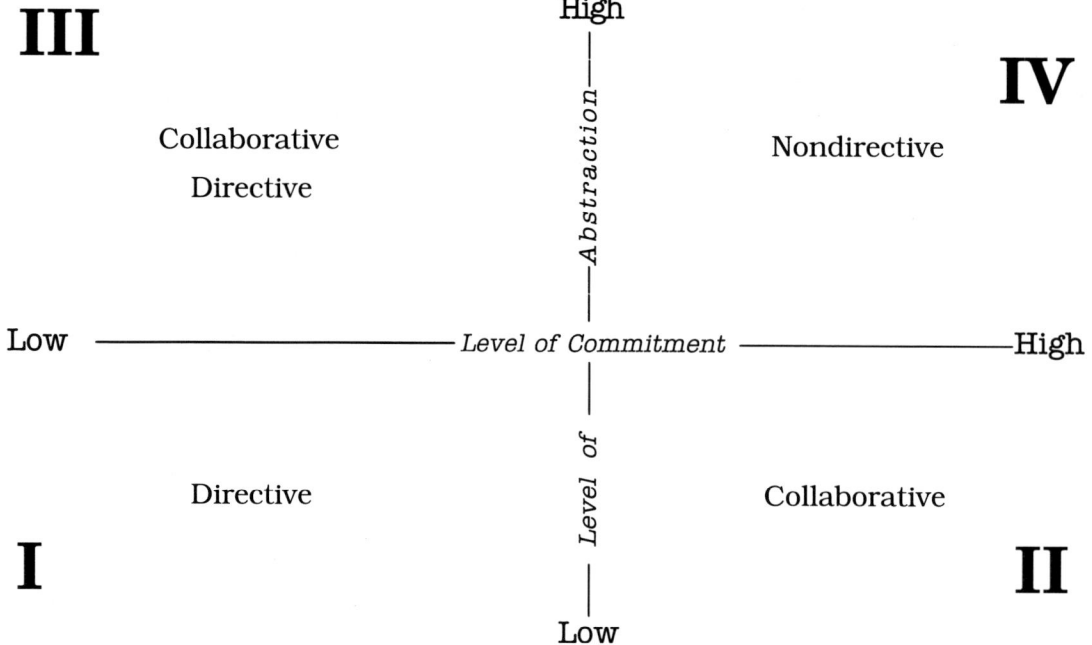

Figure 3-1*

* Adapted from Carl D. Glickman, *Leadership For Learning: How to Help Teachers Succeed.* (Alexandria, VA: Association for Supervision and Curriculum Development), p. 88. Copyright © 2002 ISED, Inc. Reprinted by permission. All rights reserved.

Since we are focusing on the teacher in need of assistance, we concentrate our examples of appropriate supervision styles for teachers in Quadrants I through III. The Quadrant IV teacher is, in general, the effective teacher.

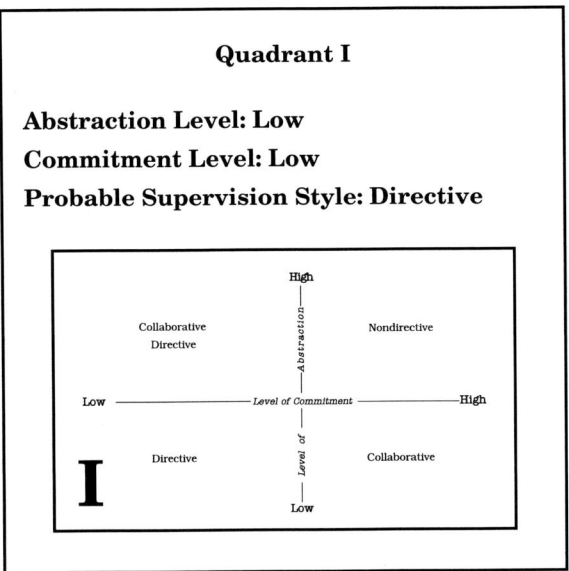

A directive style probably is most appropriate for the Quadrant I teacher. Remember, this teacher has a low level of abstraction and a low level of commitment--she has a small tool kit and may be unaware of problems, and she has a low commitment to changing/improving anything in her classroom. Consider the following scenario:

> In the post-observation conference, you tell the teacher that you observed four students passing notes. Then she responds, "Which students? When were they passing notes?" Later in the conference, you tell her that during the 45 minutes of observation three of the 28 students participated in the lesson in ways other than passive listening and note-taking. The teacher responds, "Is that a problem?" Toward the end of the conference, you ask her what changes she would make if she were to teach the same lesson again tomorrow. She replies: "I'd probably do it pretty much the same way. These remedial-level kids aren't going to do anything no matter what I do."

This teacher needs a directive style of supervision if any changes are going to occur. Her inability to see the problems in her classroom demonstrates her low level of abstraction, and even when problems are identified, she does not understand how to solve them or even acknowledge that they exist. The directive supervisory style will be the most effective approach in this situation, and the supervisor must control the issues of diagnosis, prescription, and time line.

In addition, the post-observation conference revealed that this teacher thinks the students are the problem and that not much change will take place as a result of her initiative. Clearly, her level of commitment is low; therefore, you also must control the prescription and time lines for her improvement.

Since this will be a directive conference, you will talk about your diagnosis, prescription, and time lines, and when you are finished, you will invite the teacher to say whatever she likes. You are the decision-maker; you will not be negotiating, arguing, attempting to convince, or attempting to reach consensus. That is what directive supervision is all about.

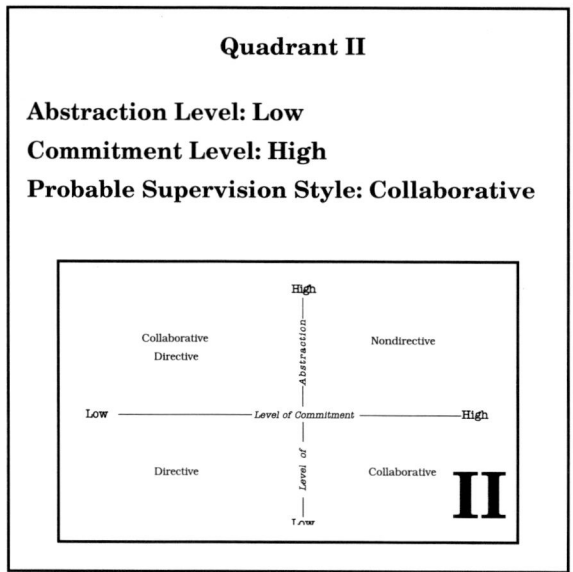

A collaborative style is probably the most appropriate for the Quadrant II teacher. Recall from our previous discussion that many beginning teachers are in this quadrant. The following scenario illustrates how to work with a teacher who has a high level of commitment but whose low level of abstraction hinders his effectiveness.

> In the post-observation conference, you share with the teacher some of the data you gathered during the observation. You tell him that when students were successful in responding to questions, he simply called on the next student and that when students were unsuccessful he provided no prompting or corrective feedback. The teacher is surprised. "I really thought I was using more positive reinforcement with the kids. I really enjoy them, and I want them to feel good when they are successful. I know I'm not very good at giving corrective feedback and prompting. I'm always so afraid I'll make them feel dumb or embarrass them if I try to help them get the right answer." When he asks you what he should be thinking about doing to improve both situations, you offer a number of alternatives. He replies, "I'd really like to attend the workshop on instructional strategies for low-achieving students and to observe Mr. Jones. He's really good at helping his kids without making them feel bad." He then asks if you can come back to observe immediately after he attends the workshop and observes Mr. Jones to see if he has improved. You suggest that maybe two weeks after the workshop and the observation of Mr. Jones' class would be a better time for you to revisit his classroom. This will give the teacher time to practice what he has learned.

This teacher is aware of some problems but not of others. In discussing the problems, he indicates that he is not quite sure how to solve them. This indicates a low level of abstraction. If the goal is to help the teacher improve, you need to share control of the diagnosis and prescription by presenting the objective data from the observation and offering a range of suggestions from which the teacher may choose or advise him to meet with an effective teacher in his area of instruction. Fortunately, this teacher has a high level of commitment. He wants to be better at both positive reinforcement and corrective feedback and even suggests one strategy for improvement. He asks you to return to the classroom to see if he has improved. You share control of the diagnosis and prescription. Because of his low level of abstraction, he needs assistance in identifying the problems and their solutions. You also share control of the time line; because he has *high* commitment, he may be inclined to overcommit to both the complexity and the speed of change.

You may find yourself supervising a Quadrant II teacher who wants to improve and who has a high level of commitment but whose level of abstraction is so low that improvement within a reasonable period of time is unlikely. In this instance, you may want to consider shifting your supervisory style from collaborative to directive.

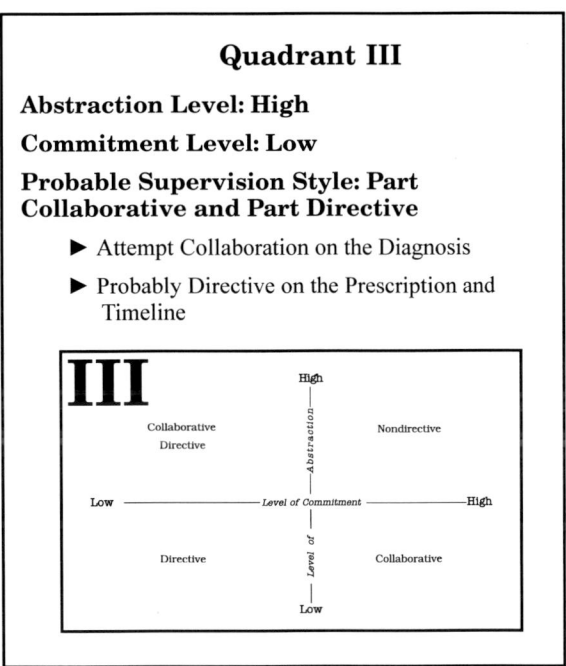

This area of supervision may be very complex. Because of the teacher's high level of abstraction, she is certainly capable of sharing control (collaborative style of supervision) of the diagnosis and prescription. Because she is low in commitment, you may learn early in the supervisory relationship that she is unwilling to accept responsibility for the ineffectiveness of her instruction. If your goal is to help the Quadrant III teacher improve, a collaborative style probably will be your first choice. If you discover that she is unwilling to acknowledge that there are problems with her instructional strategies, then a directive style may be more appropriate for diagnosis, prescription, and time lines. Here's a possible scenario.

In the post-observation conference, you tell the teacher that when you were observing her lesson, she put the term "existentialism" on the board and proceeded to talk about Jean-Paul Sartre and how he influenced a whole generation of American writers. When students were asked what Sartre's influence was on three short stories they recently had read, none of the six students called on was able to give a correct answer. When she assigned a three-paragraph in-class essay on Sartre's influence on the stories, at least nine students just sat at their desks looking at blank paper. At least six others had their hands up constantly. The teacher replied, "I know they had no idea what to do. I probably should have identified the four or five characteristics of existentialism and given them some examples before asking questions and making the writing assignment. I know from Madeline Hunter's work that abstract concepts are made more understandable and concrete for students if the critical attributes can be identified and elaborated. I will certainly need to do that in the future." Two weeks later, you observe the teacher teaching a lesson on Romanticism in American literature. She teaches this lesson in exactly the same way as she taught the lesson on existentialism and with the same effect on students.

This teacher has a high level of abstraction. She knows the problem, how to address the problem, what the options are, and the research literature. She has the ability to share control of diagnosis and prescription issues with the supervisor. In this instance, she does so accurately. However, this teacher's lack of commitment becomes apparent when her teaching style remains the same even after the need for change was discussed in the post-observation conference. The supervisor, therefore, must control the time line by reminding this teacher what she committed to do and setting a deadline for doing it.

If the supervisor determines that the teacher is unwilling to change and/or if the teacher blames the students for the problems and for her lack of effectiveness, the supervisor should choose a directive style of supervision for all three issues: diagnosis, prescription, and time lines.

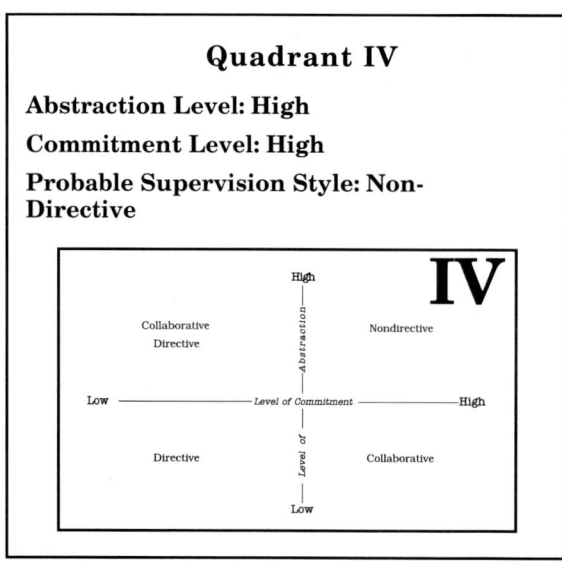

Quadrant IV

Abstraction Level: High

Commitment Level: High

Probable Supervision Style: Non-Directive

It is unlikely that you will ever need to use a directive approach with a Quadrant IV teacher. This teacher has a high level of abstraction and a high level of commitment. Consider the following scenario:

> In the post-observation conference, you ask the teacher to reflect on the mathematics lesson you observed. The teacher tells you that he is generally pleased with the way the lesson went. "The students were all engaged and almost all of them participated when I was demonstrating the algorithm on the SmartBoard. I know that's sometimes hard for them to do." When you ask the teacher what strategies he most commonly plans to maximize the level of engagement and participation, he says, "Well, I think there are several things I consider. I try to apply the concepts we study to things that are relevant to them. In this lesson, I used data from the sale of rap and pop music. There's usually more motivation to be engaged when the mathematical questions are interesting and relevant." You ask the teacher what he is considering doing in future lessons to maintain a high level of participation. The teacher replies, "I really want to move away from so much traditional paper/pencil assessment of their learning. I've been reading about problem-based learning in the math journals. That approach calls on students to produce products or performances that demonstrate that they understand and can apply the math. I'd really like to learn more about that and begin to try it out—maybe some time next semester."

A nondirective style clearly will be most appropriate because his high levels of abstraction and commitment make him effective. He recognizes what works in his class and can articulate the strategies he implements. He reads the literature in his field and is familiar with other options available to him. He is quite capable of controlling his own diagnosis and prescription. Since it reasonably can be anticipated that this teacher will take action to repeat effective behaviors and work to improve ineffective behaviors, the supervisor also should allow him to control the time lines.

Note: On rare occasions, you may encounter a teacher who is truly a Quadrant IV on almost every issue; however, there is one particular issue on which the teacher behaves as a Quadrant III. For example, the teacher is very effective and earns high ratings on almost every area of his appraisal. However, the teacher is highly resistive of the state-mandated Response to Intervention (RtI). The teacher makes comments such as "I know that some of these students need extra help and support, but a lot of them don't need separate interventions; they just need to keep up with the regular class work. It's a waste of time to design all these so-called interventions for some of these kids." He is a great teacher, but on the single issue of RtI, he disagrees with the state's requirements. You will initially attempt to use a collaborative style of supervision to persuade him of the validity of the campus RtI plan. If you are not successful, you will need to shift to a directive style and take control of the decisions on this issue. Since RtI is a state mandate, neither you nor the teacher really has any choice!

Goals of Supervision

Goal: Growth & Improvement (95%)	Goal: Contract Nonrenewal/Termination (5%)
Why This Goal: Evidence that the teacher: ▶ Wants to improve/meet expectations and ▶ Is capable of improving/meeting expectations. **Option 1:** **Nondirective Strategies and Language** ▶ Active Listening ▶ Questions using positive presuppositions ▶ Questions to probe thinking ▶ Summarizing (4 ways) ▶ Wait time for thinking and reflection **Teacher makes all the decisions (diagnosis, prescription, time lines)** **OR** **Option 2:** **Collaborative Strategies and Language** ▶ Dialogue/ Consensus-building ▶ Opportunity for teacher choices among valid options ▶ Negotiation/"Arguing" **Teacher and supervisor share decision-making (diagnosis, prescription, time lines)** **Documentation:** Notes to File—No memoranda or email to the teacher	**Why This Goal:** Evidence that the teacher: ▶ Does not want to improve/meet expectations and/or ▶ Is not capable of improving/meeting expectations. **Only One Option:** **Directive Strategies and Language** ▶ NO dialogue—"turn-talking" ▶ NO negotiation ▶ NO consensus-building ▶ NO opportunity for teacher choices among valid options ▶ NO "arguing" **Supervisor makes all decisions (diagnosis, prescription, time lines)** **Documentation:** Specific Incident Memorandum to teacher (incorporating notes to file and prior assessments, when appropriate)

As we have previously emphasized, the supervisor must know and be able to articulate the supervision goal for every employee. This chart suggests that there are only two possible goals: growth and improvement or contract nonrenewal/termination. The only other option is benign neglect: Stay out of their classrooms, be thankful for the good ones and hope they remain good, and pray that the bad ones either get better or go away! Obviously, the third option is a "non-option." Happily, most teachers (95%) want to improve and are capable of improving. That means you can spend most of your time and effort with them. Unfortunately a few do not want to/cannot meet expectations. Those are usually candidates for contract nonrenewal/termination.

The previous discussion in this chapter suggests that everyone should be supervised, but everyone should not be supervised in the same way. The chart indicates that when your goal is to help the employee get better, there are two supervision options: nondirective and collaborative.

OPTION 1: *NONDIRECTIVE STRATEGIES AND LANGUAGE*

Teacher makes all the decisions (diagnosis, prescription, time lines)

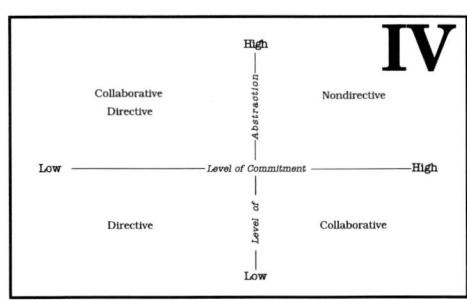

As indicated above, the nondirective supervisory style is often appropriate in cases involving teachers in Quadrant IV. The steps listed below are part of an overall strategy of collaborative supervision.

1. You may choose to conduct pre-observation conferences to discuss the teacher's plans for the lesson (e.g., the learning objective, instructional strategies, classroom management practices, techniques of presentation of subject matter, learning climate, evidence of successful student performance).

2. Conduct classroom observations, collect data, analyze the data. Do not make judgments. This will be a nondirective conference and the teacher will make whatever judgments she deems are appropriate. Your job is to coach her thinking and reflection—not judge and evaluate her practice. Observations will generally be announced—your goal is to help the teacher improve, not to play "gotcha."

3. After each observation, conduct a post-observation conference. In the conference, ask questions that encourage the teacher to analyze the lesson and the data and reflect on the lesson (or some strategy in the lesson). Remember that this is a nondirective conference—the teacher is in control of the issues: diagnosis, prescription, and time lines.

4. Diagnosis: Because the teacher has both high abstraction and high commitment, she is in control of this issue. Using the strategies and language for nondirective conversations, invite the teacher to reflect on the success of the lesson, what she believes was or was not effective.

5. Prescription: This is the teacher's decision. Using the strategies and language for nondirective conversations, invite the teacher to reflect on what she is thinking she might do differently (or repeat) in future lessons.

6. Time lines: Again, this is the teacher's decision. You might ask the teacher when she is considering acting on the changes (or repetitions) and ask her when she would like for you to come and observe again.

7. Since you believe that the teacher wants to get better (commitment) and has the capacity for getting better (abstraction), writing a specific incident memorandum

Nondirective Strategies and Language

▶ *Active Listening*
▶ *Questions using positive presuppositions*
▶ *Questions to probe thinking*
▶ *Summarizing (4 ways)*
▶ *Wait time for thinking and reflection*

would be counter-productive. In the culture of schools, receiving a written memorandum is perceived as negative. This perception may be seen as a violation of trust or as damaging to the supervisor/teacher relationship. It is advisable to write a simple note to file in the event you are wrong in your judgment about the teacher. If later, you begin to believe that the teacher does not want to/cannot improve, you have preserved the conversation and can later incorporate it into a specific memorandum.

OPTION 2: COLLABORATIVE STRATEGIES AND LANGUAGE

Teacher and supervisor share all the decisions (diagnosis, prescription, time lines)

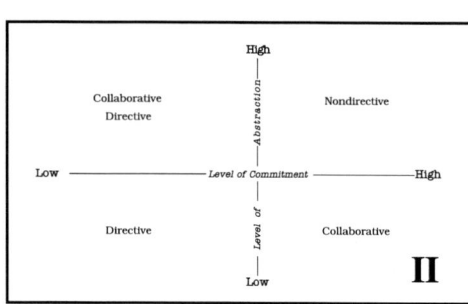

As indicated above, the collaborative supervisory style is often appropriate in cases involving teachers in Quadrant II. Collaboration might also be appropriate for the diagnosis with a Quadrant III teacher. The steps listed below are part of an overall strategy of collaborative supervision.

> **Option 2: Collaborative Strategies and Language**
>
> ▶ *Dialogue / Consensus-building*
> ▶ *Opportunity for teacher choices among valid options*
> ▶ *Negotiation / "arguing"*
>
> **Many of the Option 1, nondirective strategies may also be useful**
>
> ▶ *Active Listening*
> ▶ *Questions using positive presuppositions*
> ▶ *Questions to probe thinking*
> ▶ *Summarizing (4 ways)*
> ▶ *Wait time for thinking and reflection*

1. You may choose to conduct pre-observation conferences to discuss the teacher's plans for the lesson and agree on what the teacher will do and what you will see/ hear (e.g., the learning objective, instructional strategies, classroom management practices, techniques of presentation of subject matter, learning climate, evidence of successful student performance).

2. Conduct classroom observations, collect data, analyze the data, and make your own preliminary judgments about the practices that are effective in terms of successful student behavior/ performance and those that are not. Observations will generally be announced—your goal is to help the teacher improve, not to play "gotcha."

3. After each observation, conduct a post-observation conference. In the conference, ask questions that encourage the teacher to analyze the lesson and the data and reflect on the lesson (or some strategy in the lesson). Remember that this is a collaborative conference, so you will be sharing control of the issues: diagnosis, prescription, and time lines.

   You are sharing control of decision-making; you may be negotiating, arguing, attempting to convince, or attempting to reach consensus.

4. Diagnosis: This is a shared decision. Determine through questioning what she believes was or was not effective. Ask questions and provide data from the observation that prompt the teacher to identify teaching practices or lesson designs that were or were not effective.

5. Prescription: This is a shared decision. Ask the teacher about what changes in teaching practices or lesson design could/should occur. Offer choices (not suggestions or directives) for alternative strategies and offer choices for professional development activities to help the teacher to bring about the changes.

6. Time lines: This is a shared decision. Set reasonable time frames for changes in behavior and for completion of professional growth activities in consultation with the teacher.

7. Remember that although you have some questions about her level of abstraction, you believe that she wants to get better (commitment). Therefore, writing a specific incident memorandum may be counter-productive. In the culture of schools, receiving a written memorandum is perceived as negative. This perception may be seen as a violation of trust or as damaging to the supervisor/teacher relationship. It is advisable to write a simple note to file in the event you are wrong in your judgment about the teacher. If, later, you begin to believe that she does not want to/cannot improve, you have preserved the conversation and can later incorporate it into a specific memorandum.

STRATEGIES FOR DIRECTIVE SUPERVISION

If your goal is contract nonrenewal/termination, a directive approach is essential. Typically, these are the teachers in Quadrant I and Quadrant III. The steps listed below are part of an overall strategy of directive supervision.

Only One Option: Directive Strategies and language

▶ *NO dialogue—"turn-talking"*
▶ *NO negotiation*
▶ *NO consensus-building*
▶ *NO opportunity for teacher choices*
▶ *No "arguing"*

1. 1. You may choose to conduct pre-observation conferences to discuss the teacher's plans for the lesson and what you will expect to see (e.g., instructional strategies, classroom management practices, techniques of presentation of subject matter, learning climate, evidence of successful student performance).

2. Conduct frequent classroom observations, collect data, and analyze the data to determine which practices are effective and which are not in terms of successful student behavior/performance. Some observations may be announced; others may be unannounced "walk-through" observations. You do not simply want to see a dog-and-pony show. You want to see what is typical in this teacher's classroom.

3. After each observation, conduct a post-observation conference to provide feedback on the issues discussed in the pre-observation conference. Remember that this is a directive conference, so you will be in control (not shared control) of the issues—you will be the decision-maker for diagnosis, prescription, and

time lines. You will be the sole decision-maker about what is acceptable and what is not acceptable. This is a monologue — not a dialogue. Additionally, remember that if your goal is contract nonrenewal or termination, focus only on the observation data that show a need for improvement and your directives for improvement.

4. Diagnosis: You have control of this issue. When relying on the data from your observation(s), be very specific about what was or was not effective.

5. Prescription: You have control of this issue. Be very specific about what additional changes in his behavior must occur. Appendix C is a resource for writing specific, measurable changes in teacher behavior.

6. Time lines: You have control of this issue. Set reasonable time frames for changes in behavior and for completion of professional growth activities.

7. Write a specific incident memorandum to the teacher following each conference. (See Chapters 2 and 4.)

8. Continue to observe the teacher in the classroom, focusing on the specific changes in behavior that you directed and on evidence of successful student performance. (See Chapter 6.) These observations will probably be unannounced — you do not want to see dog-and-pony shows!

9. At some point in the supervision process, consider creating an intervention plan to formalize your judgments regarding deficiencies (diagnosis), your directives for changes in a classroom behavior (prescription), your expectations for student performance, and time lines for successful implementation of the standards. (See Chapter 6.)

Note: The teacher's failure to follow directives to change instructional behavior may become the basis for decisions to nonrenew or terminate the teaching contract.

FOCUSING ON INSTRUCTION IN THE CLASSROOM

It should be clear from our discussion so far that the supervisor responsible for marginally effective teachers will be spending considerable time in their classrooms. A teacher who resents your increased attention may accuse you of harassment, claiming that she is the subject of "arbitrary and capricious treatment." Why else would you be spending so much time in her classroom in comparison with the time spent in the classrooms of other teachers? Claims of harassment are unlikely to be given much credence when the rationale for stepped-up classroom visitations is objectively clear. There are a number of tactics you can use to forestall allegations of harassment and arbitrary and capricious treatment. Begin by making certain that you do, in fact, have objective reasons for visiting the teacher's classroom more frequently. The following list includes sample reasons for spending more time in a classroom. Whether they apply in a given school will depend on your district's or charter school's policies.

- Deficiencies apparent in previous classroom observations.
- Need to monitor compliance with directives and/or the requirements set forth in an intervention plan.
- Failure rates that exceed the norm for your campus.
- Complaints from parents, students, or other staff members.
- Low student performance indicated by the results of STAAR, TPRI, AP, mCLASS tests.
- Uniform treatment of an entire "class" of teachers (e.g., all probationary contract teachers, all teachers in their first year of assignment to your campus); if your campus plan has targeted raising math scores, the "class" of teacher may be all math teachers.

Note that these issues are not reasons for contract nonrenewal or termination. They are reasons for being in the teacher's classroom more frequently.

When your supervision goal is growth and improvement, explain to the teacher that your purpose is to help, not hurt. Comments such as these might be useful:

> As you know, Ms. Jones, my observations have revealed some concerns about teaching and learning in your classroom. I am going to devote as much of my time as possible to helping you address those concerns. I will be visiting your classes periodically to learn what else we might do. Please don't be upset by my visits. My purpose is to help you to address these concerns so that you can realize your full potential as a teacher on this campus.

It is true, of course, that you may eventually conclude that Ms. Jones will never be an effective teacher. Because of low abstraction and/or commitment levels, some marginally effective teachers cannot and/or will not respond favorably to guidance and principles of good developmental supervision. In these instances, it may become necessary for you as the supervisor to adopt a directive style of supervision that does not include encouragement to improve, because your goal is now to assemble sufficient evidence of ineffective teaching and/or of failure to follow your directives for behavior change to support a recommendation for contract nonrenewal or termination.

SUMMARY

In this chapter we have addressed the sources of weak instructional behaviors — low levels of abstraction and commitment — and discussed the supervisory issues and approaches that affect and support instructional improvement and professional growth in teachers in need of assistance. In the next chapter we will provide information and models for collecting data on classroom behavior and writing specific incident memoranda related to instruction. In Chapter 6, we will address the development of intervention plans that clearly communicate directives for change and specify techniques designed to facilitate better instructional behaviors and improved student outcomes.

REFERENCES

Costa, A.L., & Garmston, R. J. (2002). Cognitive coaching: a foundation for renaissance schools. Norwood, MA: Christopher Gorden.

Glickman, C.D. (2002). Leadership for learning: How to help teachers succeed. Alexandria, VA: Association for Supervision and Curriculum Development.

Kee, Katheryn et al. (2012) RESULTS coaching: The new essential for school leaders. Thousand Oaks, CA: Corwin.

Marzano et al. (2012). Becoming a reflective teacher (Classroom Strategies). Marzano Research Laboratory: Bloomington, IN.

Taggart, G. (2005). Promoting reflective thinking in teachers: 50 action strategies. Thousand Oaks, CA: Corwin Press.

York-Bar, J. et al. (2006). Reflective practice to improve schools: An action guide for educators. Thousand Oaks, CA: Corwin Press.

CHAPTER FOUR: DOCUMENTING INSTRUCTION

As discussed in Chapter 1, Education Code Section 21.3541 establishes the standards for the evaluation of principals and other administrators: Texas Principal Evaluation and Support System (T-PESS). Standard 1 (Instructional Leadership) sets the standard that "the principal is responsible for ensuring every student receives high quality instruction." Standard 2 (Human Capital) extends on Standard 1: "The principal is responsible for ensuring there are high quality teachers and staff in every classroom and throughout the school." High quality teachers planning and delivering high quality teaching and learning are clearly among the most important responsibilities for campus administrators. In order to fulfill those responsibilities, administrators must frequently be in classrooms to determine the quality of teaching and learning. If deficiencies are identified, the administrator must gather objective data about the teaching and learning process and, as discussed in Chapter 3, be prepared to work with the teacher toward growth and improvement or contract nonrenewal or termination.

The classroom data-gathering and documentation process described in this chapter both complements, and may be independent of, the appraisal process using the Texas Teacher Evaluation and Support System (T-TESS), or a locally developed system, including the Professional Development and Appraisal System (PDAS). The process complements these systems in that it provides a means of gathering cumulative data between formal assessments that can be incorporated into the overall teacher appraisal so long as the necessary time lines and other relevant procedures of the district's appraisal system are followed.

When documentation is tied to the teacher's appraisal, regardless of the rating, that rating needs to be supported by some data and shared with the teacher. This is the thrust of a 2015 Texas Commissioner of Education decision. In this case, the teacher contested her rating in Domain V of the PDAS Summative Annual Appraisal Report as not being supported by cumulative data. The school district noted that she was rated as proficient in this domain so no cumulative data had to be reported. The commissioner disagreed, saying "19 Texas Administrative Code Section 150.1003(f) requires cumulative [data] to be shared and makes no exception when a teacher is rated proficient in a domain. Since cumulative data does not support the ratings in Domain V, such ratings are arbitrary and capricious."[1]

The section of the code that the commissioner referred to is carried over to the new appraisal rules for T-TESS. The section number is still the same and reads in part: "Any documentation that will influence the teacher's summative annual appraisal report must be shared in writing with the teacher within 10 working days of the certified appraiser's knowledge of the occurrence. The principal shall also be notified in writing of the cumulative data when the certified appraiser is not the teacher's principal." Thus, there always must be data to support an appraisal rating and those data must be shared with the teacher.

The classroom documentation process described in this chapter also can be used as an independent assessment system for the marginally effective teacher, dependent upon local policy. As we saw in Chapter 1, the Texas Commissioner of Education has issued decisions indicating that satisfactory ratings on an overall appraisal system do not necessarily insulate a teacher from contract nonrenewal or termination. This is particularly true where overall domain scores on an appraisal instrument mask serious deficiencies in classroom performance. It also is true with regard to the probationary contract teacher where the development of appraisal-based growth plans may not be feasible. It is important to emphasize that we are focusing in this chapter on the marginally effective teacher who needs considerable supervisory attention and who may be a candidate for contract nonrenewal or termination. Our assumption is that your time is valuable and that you can realistically concentrate only on one or two marginally effective teachers at a time.

In Chapter 2, principal Ima Leader documented the out-of-classroom behavior of Melba Toast, a teacher on her faculty, who disparaged Ima's leadership in a public and unprofessional manner. Melba's conduct went well beyond complaining and criticizing. She flatly refused to implement Ima's discipline policy in the classroom. Though she later did comply with the policy, the unprofessional manner in which she addressed Ms. Leader was the focus of the last chance memorandum that Ima wrote.

Your memorandum may, however, have an altogether different focus. Suppose that a teacher on your staff — we will call him Benson Burner — is marginally effective or ineffective because of his poor teaching. You have worked with Mr. Burner over a period of time, and you are beginning to believe that he cannot (level of abstraction) and/or will not (level of commitment) improve. Your task now is to document one or more of Mr. Burner's ineffective instructional practices from information you gather during classroom observations.

METHODS OF GATHERING DATA IN CLASSROOM OBSERVATION

Before you can document inadequacies in the teaching/learning process, you first must go into the classroom to observe and collect data. Your ability to write effective documentation related to instruction is directly related to your ability to gather objective information in the teacher's classroom. Otherwise, you would have nothing to document except your own opinion— never a good idea. There are several effective ways to do this. Your choice of methods depends both on why you are observing and on how many different decisions you need to make following an observation. There are four primary methods of gathering and recording information during an observation: scripting, writing an anecdotal record, electronic recording, and using focused observation instruments.

A script is a word-for-word transcript of what the teacher and students say. Imagine that you have come to Mr. Burner's classroom to observe and you choose to employ the scripting technique. Here is an excerpt from your script notes:

Scripting

▶ Word-for-word script of everything teacher and students say and do

▶ Limitations:
  - Difficult
  - Potentially miss nonverbals

Teacher: OK, Noah, what's the difference between work and energy?
Noah: (is not successful)
Teacher: No, not exactly. (calls on Mariana)
Mariana: (successful response) Exactly. Great answer.
Teacher: Calls on Nari. If you are pushing against a wall and sweat & your muscles ache, are you doing any work?
Nari: I don't know.
Teacher: Why not? There's a picture in the book. Didn't you read the assignment?
(calls on Jacob)

Scripting is useful when you are conducting a lengthy classroom observation after which you will go back to your office and make many decisions about the lesson (how to rate the teaching and learning issues within your teacher appraisal system, for example). Scripting is a good option when you need detailed documentation of everything that was said and done during the lesson.

An advantage of the detailed word-for-word account of the lesson obtained by scripting is that it helps you to determine precisely why certain aspects of a lesson were significant. For example, the details you transcribed can tell why the lesson was extremely successful or was not at all successful.

The disadvantages of scripting are obvious. You are so busy writing (with your head down, most likely) that you may miss important non-verbal student and teacher behavior. You also might find that completeness and accuracy are very difficult to attain.

Anecdotal Record
- ▶ *Objective, descriptive notes*
- ▶ *Easier and faster than scripting*
- ▶ *Limitation: may miss some details of the lesson*

Writing an anecdotal record differs from scripting in that the observer takes descriptive notes about what is observed rather than trying to record each word. The exchange in the example above would appear this way if written as an anecdotal record:

Mr. Bruner called on Noah. He gave incorrect response. No corrective feedback. Teacher called on Mariana. She was successful.

Like scripting, the anecdotal record is useful when you are conducting a lengthy classroom observation upon which many decisions will be based and for which you will need information about every aspect of the lesson. It is appropriate to use anecdotal records rather than scripting when you do not need a verbatim record of the teacher monologue and student/teacher interaction.

Taking notes for the anecdotal record is faster and easier than scripting, allows the observer to note non-verbal teacher and student behaviors, and provides a great deal of information about many different aspects of the teaching/learning process. On the other hand, it does not provide details about what was said by teachers or by students.

Electronic Recording
- ▶ *Audio or video recording*
- ▶ *Incontrovertable evidence*
- ▶ *Limitations*
  - *Poor quality equipment*
  - *Disruption caused by equipment*

You may choose to record a lesson with audio or video equipment when the observation will be lengthy, when it will form the basis for many decisions, and when you need incontrovertible evidence of what was said or done during the lesson. You may also choose to record electronically when you decide that your skills at scripting or note-taking are not good enough to give you the information you need.

An obvious advantage of electronic recording is that you have a word-for-word record of the lesson with detailed verbal (and with video, nonverbal) information for use in analyzing the lesson and its effectiveness. You also have incontrovertible proof of what occurred in the classroom.

There are several disadvantages of electronic recording. As noted in Chapter 1, if audio or video recording is being done as part of teacher assessment, then parent permission for each student in the class should be obtained before doing so in order to avoid a privacy issue arising under Texas Education Code Section 26.009. Then too the video or audio recording equipment often available in schools may be of poor quality. Audio recording omits critical non-verbal behaviors while video recording sees only what the camera beholds (and the camera is often pointed at the wrong place).

Another very important drawback to electronic recording is that the disruption created by the equipment in the classroom is greater than that created by the observer alone. Moreover, the presence of the equipment may aggravate the teacher's anxiety and resistance. While teachers can be audio recorded or video recorded in the classroom over their objections as noted in Chapter 1, it would be best to get their buy-in by telling them how much they can learn about what works and what does not in their teaching. Another detriment to audio recording is that the transcript as written following the recording is detailed and fairly complete—the result of nonstop note-taking in the classroom itself or of a long series of write, rewind, write, rewind, write, etc., from a recorded source, which may take much longer than the original 25-minute observation. The focused observation instruments that follow are designed to minimize the time spent recording data by sharpening the observer's focus.

What might be your focus for the observation/data collection?
How might T-TESS organization and language
help focus the observation/data collection?

Focused Observation Instruments
▶ *Checklists/charts*
▶ *Focus data collection on a few issues rather than capturing everything that is said and done*
▶ *Limitation: will not produce data beyond the focus of the instrument*

Suppose you want to visit a teacher's classroom specifically to observe two or three aspects of the planning/teaching/learning process—instruction, for example. When you are concerned only with one or two issues during a classroom visit, you should use a focused observation instrument such as a check list, seating chart, or short question-answer list for gathering information. In the case of student participation, for example, a seating chart similar to the one shown in Figure 4-1 on p. 4-37 will prove helpful. The chart will make it easy to document the interchange between the teacher and students.

Focused observation instruments that target only a particular aspect of instruction are easy to use because they do not require a great deal of writing. Not burdened by taking notes, you are free to detect non-verbal behaviors and can gain a great deal of information about the issue or issues you came to observe. Recognize, however, that focused observation instruments should not be used for formal appraisals or for gathering data upon which many decisions will be made, because they do not address all aspects of the lesson.

GATHERING DATA IN THE MARGINAL TEACHER'S CLASSROOM

In Chapter 3 we described the marginally effective teacher and made a series of recommendations for appropriate supervision practices. Recall that the marginally effective teacher is one who has some competence but who also has one or more deficiencies in instructional practice. More importantly, these deficiencies impede his or her performance, as evidenced in student misbehavior, lack of success, or other factors.

Suppose that you have decided that you no longer can ignore the teacher's inadequacies. The action that you take as his supervisor may assist him to improve. Or, despite your best efforts, he may not improve beyond his marginal effectiveness, and you may eventually recommend a negative employment decision.

Your best approach may be to conduct a series of 15 to 30 minute observations in his classroom and direct your data collection efforts toward his weak planning and instructional areas.

The history of teacher evaluation in Texas has included three different appraisal systems:

- Texas Teacher Appraisal System (TTAS)
- Professional Development and Appraisal System (PDAS)
- Texas Teacher Evaluation and Support System (T-TESS)

Although each iteration of teacher appraisal has changed the rules, process, and scoring/ rating, the basic criteria for effective teaching and learning have not changed. In the areas ad- dressing teaching and learning, any researched-based teacher appraisal process will include a consistent set of common themes. Those themes may be organized and articulated differently. Language describing varying levels of proficiency may also change. The teaching/learning themes, however, have been consistent over the 27 year history of the state's formal appraisal processes. Whether your district uses PDAS, T-TESS, or a locally adopted process, it is likely that your system will in some way address these issues.

Many of the themes overlap each other. For example, the T-TESS planning dimension significantly overlaps the instruction dimension. Planning student-centered activities is essential before seeing student-centered activities appear in the classroom. The chart below provides some guidance in how T-TESS is structured around these universally accepted best practices.

| **T-TESS Domains With Subsets Common to Best Practice and All Texas Teacher Evaluation Systems** ||
T-TESS Domains	**Best Practices Found in All Teacher Evaluation Systems**
1. Planning: Alignment of Curriculum, Instruction, and Assessment	a. Data-Driven b. Alignment of Curriculum Objectives, Activities, and Resources c. Quality of Learning Activities d. Recognition of Unique Needs and Characteristics of Students e. Reflects an Intentional, Organized Plan to Address the Instruction and Learning Environment
New Alternate 1. Lesson Internalization: Alignment of Curriculum, Instruction, and Assessment	

With the availability of High Quality Instructional Materials, teachers may be required to internalize the available lesson design and use of resources rather than develop their own lesson plans. School systems will have the option to use the newly adopted Alternate Domain I: Lesson Internalization. This domain is applicable and may be used for appraisals when a teacher's instructional preparation shifts from lesson planning to lesson internalization.

2. Instruction	a. b. c. d. e. f. g. h. i.	Student Participation and Success Content Knowledge and Expertise Communication Depth/Complexity of Learning Connectivity of Learning (student experience, prior learning, other disciplines, world beyond the class) Learning/Lesson Design Differentiation Based on Unique Needs/Characteristics of Students Monitoring/Formative Assessment, Feedback to Students, Adjustment When Needed Integration of Technology (when available and appropriate)
3. Learning Environment	a. b. c. d. e.	Physically and Psychologically Safe and Supportive Students Participate and Manage with Very Limited Teacher Direction Intrinsic Student Motivation for Learning and Behavior (student interest/relevancy, differentiation of learning, students participate and manage with very limited teacher direction) Classroom Management/Organization (time, materials, activities, student behavior) Classroom Culture

The next chart below illustrates how the T-TESS Scoring Rubric organizes these themes and assesses a teacher around "domains" and their subsets, referred to as "dimensions":

Four Domains of the T-TESS Rubric

▶ First three domains address teaching and learning
- The three teaching/learning domains have a total of twelve subsets (called "dimensions")
- Each dimension is scored separately

▶ One domain (4) addresses professional practices and responsibilities
- This domain has four dimensions
- Each dimension is scored separately

Domain 1: Planning or Alternate Domain 1: Lesson Internalization 1.1 Standards and Alignment 1.2 Data and Assessment 1.3 Knowledge of Students 1.4 Activities	**Domain 2: Instruction** 2.1 Achieving Expectations 2.2 Content Knowledge and Expertise 2.3 Communication 2.4 Differentiation 2.5 Monitor and Adjust
Domain 3: Learning Environment 3.1 Classroom Environment, Routines and Procedures 3.2 Managing Student Behavior 3.3 Classroom Culture	**Domain 4: Professional Practices and Responsibilities** 4.1 Professional Demeanor and Ethics 4.2 Goal Setting 4.3 Professional Development 4.4 School Community Involvement

Transitioning from one appraisal system to another is frequently challenging. For example, in many instances, the Teacher Self-Report in PDAS had become a mere formality. In T-TESS, emphasis on teacher self-assessment, goal-setting, professional development, and coaching conferences is very serious and is central to the process. Arguable, the two systems (T-TESS and PDAS) have a very different focus. "...(T)hey are different systems and trying to side-by-side them will send the wrong message (emphasis added)." (*TEA Evaluation Refinement Year Newsletter*; Texas Education Agency, September, 2015.)

There is, however, a body of research on which most teacher evaluation systems are based. This research tends to lead any system to the same criteria: planning, instructional design, classroom management, learning environment, active student participation, student success, depth/ complexity of learning, etc. T-TESS and PDAS are no different; each relies on the same body of research and best practices. While there are differences in the focus and scoring rubric of each system, the criteria for each are the same.

For a more detailed understanding of how the common criteria and accompanying descriptive language of PDAS and T-TESS correlate with each other as well as with research-based accepted best practices, see the correlation chart at the end of this chapter.

In order to capture objective data on a limited number of teaching/learning issues, we offer three focused observation instruments. They are designed to be used during classroom observations, before and/or after the formal appraisal observation. Regardless of how your specific appraisal system is organized, the teaching/learning process is highly complex and integrated. Issues in one area tend to overlap and impact other areas. For example, in T-TESS, active student participation and connections to students' prior knowledge and experiences must be planned for in both the original Domain I (Planning) and in the Alternate Domain I (Lesson Internalization). In addition, active student participation is observable evidence of whether the planning resulted in active student behavior during the lesson (Domain 2: Instruction).

A Note on the Lesson Scenario

In order to illustrate how the focused observation instruments work, we have provided a lesson scenario and examples of how each of the three focused observation instruments might look, based on that scenario. The lesson below is a teacher-centered lesson. Both T-TESS and PDAS have qualitative biases in their evaluation scales. For example, in T-TESS, the "continuum for scoring" rubrics are based on "teacher-centered actions" at the Improvement Needed and Developing score points. The rubrics for Accomplished and Distinguished score points are based on "student-centered actions." In other words, the more student-centered the classroom is, the more likely it is that the teacher will receive a higher score. As Texas Education Agency has pointed out, "...you can watch two teachers teach the exact same lesson the exact same way, and one lesson can rate Developing and one can rate Accomplished because what really matters is how the students respond to the learning" (*TEA Evaluation Refinement Year Newsletter*; Texas Education Agency, September, 2015.)

Likewise, PDAS follows the same line of qualitative reasoning. If (1) the students are doing most of the work and thinking and (2) the work and student learning reflect depth and complexity, the teacher is likely to receive a better appraisal score.

Since our emphasis here is on the marginally effective teacher who may be a candidate for contract nonrenewal or termination, the scenario is intentionally designed to reflect a teacher-centered lesson and to surface deficiencies in multiple domains.

Additionally, coauthor John Crain has analyzed anecdotal data from more than 2,000 walk-through observations. Unfortunately, more than 70% of these observations reflected teacher-centered lessons in which most students were not actively participating in the lesson.

> "... you can watch two teachers teach the exact same lesson the exact same way, and one lesson can rate Developing and one can rate Accomplished because what really matters is how the students respond to the lesson."

We have intentionally chosen science as the content of the lesson. Frequently, supervisors are uncomfortable when a lesson's academic content is outside their own area of specialization. The point to recognize is that you do not have to be a content expert in order to be an expert supervisor/evaluator. The teacher is the content expert; you are the expert on teaching and learning. The scenario is designed to make that point. If you have concerns about the teacher's knowledge of subject matter or if you receive complaints from other teachers or parents about inaccurate content, take a content expert with you to do a classroom observation. This issue is discussed and illustrated in more detail later in this chapter. The following scenario involves a marginally effective teacher, focused observation instruments based on the scenario, and accompanying memoranda to the teacher.

```
Class:      9th grade History
Teacher:    Mr. Bill Laze
Date:       November 8, 2023
Time:       8:30-8:55
Number of students:  30
```

(As you enter the room and sit down, you note the following objective written on the whiteboard: 6.8 Force, motion, and energy. The student knows force and motion are related to potential and kinetic energy. The student is expected to: (A) compare and contrast potential and kinetic energy. On your iPad you verify that this is one of the curriculum objectives for this six-weeks. You also note that student desks are arranged in pairs, all facing the front of the room.)

(Students are entering room. Bell rings. Four students enter after the tardy bell. Mr. B. is talking to two students at his desk. Mr. B. does not say anything to four students who enter late. Roll-taking, management tasks, and the teacher walking around the room to give each student a one-page handout take six minutes. Teacher stands behind his lectern.

Teacher: OK. Open your science books to page 87. Today we're going to be talking about the differences between kinetic and potential energy. You were supposed to read this chapter as part of last night's assignment. You need to be sure and take notes from the Power Point and on the handout, because some of this is not in your chapter.

Teacher: OK. Let's start with energy. As you see on the handout, energy is the ability to do work. Work happens when force causes an object to change or move. Because work and energy are so closely related, they are expressed in JOULES (J). When a given amount of work is done, the same amount of energy is involved. So, Noah what's the difference between work and energy?

Noah: Well, I guess work is labor, like my uncle does at the factory where he works. Uh, and I guess energy is what he needs to do the work.

Teacher: No, not exactly. Mariana, do you know?

Marianna: I think, like it says on the handout, anytime an outside force causes something to change or move, that's work. The force that causes the change or move is energy.

Teacher: Exactly right. Great answer.

Teacher: Now, Nari, if you are pushing against the wall over there and you are pushing so hard that that you start to sweat and the muscles in your arms begin to ache, are you doing any work?

Nari: I don't know.

Teacher: Why not? There's a picture like that right there in the book. Didn't you read the assignment? Jacob?

Jacob: Well, sure. If you are pushing and sweating and your muscles ache, you are working really hard and using a bunch of your energy.

Teacher: Oh, my gosh. You are completely missing the point, as usual. Mariana, can you bail him out?

Mariana: It doesn't matter how hard you are pushing. If the wall does not move, no work is being done. That's kinda the definition: work is happening only if the object changes or moves.

Teacher: You nailed it again, Mariana. That's exactly the point. If you are pushing and sweating and achy but the wall does not move, there's no work being done.

(Teacher: continues to stand behind lectern. Refers to the handout and tells students that there are eight types of energy and verbally defines each one.)

Teacher: Be sure you got all those definitions down on your handout because they are probably going to be on the test and the definitions in your textbook are a little different.

Teacher: Now let's focus just on mechanical energy because mechanical energy can be all potential energy, all kinetic energy, or both—that's right there on slide 4. So let's think about kinetic energy for a minute. All right Aaron, I'm going to give you another chance. (Teacher picks up a hammer from the lectern and holds it up in a stationary position.) Does this hammer have kinetic energy?

Aaron: Sure. You can use that hammer to pound nails, or break up concrete—all kinds of work. And you said work and energy were basically the same thing.

Teacher: Not hardly, Aaron—you completely missed the point. Does anybody know?

(Aaron closes his book and puts down his pen. Pause. No hands are raised. Mr. B. is still standing at lectern. (Teacher sighs)

Teacher: You duds are going to have to start reading the assignment if you ever expect to pass my class. (Mariana raises her hand.) Yeah, Mariana.

Mariana: When you hold the hammer over your head like that, it has potential energy. But until you start to move the hammer by swinging it, then it has kinetic energy. The book says that on page 90.

Teacher: That's another great answer. Did everybody get that? The hammer has potential energy—not kinetic energy. It doesn't have kinetic energy until you start to move it.

(Mr. B. is still standing behind lectern, lecturing from Slide 5 about gravitational potential energy and how it can be expressed by a mathematical formula.)

Teacher: Now tomorrow I am going to show you how to work some of these problems so you can measure potential energy. But we're not going to do that until tomorrow.

(At 8:45: Six students are taking notes. All others are not taking notes. Mr. B. continues to stand at lectern. Nothing has been written on board. Other than the hammer, no objects or pictures have been used. Three students in the back — Aaron, William, Ava — are whispering. Mr. B. still at lectern and begins talking about potential energy.)

Teacher: I forgot to put the definition of potential energy on the handout, so be sure to get this down in your notes. Potential energy is stored energy. It has the potential to do work.

(Five students write something on their handout. None of the other students do.)

Teacher: Imagine a roller coaster stopped at the top of a ramp. It has potential energy when it is high in the air. An object high up has the potential for energy due to gravity. When the roller coaster begins to move, its potential energy is transformed into kinetic energy. So, Matt, what's the difference between mechanical potential energy and mechanical kinetic energy?

Matt: I don't have a clue.

Teacher: You rarely do. Jacob? Jacob: What's the question?

Teacher: What's the difference between mechanical potential energy and mechanical kinetic energy?

Jacob: An object at rest has potential energy. When the object starts to move it has kinetic energy.

Teacher: Finally, Jacob. Somebody gets it.

(Observation ends at 8:55. Mr. B. is still at lectern lecturing about the conservation of energy. Angel is helping Jason sort papers. Luciana and Reggie are talking. Liam and Mia are watching me.)

GATHERING AND TRANSCRIBING DATA

Focused Observation #1 Planning /Internalization and Instruction
Primary Focus:

▶ *Student participation & Success/Mastery*

▶ *Feedback to / Interaction with Students*

▶ *Depth/Complexity/ Creativity of Learning*

▶ *Alignment: Objective, Activities, Materials*

Focused Observation Instrument #1: Planning/ Internalization and Instruction (Primary Focus #1)

You will notice that this instrument relates to both the planning and instruction domains. Who is doing most of the work and thinking? Are students successfully engaged in learning that reflects depth, complexity, and/or creativity? Is there alignment among objectives, activities, materials, and the needs/characteristics of students?

Are students responding to and participating in instruction because the teacher has selected instructional strategies, activities, and materials that motivate and engage the students, or is student participation merely mechanical and compliant?

This instrument has the potential to yield objective data on several different issues related to both planning and instruction.

FOCUSED OBSERVATION INSTRUMENT #1: Planning /Internalization and Instruction

- ✔ Student Participation & Success
- ✔ Feedback to / Interacftion with Students
- ✔ Depth/Complexity/Creativity of Learning
- ✔ Alignment: Objective, Activities, Materials

Name of Teacher: Benson Burner
Subject/Grade Level: 6th grade science
Specific Content/Activity: Compare and contrast potential and kinetic energy

Date of Observation: 11/8/21
Time of Observation: Begin: 8:30   End: 8:55
Number of Students in Class: 26

(1)

For **whole-group, teacher-centered instruction**, record the names (descriptions, seat assignment) of students who participated in ways other than passive listening. Record the question/prompt from the teacher. Circle the + beside the name(s) of students whose participation was successful. Circle the – beside the name(s) of students whose participation was not successful. Circle a ? if you cannot determine student success. Record the teacher's response to the student's response/performance/demonstration.

STUDENT	QUESTION	SUCCESSFUL/UNSUCCESSFUL	TEACHER RESPONSE TO STUDENT
1. Noah	What's the difference between work and energy	+ ⊖ ?	No, not exactly. (Calls on Marina)
2. Mariana	(same question)	⊕ – ?	Exactly. Great answer.
3. Nari	If you are pushing against a wall and sweat and your muscles ache, are you doing any work?	+ ⊖ ?	Why not? There is a picture right there in the book. Didn't you read the assignment? (Calls on Jacob)
4. Jacob	(same question)	+ ⊖ ?	Oh my gosh. You are missing the point, as usual. (Calls on Mariana)
5. Mariana	(same question)	⊕ – ?	You nailed it again, Mariana. That's exactly the point.
6. Aaron	(T. holds up a hammer) Does this hammer have kinetic energy?	+ ⊖ ?	Not hardly, Aaron. You completely missed the point.
7. To class	Does anybody know?	+ ⊖ ?	(No hands raised. Aaron closes his book puts down pen. T. sighs) You duds are going to have to start reading the assignment if you are going to pass my class
8. Mariana	Yeah Mariana (same hammer question	⊕ – ?	That's another great answer. Did everybody get that?
9. Matt	What is the difference between potential energy and mechanical energy?	+ ⊖ ?	(Matt says, "I don't have a clue.") T: You rarely do. (Calls on Jacob)
10. Jacob	(same question)	⊕ – ?	Finally, somebody gets it. Good job, Jacob
11.		+ – ?	
12.		+ – ?	
13.		+ – ?	

(2)

4-12

Evidence of Activities Planned and Implemented to Promote
Participation, Success, Complex/Creative Learning, and/or Connectivity

Check any techniques that the teacher used to promote active, successful student participation, complex learning, and/or connectivity of learning. Checking the technique does not necessarily mean that the technique was used effectively — it simply means that the technique was used. Make any specific notes that will help you remember what the teacher did/failed to do.

____ Used strategies that provided for students to make connections of new learning (e.g., prior/future learning within the discipline, own interests/experiences, other disciplines, world beyond the classroom)	____ Sent students to board/chart/map (3)
	____ Varied activities
	____ Provided activities/materials that made lesson relevant/interesting to students
____ Provided opportunities for students to interact with each other	____ Provided application/lab activity
X Provided opportunities for students to volunteer, offer feedback, make independent choices *1 whole group question - no responses*	____ Instructional activities allowed/ encouraged students to interact with each other around the learning
X Asked questions/assigned tasks at the application level or higher (Bloom's Taxonomy) *2 students successful*	X Positively reinforced student participation and/or success *2 students*
____ Instructional activities provided for students to produce products that represent complex learning	____ Recognized when students become confused or disengaged and responds to student learning or social/emotional needs
____ Designed inductive learning for students to explore/research	____ Addresses student mistakes and follows through to ensure student mastery
____ Used pair/share, elbow partners, quick-write, etc.	____ Other technique/strategy
____ Used group discussion	____ Other technique/strategy
X Used random calling *6 students*	____ Other technique/strategy

Evidence of Student Engagement/No Engagement
8:45: Six students taking notes. All others are not taking notes. T. continues to stand at lectern. Other than the hammer, no objects or pictures have been used. Three students in the back - Aaron, William, Ava - are whispering. Mr. B. still at lectern and begins talking about potential energy. (Observation ends at 8:55. Mr. B. is still at lectern lecturing about the conservation of energy. Angel is helping Jason sort papers. Luciana and Reggie are talking. Liam and Mia are watching me.)

(4)

Summary of Data and Preliminary Judgments on Planning /Internalization and Instruction

In the space below, summarize the data from the previous two pages and make judgments about the quality of instructional strategies. **(5)**

Active, Successful Student Participation

▶ How many students participated? __6__ of __26__ participated.
  (total # of students)
▶ How many students did not participate? __20__
▶ How many students were successful? __2__
▶ How many students were unsuccessful? __4__
▶ What was the learning/curriculum objective? _Compare and contrast potential and kinetic energy_

▶ What instructional activities, strategies, and materials/resources were used in teaching this lesson?
Lecture (from behind lectern entire period). Question/answer. Textbook, hammer, handout

Based on the data, circle YES if the statement describes what you say/heard. Circle NO if the statement does not describe what you saw/heard. If you have no data or insufficient data, do not circle anything. In making judgments, rely on the preponderance of the data/ evidence. **(6)**

All descriptions, unless otherwise noted, are based on the Proficient language of the Texas Teacher Evaluation and Support System (T-TESS). For corresponding language from the Professional Development and Appraisal System, see the correlation chart at the end of this chapter.

PLANNING & INSTRUCTION: Student Participation & Success	**PLANNING AND INSTRUCTION: Depth and Complexity of Learning**
• Most students demonstrate mastery of the objective YES **(NO)**	• Insured high levels of learning, social emotional development and achievement for all students YES **(NO)**
• Engaged all students in relevant, meaningful learning YES **(NO)**	• Lesson was flexible and encouraged higher-order thinking, persistence, and achievement YES **(NO)**
• Addressed student mistakes and followed through to ensure student mastery YES **(NO)**	• Asked questions that encouraged all students to engage in complex, higher-order thinking YES **(NO)**
• Led a mutually respectful and collaborative class of actively engaged learners YES **(NO)**	
• Recognized when students become confused or disengaged and responds to student learning or social/emotional needs YES NO	**PLANNING AND INSTRUCTION: Alignment**
• Established classroom practices that provided opportunities for most students to communicate effectively with the teacher and their peers YES NO	• All goals were aligned to state content standards. **(YES)** NO
• Used probes to clarify, elaborate thinking. YES **(NO)**	• Activities, resources, technology and instructional materials are all aligned to instructional purposes (objectives) YES **(NO)**
• Asked remember, understand and apply level questions that focus on the objective of the lesson and provoke discussion **(YES)** NO	• All activities were sequenced and relevant to students YES **(NO)**
• Students worked respectfully individually and in groups YES **(NO)**	• The lesson integrated learning objectives with other disciplines YES **(NO)**
• Anticipates possible student misunderstandings. YES **(NO)**	• Lesson accurately reflected how the lesson fits within the structure of the discipline and state standards. YES **(NO)**
• Interacted with students in respectful ways at all times (Teacher Standard 4: Learning Environment) YES **(NO)**	• Provided opportunities for students to use different types of thinking (e. g., analytical, practical, creative and research-based) YES **(NO)**

The evidence of the quality of the planning will most likely be found in the actual implementation of the instruction and its impact on students.

Commentary and Rationale

(1) The first section of the instrument provides essential information that you will need when you are ready to write your memorandum to Mr. Burner (e.g., date and time of the observation, length of the observation, etc.). In order to make decisions about fidelity to the district curriculum and alignment of instruction, materials and students, it is essential to capture the curriculum objective. If the objective is not posted in the classroom, you will need to check the teacher's lesson plans and/or the district curriculum scope-and-sequence.

(2) In this section, you record each teacher/student interaction as it occurs. Noah's response was incorrect, Mr. Burner responded, "No not exactly" and called on Mariana. When Mariana answered correctly, Mr. Burner responded, "Exactly. Great answer" and called on Nari. Note that all information is presented in objective, non-judgmental terms. Never write judgmental or editorial comments. Mr. Burner responds to Jacob, "Why not? There's a picture like that right there in the book. Didn't you read the assignment?" Write down his exact words rather than the inappropriate judgment "put-down comment by teacher." In recording observation data and writing documentation, stick to the facts—what the teacher said and did; what students said and did.

(3) This section of the instrument is completed whenever you have the opportunity: as the teacher uses a technique/strategy or during downtime, that is, when there are few teacher/student interactions and when you have time to consider other things going on in the classroom. The form indicates by an X that the teacher used random calling and you noted that the teacher called on six students. Use of positive reinforcement also is checked, with the added note that Mariana's responses were reinforced. Providing students opportunities to volunteer is also checked because the teacher asked the whole class "Does anybody know?" Note that checking a technique does not necessarily mean that the technique was used effectively; it simply means that the technique was used. You may later make the judgment whether or not these techniques were effective. During the observation, however, record only that these techniques were used. Notice that there are very few items that are marked X. This is, in and of itself, important. Sometimes no data are data.

(4) In this section, you have captured evidence related to student engagement.

(5) The final page of the focused observation instrument should be completed back in your office. It consists of a summary of the data and preliminary judgments from the previous two sections of the instrument. Remember that the preceding data were factual and objective—no judgments were made about the quality or effectiveness of the teaching behaviors. In completing

this section, you summarize the data from the first two pages. In the case of Mr. Burner, the summary reveals the following:

- Six of the 26 students participated.
- Two of the six students who participated (Mariana and Jacob) were successful.
- Twenty students did not participate.
- Three of the four correct responses came from Mariana. The observer is concerned with how many students gave correct responses, not with how many responses were correct.
- You have copied the curriculum objective from the first page and listed the activities, strategies, and resources that were used in the lesson.

Note that everything summarized up to this point has been reported objectively—no judgments or conclusions.

(6) The bottom of the page consists of preliminary judgments, based on the data. You should only make judgments if the preponderance of evidence from the first two pages can convincingly support the judgments.

- Unless otherwise noted, all judgments use language from the Proficient description in T-TESS. If your district or charter school uses a different teacher appraisal system, you will want to use the Proficient description from your system.
- Two judgments were marked "Yes," indicating that the data on the first two pages showed that "goals were aligned to state content standards" and that "the teacher asked remember, understand and apply level questions that focused on the objective of the lesson." Although these questions did not "provoke discussion," you are giving the teacher some credit here.
- Seventeen judgments were marked "NO". This indicates that the observer had data from the first two pages that warranted a NO response.

FORMAL DOCUMENTATION

> **Be Focused and Selective**
>
> ▶ *What are the most significant deficiencies?*
>
> ▶ *On which issues do you have the strongest data?*
>
> ▶ *What issues are most closely aligned with the focus of this observation?*
>
> ▶ *What issues are sufficiently related that you can combine them?*
>
> ***Don't major in the minors.***

After the observation, you will schedule a conference with the teacher. Recall the three sequential steps: observe, talk, write. If this is a Quadrant II teacher (see the diagram on page 8 in Chapter 3) and your goal is growth and improvement, you will use a collaborative style of supervision. If your goal is contract nonrenewal/ termination, you will use a directive style. In this scenario, we are assuming that you have already had a number of conversations with the teacher about your concerns. One of your dilemmas in this scenario is that you have marked 17 judgments as NO. This presents several prob- lems for you. If you elect to include all 17 issues in the conference, you have the effect of completely overwhelming the teacher. If you are on the road toward a recommendation of contract termination or nonrenewal, you should anticipate that you may be accused of just "being out to get the teacher." Citing 17 areas of concern may strengthen that accusation.

All 17 issues may not be of equal importance. "Lesson integrated learning objectives with other disciplines" may not be as critical as "Addressed student mistakes and followed through to ensure student mastery." You must decide what the priority issues are for you, the campus, and this teacher. A general rule of thumb is that no more than 3-4 issues will be discussed and documented. After the conference with the teacher, you are now ready to write a memorandum to communicate the information and judgments to Mr. Burner and to preserve the information if:

- you contemplate revisiting the Goal-Setting and Professional Development plan (GSPD) to modify it to reflect your concerns. This will be necessary if your remediation directives require additional paper work by the teacher.
- you later need to document failure to comply with administrator directives that will be a part of this memorandum and/or
- you later need to justify developing an intervention plan (IP) as discussed in Chapter 6

To be consistent with terminology introduced in Chapter 2, we are calling this instructional memorandum a "specific incident memorandum," since it has the same essential elements. In this case, the "specific incident" is your observation in the teacher's classroom and the teacher and student behaviors that you observed.

Directives for professional development activities are not necessarily requirements in a specific incident memorandum. However, you may sometimes want to include them in order to demonstrate your commitment to support the teacher. When you write directives for changes in teacher behavior, we recommend using the language of your teacher appraisal system. This may remove some of the possible negative emotion and minimize potential accusations of personal bias. You are, after all, simply directing the teacher to do what the district has defined as the behavior of a proficient teacher.

Recall from Chapter 2 the essential elements of a specific incident memorandum:

- Letterhead Stationery
- Date
- Subject
- Allegation and Investigation
- Findings of Fact
- Conclusions
- Directives
- Opportunity to Respond
- Dated Employee Signature

From the 17 judgment marked NO on the focused observation instrument, we have selected four to discuss in the conference with the teacher and to include in the memorandum. These four were selected, in part, because they were the focus of the observation and there were significant findings indicating that there are problems in all four areas.

1. Engagement of all students in relevant, meaningful learning
2. Student mastery of the objective

3. Responding to students who become confused or disengaged
4. Teacher interaction with students

As we noted previously, your professional judgment may lead you to a different prioritization of the problems. Using the data from the focused observation instrument, our specific incident memorandum might look like the following. Note that for illustrative purposes, we have included on the left side of the memorandum the essential elements of a specific incident memorandum. You would not include these in the actual memorandum you send to the teacher.

ESSENTIAL ELEMENTS	
Letterhead	**BESTEVER ISD** **1234 Sunny Lane** **Bestever, TX 70000**
Date	TO: Mr. Benson Burner FROM: Dr. Great Principal DATE: November 10, 2023 SUBJECT: Classroom Observation on November 8 and Conference on November 10
Nature of Allegation and Investigation	This memorandum will formally communicate information gathered during my observation in your classroom on November 8, 2023 and discussed with you in our conference on November 10, 2023. I observed from 8:30 to 8:55. You were conducting a lesson on comparing and contrasting potential and kinetic energy using lecture, question/answer, the textbook, a handout, and a hammer with a group of 26 sixth graders.
Findings of Fact	The observation revealed the following information in the context of T-TESS, our district's assessment system.

<u>Engagement of All Students in Relevant, Meaningful learning
Student Mastery of the Objective</u>

- The lesson was a whole-group, teacher-centered
- Six of 26 students participated
- Twenty students did not participate
- Two of the six who participated were successful

<u>Responding to Students Who Become Confused or Disengaged
Teacher Interaction with Students</u>

When students were not successful, you responded:

- (to Noah) "No, not exactly." You then called on Mariana.
- (to Nari) "Why not? There's a picture like that right there in the book. Didn't you read the assignment?" You then called on Jacob.
- (to Jacob) "Oh my gosh. You are completely missing the point, as usual." Then you called on Mariana.
- (to the whole class when no one volunteered to respond to a question) "You duds are going to have to start reading the assignment if you ever expect to pass my class." (Jacob closed his book)

| ESSENTIAL ELEMENTS |

- (to Matt when he responded to your question saying "I don't have a clue" you said "You rarely do."

You provided no prompting, clarification, or corrective feedback to these students.

Conclusions

Based on these data, I have concluded that you are not meeting the district's expectations of a proficient teacher as set forth in the Domains and Dimensions of T-TESS. These include:

1. Most of the students were not engaged in relevant, meaningful learning (Domain 2, Dimensions 4; Domain 3, Dimension 3).

2. Most students did not master the objective (Domain 2, Dimensions 1 and 4; Domain 3, Dimension 3).

3. When students were confused and unsuccessful, you did not alter the instruction to address their learning gaps (Domain 1, Dimension 3), recognize student misunderstanding and respond with an array of teaching techniques to clarify concepts (Doman 2, Dimension 3), or address their mistakes by following through to ensure student mastery (Domain 2, Dimension 1).

Directives for Changes in Behavior

4. When you responded to students who had become confused or disengaged you did not interact with them in respectful ways (Teacher Standard 4: Learning Environment).

In all future lessons you will plan and implement all lessons in such a way that:

1. All students are engaged in relevant, meaningful learning.

2. Most students demonstrate mastery of the objective.

3. You recognize when students become confused or disengaged and address student mistakes by following through with corrective feedback, prompting, and/or adjusting the lesson to ensure student mastery.

Opportunity to Respond

4. All of your interactions with students are respectful at all times.

Dated Signature of Employee

I have received a copy of this memorandum. I understand that my signature does not necessarily indicate that I agree with its content. I further understand that I have a right to respond in writing within 10 days.

_____

/s/ Benson Burner   Date

NOTE: This memorandum contains comprehensive directives for changes in behavior. The directives are written in the form described in Chapter 6 and in Appendix C. While such comprehensive directives are not essential in a specific incident memorandum, you may choose to include them for the reasons previously expressed. This memorandum does not include directives for professional growth activities; they are optional in a specific incident memorandum related to instruction.

GATHERING AND TRANSCRIBING DATA

Focused Observation Instrument #2: Planning/Internalization and Instruction (Primary Focus # 2)

> **Focused Observation #2**
> **Planning / Internalization and Instruction**
> *Primary Focus:*
> ▶ *Student Mastery*
> ▶ *Monitoring*
> ▶ *Feedback to Students*
> ▶ *Instructional Adjustment*
> ▶ *Differentiation*
> ▶ *Re-teaching*

This instrument relates to a different aspect of both planning and instruction. Are assessment strategies aligned with the objectives and with the varied needs/characteristics of students? Do students receive appropriate reinforcement and corrective feedback on their learning?

Is the teacher monitoring student learning? How? Is there evidence that the teacher is formatively assessing student learning and providing feedback? Do the results of the monitoring lead to differentiation and/or adjusting the instruction? Based on the learning objective, are students achieving the expectations as described by the learning objective?

This instrument has the potential to yield objective data on several different issues related to both planning and instruction. The evidence of the quality of the planning will most likely be found in the actual implementation of the instruction and its impact on students.

FOCUSED OBSERVATION INSTRUMENT #2: Planning/Internalization and Instruction

- ✔ Student Mastery
- ✔ Monitoring
- ✔ Feedback to Students
- ✔ Instructional Adjustment
- ✔ Differentiation
- ✔ Re-teaching

Name of Teacher: Benson Burner
Date of Observation: 11/8/23
Subject/Grade Level: 6th grade science
Time of Observation: Begin: 8:30
Specific Content/Activity: Compare and contrast potential and kinetic energy
End: 8:55
Number of Students in Class: 26   **(1)**

For **whole-group, teacher-centered instruction**, record the names (descriptions, seat assignment) of students who participated in ways other than passive listening. Record the question/ **(2)** prompt from the teacher. Circle the + beside the name(s) of students whose participation was successful. Circle the – beside the name(s) of students whose participation was not successful. Circle a ? if you cannot determine student success. Record the teacher's response to the student's response/performance/demonstration.

STUDENT	QUESTION	SUCCESSFUL/ UNSUCCESSFUL	TEACHER RESPONSE TO STUDENT
1. Noah	What's the difference between work and energy	+ ⊖ ?	No, not exactly. (Calls on Marina)
2. Mariana	(same question)	⊕ – ?	Exactly. Great answer.
3. Nari	If you are pushing against a wall and sweat and your muscles ache, are you doing any work?	+ ⊖ ?	Why not? There is a picture right there in the book. Didn't you read the assignment? (Calls on Jacob)
4. Jacob	(same question)	+ ⊖ ?	Oh my gosh. You are missing the point, as usual. (Calls on Mariana)
5. Mariana	(same question)	⊕ – ?	You nailed it again, Mariana. That's exactly the point.
6. Aaron	(T. holds up a hammer) Does this hammer have kinetic energy?	+ ⊖ ?	Not hardly, Aaron. You completely missed the point.
7. To class	Does anybody know?	+ ⊖ ?	(No hands raised. Aaron closes his book, puts down pen. T. sighs) You duds are going to have to start reading the assignment if you are going to pass my class
8. Mariana	Yeah, Mariana (same hammer question)	⊕ – ?	That's another great answer. Did everybody get that?
9. Matt	What is the difference between potential energy and mechanical energy?	+ ⊖ ?	(Matt says, "I don't have a clue.") T: You rarely do. (Calls on Jacob)
10. Jacob	(same question)	⊕ – ?	Finally, somebody gets it. Good job, Jacob
11.		+ – ?	
12.		+ – ?	
13.		+ – ?	

Instructional Strategies Used to Monitor, Provide Feedback, and Differentiate/Reteach (3)

Check any techniques that the teacher used. Checking the technique does not necessarily mean that the technique was used effectively — it simply means that the technique was used. Make any specific notes that will help you remember what the teacher did/ failed to do.

Monitoring	Notes on Teacher/Student Behavior (impact on students)
X Verbally monitoring/assessing *individual students* (random questioning, interacting during group/seat work)	6 of 26 students verbally monitored; no physical monitoring (moving around the classroom)
_____ Physically monitoring *individual* students (walking around, examining work)	
X Verbally monitoring/assessing *groups* of students (choral response, signal response)	T. standing at lectern entire period. 1 group question
_____ Physically monitoring *groups* of students	
_____ Use of formative assessments (paper/pencil, performances, demonstrations)	

Feedback

X Used positive reinforcement of successful responses/ performances (verbal and/or non-verbal)	2 students
_____ Used specific corrective feedback to students who are unsuccessful	No corrective feedback to unsuccessful students; 1 student closed book and put down pen; 6 students took notes.
_____ Prompted/assisted students who are having difficulty responding	
_____ Probed to clarify, elaborate thinking	
_____ Clarified/extended learning in response to monitoring/ assessment	

Differentiation/Corrective Teaching/Re-teaching

_____ Adjusted instruction and activities to maintain student engagement.	1 activity for all students: lecture/ Q&A; no change or adjustment in lesson
_____ Adjusted instruction/clarifies in response to monitoring/assessing	
_____ Recognized when students become confused or disengaged and responded to student learning or social/emotional needs	
_____ Provided differentiated instructional methods and content to ensure students have the opportunity to master what is being taught	
_____ Adapted lessons to address individual needs of all, especially when they are not being successful	
_____ Utilized instructional adjustments to address strengths and gaps in background knowledge, life experiences and skills of all students	
_____ Invited input from students in order to monitor and adjust instruction	
_____ Re-taught the lesson (some or all students)	

_____ Other technique/strategy
_____ Other technique/strategy
_____ Other technique/strategy

Summary of Data and Judgments on Monitoring and Assessing

In the space below, summarize the data from the previous two pages and make judgments about the quality of instructional strategies.

(4)

- How many students participated? __6__ of __26__ participated. *(total # of students)*
- How many students did not participate? __20__
- How many students were successful? __2__
- How many students were unsuccessful? __4__
- What was the learning/curriculum objective?
  Compare and contrast potential and kinetic energy
- What instructional activities, strategies, and materials/resources were used in teaching this lesson?
  Lecture (from behind lectern entire period). Question/answer. Textbook, hammer, handout

Based on the data, circle YES if the statement describes what you say/heard. Circle NO if the statement does not describe what you saw/heard. If you have no data or insufficient data, do not circle anything. In making judgments, rely on the preponderance of the data/evidence.

(5)

All descriptions, unless otherwise noted, are based on the Proficient language of the Texas Teacher Evaluation and Support System (T-TESS). For corresponding language from the Professional Development and Appraisal System, see the correlation chart at the end of this chapter.

PLANNING & INSTRUCTION: Monitoring/Feedback

- Used formal and informal assessments to monitor progress of all students   YES **(NO)**
- Provided substantive, specific and timely feedback to students, families and other school personnel while maintaining confidentially.   YES   NO
- Used probes to clarify, elaborate thinking   YES **(NO)**
- Monitored student behavior and responses for engagement and understanding   YES   NO

PLANNING AND INSTRUCTION: Achieving Expectations

- Addressed student mistakes and followed through to ensure mastery   YES **(NO)**
- Recognized students misunderstanding and responded with an array of techniques to clarify concepts   YES   NO
- Used positive reinforcement of successful responses/performances (verbal and/or nonverbal)   **(YES)**   NO
- Recognized when students became confused or disengaged and responded to student learning or social/emotional needs   YES   NO
- Interacted with students in respectful ways at all times (Teacher Standard 4: Learning Environment)   YES **(NO)**

PLANNING AND INSTRUCTION: Differentiation & Communication

- Adjusted instruction to address strengths and gaps in background knowledge, life experiences and skills of all students   YES **(NO)**
- Adjusted instruction and activities to maintain student engagement   YES **(NO)**
- Implemented activities, resources, technology and instructional materials that were aligned to instructional purposes/objective   YES **(NO)**
- Persisted with the lesson until there was evidence that most students demonstrate mastery of the objective   YES **(NO)**
- Provided opportunities for students to use different types of thinking (e.g., analytical, practical, creative and research-based)   YES **(NO)**
- Provided differentiated instructional methods and content to ensure students had the opportunity to master what was being taught   YES **(NO)**
- Recognized when students became confused or disengaged and responded to student learning or social/emotional needs   YES   NO   YES **(NO)**

Other Judgments

Interactions with students were not respectful

Commentary and Rationale

(1) The first section of the instrument provides essential information that you will need when you are ready to write your memorandum to Mr. Burner (e.g., date and time of the observation, length of the observation, etc.). In order to make decisions about monitoring/feedback, student mastery, and differentiation, it is essential to capture the curriculum objective. If the objective is not posted in the classroom, you will need to check the teacher's lesson plans and/or the district curriculum scope-and-sequence.

(2) You will recognize that the first page of this instrument collects exactly the same data as the first focused observation instrument. However, the second and third pages are significantly different. That is because your focus has changed to different areas of concern: monitoring, feedback, student mastery, and differentiation. The previous focused observation instrument and the next one focus on different matters. In this section, you record each teacher/student interaction as it occurs. Noah's response was incorrect, Mr. Burner responded, "No, not exactly" and called on Mariana. When Mariana answered correctly, Mr. Burner responded, "Exactly. Great answer." and called on Nari. Note that all information is presented in objective, non-judgmental terms. Never write judgmental or editorial comments. Mr. Burner responds to Nari, "Why not? There's a picture like that right there in the book. Didn't you read the assignment?" You wrote down his exact words rather than the inappropriate judgment "put-down comment by teacher." In recording observation data and writing documentation, stick to the facts—what the teacher said and did, what students said and did.

(3) This section of the instrument is completed whenever you have the opportunity: As the teacher uses a technique/strategy or during downtime, that is, when there are few teacher/student interactions and when you have time to consider other things going on in the classroom. Note that the possible techniques/strategies are different because your focus is different. Note also that you have recorded objective comments that all relate to the area of focus for this instrument. For example, T. standing at lectern entire period; No corrective feedback to unsuccessful students; 1 student closed book and put down pen; 1 activity for all students: lecture/Q&A; no change or adjustment in lesson.

Remember that checking a technique does not necessarily mean that the technique was used effectively; it simply means that the technique was used. You may later make the judgment whether or not these techniques were effective. During the observation, however, record only that the techniques were used. Notice that there are very few items that are marked X. This is, in and of itself, important. Sometimes no data are data. That is particularly true in this lesson. None of the strategies in the category of Differentiation/ Corrective Teaching/Re-teaching is marked. That, in and of itself, is data.

(4) The final page of the focused observation instrument should be completed back in your office. It consists of a summary of the data and preliminary judgments from the previous two sections of the instrument. Remember that the preceding data were factual and objective—no judgments were made about the quality or effectiveness of the teaching behaviors. In completing this section, you summarize the data from the first two pages. In the case of Mr. Burner, the summary reveals the following:

- Six of the 26 students participated.
- Two of the six students who participated (Mariana and Jacob) were successful.
- Twenty students did not participate
- Three of the four correct responses came from Mariana. The observer is concerned with how many students gave correct responses, not with how many responses were correct.
- You have copied the curriculum objective from the first page and, in bulleted form, listed the activities, strategies, and resources that were used in the lesson.

Note that everything summarized up to this point has been reported objectively—no judgments or conclusions.

(5) The bottom of the page consists of preliminary judgments, based on the data. You should only make judgments if the preponderance of evidence from the first two pages can convincingly support the judgments.

- Unless otherwise noted, all judgments use language from the Proficient de- scription in T-TESS. If your district or charter school uses a different teacher appraisal system, you will want to use the Proficient description from your system.
- One judgment was marked "Yes," indicating that the data on the first two pages showed that the teacher "used positive reinforcement." You may or may not agree that the evidence supports this judgment.
- One judgment was not marked: provided substantive, specific and timely feedback to students, families and other school personnel while maintaining confidentially. This judgment is probably broader than a single observation would warrant.
- Fourteen judgments were marked "NO". This indicates that you had data from the first two pages that warranted a NO response. Additionally, you added a judgment about respectful interaction with students.

FORMAL DOCUMENTATION

After the observation, you will schedule a conference with the teacher. Recall the three sequential steps: observe, talk, write. If this is a Quadrant II teacher (see the diagram on page 8 in Chapter 3) and your goal is growth and improvement, you will use a collaborative style of supervision. If your goal is contract nonrenewal/ termination, you will use a directive style. In this scenario, we are assuming that you have already had a number of conversations with the

> **Be Focused and Selective**
>
> ▶ *What are the most significant deficiencies?*
>
> ▶ *On which issues do you have the strongest data?*
>
> ▶ *What issues are most closely aligned with the focus of this observation?*
>
> ▶ *What issues are sufficiently related that you can combine them?*
>
> ***Don't major in the minors.***

teacher about your concerns. One of your dilemmas in this scenario is that you have marked 14 judgments as NO. This presents several problems for you. If you elect to include all 14 issues in the conference, you have the effect of completely overwhelming the teacher. If you are on the road toward a recommendation of contract termination or nonrenewal, you should anticipate that you may be accused of just "being out to get the teacher." Citing 14 areas of concern may strengthen that accusation.

All 14 issues may not be of equal importance. "Used formal and informal assessments to monitor progress of all students" may not be as critical as "provided differentiated instructional methods and content to ensure students had the opportunity to master what was being taught." You must decide what the priority issues are for you, the campus, and this teacher. A general rule of thumb is that no more than 3-4 issues will be discussed and documented.

After the conference with the teacher, you are now ready to write a memorandum to communicate the information and judgments to Mr. Burner and to preserve the information if:

- you contemplate revisiting the Goal-Setting and Professional Development plan (GSPD) to modify it to reflect your concerns. This will be necessary if your remediation directives require additional paper work by the teacher.

- you later need to document failure to comply with administrator directives that will be a part of this memorandum and/or

- you later need to justify developing an intervention plan (IP)

To be consistent with terminology introduced in Chapter 2, we are calling this instructional memorandum a "specific incident memorandum," since it has the same essential elements. In this case, the "specific incident" is your observation in the teacher's classroom and the teacher and student behaviors that you observed.

Directives for professional development activities are not necessarily requirements in a specific incident memorandum. However, you may sometimes want to include them in order to demonstrate your commitment to support the teacher. When you write directives for changes in teacher behavior we recommend using the language of your teacher appraisal system. This may remove some of the possible negative emotion and minimize potential accusations of personal bias. *You are, after all, simply directing the teacher to do what the district has defined as the behavior of a proficient teacher.*

From the 14 judgments marked NO on the focused observation instrument, we have selected five to discuss in the conference with the teacher and to include in the memorandum. These five were selected, in part, because they were the focus of the observation and there were significant data indicating that there are problems

1. Student mastery of the objective

2. Monitored student behavior and responses for engagement and understanding

3. Recognized students misunderstanding and responded with an array of techniques to clarify concepts

4. Adjusted instruction and activities to maintain student engagement and mastery of the objective
5. Responses to students who become confused or disengaged

As we have noted previously, your professional judgment may lead you to a different prioritization of the problems. Sometimes you will want to combine judgments that are closely linked. Judgments 3-4 both relate to various ways to address adjustment/differentiation are examples of those linkages.

Using the data from the focused observation instrument, our specific incident memorandum might look like the following. Note that for illustrative purposes, we have included on the left side of the memorandum the essential elements of a specific incident memorandum. You would not include these in the actual memorandum you send to the teacher.

ESSENTIAL ELEMENTS	
Letterhead Stationery	**BESTEVER ISD** **1234 Sunny Lane** **Bestever, TX 70000**
Date	TO: Mr. Benson Burner FROM: Dr. Great Principal DATE: November 10, 2023 SUBJECT: Classroom Observation on November 8 and Conference on November 10
Allegation and Investigation	This memorandum will formally communicate information gathered during my observation in your classroom on November 8, 2023 and discussed with you in our conference on November 10, 2023. I observed from 8:30 to 8:55. You were conducting a lesson on comparing and contrasting potential and kinetic energy using lecture, question/answer, the textbook, a handout, and a hammer with a group of 26 sixth graders.
Findings of Fact	The observation revealed the following information in the context of T-TESS, our district's assessment system. **Student Mastery of the Objective** • Lesson was whole-group, teacher-centered • Six of 26 students participated • Twenty students did not participate • Two of the six who participated were successful **Monitoring Student Responses for Engagement and Understanding** • You stood behind the lectern for the entire class period • Six of the 26 students were verbally monitored (asked questions) **Instructional Adjustments and Differentiation** • You used a single instructional activity: lecture/question/answer

ESSENTIAL ELEMENTS	• When students were confused unsuccessful, you continued the single strategy and did not adjust or differentiate the instruction

Responses to Students Who Were Confused and/or Disengaged

When students were not successful, you responded:

- (to Noah) "No, not exactly." You then called on Mariana.
- (to Nari) "Why not? There's a picture like that right there in the book. Didn't you read the assignment?" You then called on Jacob.
- (to Jacob) "Oh my gosh. You are completely missing the point, as usual." Then you called on Mariana.
- (to the whole class when no one volunteered to respond to a question) "You duds are going to have to start reading the assignment if you ever expect to pass my class."
- (to Matt when he responded to your question: "I don't have a clue." "You rarely do."

Conclusions

Based on these data, I have concluded that you are not meeting the district's expectations of a proficient teacher as set forth in the Domains and Dimensions of T-TESS. These include:

1. Most students did not master the objective (Domain 2, Dimensions 1 and 4).
2. You did not monitor the engagement and understanding of most students (Domain 2, Dimension 5).
3. There was no evidence of any differentiation in the lesson. When students were confused and unsuccessful, you did not adjust the instruction to address their learning gaps (Domain 1, Dimension 3), recognize student misunderstanding and respond with an array of teaching techniques to clarify concepts (Doman 2, Dimension 3), or address their mistakes by following through to ensure student mastery (Domain 2, Dimension 1).
4. When you responded to students who had become confused or disengaged you did not interact with them in respectful ways (Teacher Standard 4: Learning Environment).

Directives

In all future lessons you will:

1. Plan and implement all lessons in such a way that most students demonstrate mastery of the objective.
2. Monitor the engagement and understanding of all students.
3. Plan and implement each lesson to incorporate multiple, differentiated activities, positive corrective feedback, prompting, and adjusting the lesson so that most students master the lesson objective.
4. Interact with students in respectful ways at all times.

Opportunity to Respond

I have received a copy of this memorandum. I understand that my signature does not necessarily indicate that I agree with its content. I further understand that I have a right to respond in writing within 10 days.

Dated Signature of Employee

/s/ Benson Burner   Date

NOTE: This memorandum contains comprehensive directives for changes in behavior. The directives are written in the form described in Chapter 6 and in Appendix C. While such comprehensive directives are not essential in a specific incident memorandum, you may choose to include them for the reasons previously expressed. This memorandum does not include directives for professional growth activities; they are optional in a specific incident memorandum.

GATHERING AND TRANSCRIBING DATA

Focused Observation #3 Classroom Environment Primary Focus:

▶ *Environment*

▶ *Routines and Procedures*

▶ *Classroom Culture*

▶ *Managing Student Behavior*

▶ *Student Self-directed Management*

▶ *Engagement of All Students in Relevant, Meaningful Learning*

Focused Observation Instrument #3: Classroom Environment, Routines and Procedures, Culture

This instrument focuses on data collection on classroom environment, routines and procedures, and culture. Are routines and procedures clear and efficient? Who is in charge of routines and procedures? How is time utilized? What is the evidence that students are managing their own behavior? If there is off-task or inappropriate behavior, how does the teacher address the behavior and how do students respond?

This instrument has the potential to yield objective data on several different issues related to the overall theme of learning environment. The evidence of the quality of the planning will most likely be found in the actual implementation of the instruction and its impact on students.

FOCUSED OBSERVATION INSTRUMENT #3:
Classroom Environment, Routines and Procedures, Culture

- ✔ Environment
- ✔ Routines and Procedures
- ✔ Classroom Culture
- ✔ Managing Student Behavior
- ✔ Student Self-Directed Management
- ✔ Engagement of All Students In Relevant, Meaningful Learning

Name of Teacher: Benson Burner (1)
Date of Observation: 11/8/23
Subject/Grade Level: 6th grade science
Time of Observation: Begin: 8:30   End: 8:55
Specific Content/Activity: Compare and contrast potential and kinetic energy
Number of Students in Class: 26

TIME	DESCRIPTION OF TEACHER/STUDENT BEHAVIOR	TEACHER RESPONSE/BEHAVIOR
8:30	Tardy bell rings	
	4 students enter after tardy bell	No response
	T. takes roll; passes handout to each individual student (6 minutes)	
8:36	T. standing behind lectern	
	T. begins lesson; tells students to open science books	
	Some students open science books, most do not	No redirection to other students
	6 students taking notes	No redirection to other students
8:38	T. refers to handout (side 1)	No redirection to other students
	6 students taking notes on handout	
8:40	T. behind lectern; asks Nori about pushing against a wall; she is unsuccessful	Oh my gosh. You are missing the point, as usual.
8:43	T. behind lectern; refers to handout slide 3	
8:44	T. behind lectern; holds up hammer; asks Aaron a question; Aaron is incorrect	Not hardly, Aaron
		You completely missed the point.
		Aaron closes book; puts down pen.
	Question to whole class; no one responds	You duds are going to have to start reading the assignment if you are going to pass my class.
8:47	6 students taking notes; T. at lectern	No redirection to other students
	3 students in back (Aaron, William, Ava)	No redirection
8:55	Observation ends; T. still at lectern	
	Angel is helping Jason sort papers; Luciana and Reggie are talking; Liam and Mia are watching me; same 6 taking notes	No redirection

(2)

Evidence of Effective Practices for Classroom Environment, Routines and Procedures, Culture

Check any techniques that the teacher used to promote Effective Practices for Classroom Environment, Routines and Procedures, Culture. Checking the technique does not necessarily mean that the technique was used effectively — it simply means that the technique was used. Make any specific notes that will help you remember what the teacher did/failed to do.

(3)

_____ Implemented clear and efficient routines, procedures and transitions

__X__ Created safe and accessible classroom

_____ Implemented campus/classroom behavior system   *4 students enter after tardy bell - no response from T.*

_____ Most students meet expected classroom behavior standards

_____ Successfully and respectfully intervenes to stop/ redirect off-task/inappropriate behavior

_____ Used best practices instructional strategies so that most students engaged in relevant, meaningful learning

_____ Students are worked respectfully in groups/individually

_____ Procedures were in place for students to manage supplies and equipment with very limited direction from teacher

_____ Materials are organized and managed in ways that consume very little instructional time

_____ All instructional time is used for learning

_____ Other techniques (specify _____)

_____ Other techniques (specify _____)

_____ Other techniques (specify _____)

T. begins lesson; tells students to open science books. Some students open science books; most do not

3 students at back (Aaron, William, Ava) whispering - no redirection from T.

Angel is helping Jason sort papers; Luciana and Reggie are talking; Liam and Mia are watching me; some 6 students taking notes - No redirection from T.

4-31

Summary of Data and Judgments About
Classroom Environment, Routines and Procedures

Summary of Student Behavior

▶ at least
  _18_ students were off-task/disengaged from the lesson
  (number)
  Describe: Most did not open textbook when directed; 20 students never took notes **(4)**
  as directed; 7 students talking or sorting papers

▶ _5_ students behaved inappropriately/disruptively
  (number)
  Describe: Inappropriate: 5 students were talking while teacher was lecturing and asking questions

▶ What was the learning/curriculum objective?
  Compare and contrast potential and kinetic energy

▶ What instructional materials, resources, and procedures were used in teaching this lesson?
  How were they managed? Textbook; 1-page handout; hammer; no other materials (pictures, objects) were used; T. spent 6 minutes passing the handout to each individual student.

Based on the data, circle YES if the statement describes what you say/heard. Circle NO if the statement does not describe what you saw/heard. If you have no data or insufficient data, do not circle anything. In making judgments, rely on the preponderance of the data/ evidence.

All descriptions, unless otherwise noted, are based on the Proficient language of the Texas Teacher Evaluation and Support System (T-TESS). For corresponding language from the Professional Development and Appraisal System, see the correlation chart at the end of this chapter.

Classroom Environment, Routines and Procedures

- All procedures, routines and transactions were clear and efficient   YES **NO**
- Students actively participated in groups, manage supplies and equipment with very limited teacher direction   YES **NO**
- The classroom was safe and organized to support learning objectives and is accessible to most students   **YES** NO
- Other conclusions/judgments

Classroom Culture

- Teacher led a mutually respectful and collaborative class of actively engaged learners   YES **NO**
- Engaged all students in relevant, meaningful learning   YES **NO**
- Students worked respectfully individually/in groups   YES NO
- Teacher interacted with students in respectful ways at all times (Standard 4: Learning Environment, Section 21.351 of the Education Code)   YES **NO**
- Other conclusions/judgments
- Other conclusions/judgments

Managing Student Behavior

- The teacher established, communicated and maintained clear expectations for student behavior   YES **NO**
- Consistently implemented the campus and/or classroom behavior system efficiently   YES NO
- Most students met expected classroom behavior standards (e.g., are on task, behave appropriately, follow classroom rules/procedures—PDAS)   YES **NO**
- Teacher successfully stopped/redirected off-task, inappropriate/disruptive behavior (PDAS)   YES **NO**
- Other conclusions/judgments
- Other conclusions/judgments

(5)

Commentary and Rationale

(1) The first section of the instrument provides essential information that you will need when you are ready to write your memorandum to Mr. Burner (e.g., date and time of the observation, length of the observation, etc.). In order to make decisions about environment/classroom culture, routines and procedures, managing student behavior, student self-direction/management, and engagement of all students in relevant, meaningful learning, it is essential to capture the curriculum objective. If the objective is not posted in the classroom, you will need to check the teacher's lesson plans and/or the district curriculum scope-and-sequence.

(2) In this section, there are three columns in order to track student and teacher behavior. Unlike the two previous observation instruments, the time is important in order to capture data on the frequency and duration of teacher and student behavior (e.g., how long the teacher took to hand out materials and stood behind the lectern). The second column is for anecdotal comments about what the students and teacher were doing/not doing. The third column is for anecdotal notes about how both the teacher and students responded to the behavior in the second column. In recording observation data and writing documentation, *stick to the facts—what the teacher said and did; what students said and did.* For example, at 8:47 you noted three students at back (Aaron, William, Ava) whispering, not three students off-task; the former is factual; the second is judgmental.

(3) This section of the instrument is completed whenever you have the opportunity: as the teacher uses a technique/strategy or during downtime, that is, when there are few teacher/student interactions and when you have time to consider other things going on in the classroom. The instrument indicates with an X that there was a "safe and accessible classroom."

Note that checking a technique does not necessarily mean that the technique was used effectively; it simply means that the technique was used. You may later make the judgment whether or not these techniques were effective. During the observation, however, record only that these techniques were used. Notice that there are very few items that are marked X. This is, in and of itself, important. Sometimes no data are data.

(4) The final page of the focused observation instrument should be completed back in your office. It consists of a summary of the data and preliminary judgments from the previous two sections of the instrument. Remember that the preceding data were factual and objective—no judgments were made about the quality or effectiveness of the teaching behaviors. In completing this section, you summarize the data from the first two pages. In the case of Mr. Burner, the summary reveals the following:

- At least 18 students were off-task/disengaged from the lesson
- Most students did not open their textbooks when directed

- Twenty students never took notes as directed
- Seven students were talking or sorting papers
- Five students behaved inappropriately/disruptively—they were talking while teacher was lecturing and asking questions
- Teacher did not intervene to stop or redirect the off-task and inappropriate behavior
- Teacher spent six minutes passing the handout to each individual student

Note that everything summarized up to this point has been reported objectively—no judgments or conclusions.

(5) The bottom of the page consists of preliminary judgments, based on the data. You should only make judgments if the preponderance of evidence from the first two pages can convincingly support the judgments.

- Unless otherwise noted, all judgments use language from the Proficient description in T-TESS. If your district or charter school uses a different teacher appraisal system, you will want to use the Proficient description from your system.
- One judgment was marked YES indicating that the data on the first two pages showed that "the classroom is safe and organized to support learning objectives and is accessible to most students."
- One judgment was marked neither YES or NO: "students work respectfully individually/in groups" since students did not work in groups.
- Nine judgments were marked NO. This indicates that the observer had data from the first two pages that warranted a NO response

FORMAL DOCUMENTATION

Be Focused and Selective

▶ *What are the most significant deficiencies?*

▶ *On which issues do you have the strongest data?*

▶ *What issues are most closely aligned with the focus of this observation?*

▶ *What issues are sufficiently related that you can combine them?*

Don't major in the minors.

After the observation, you will schedule a conference with the teacher. Recall the three sequential steps: observe, talk, write. If this is a Quadrant II teacher (see the diagram on page 8 in Chapter 3) and your goal is growth and improvement, you will use a collaborative style of supervision. If your goal is contract nonrenewal/termination, you will use a directive style. In this scenario, we are assuming that you have already had a number of conversations with the teacher about your concerns. One of your dilemmas in this scenario is that you have marked nine judgments as NO. This presents several problems for you. If you elect to include all nine issues in the conference, you have the effect of completely overwhelming the teacher. If you are on the road toward a recommendation of contract termination or nonrenewal, you should anticipate that you may be accused of just "being out to get the teacher." Citing nine areas of concern may strengthen that accusation.

All nine issues may not be of equal importance. You must decide what the priority issues are for you, the campus, and this teacher. A general rule of thumb is that no more than 3-4 issues will be discussed and documented.

After the conference with the teacher, you are now ready to write a memorandum to communicate the information and judgments to Mr. Burner and to preserve the information if:

- you contemplate revisiting the Goal-Setting and Professional Development plan (GSPD) to modify it to reflect your concerns. This will be necessary if your remediation directives require additional paper work by the teacher.
- you later need to document failure to comply with administrator directives that will be a part of this memorandum and/or
- you later need to justify developing an intervention plan (IP)

To be consistent with terminology introduced in Chapter 2, we are calling this instructional memorandum a "specific incident memorandum," since it has the same essential elements. In this case, the "specific incident" is your observation in the teacher's classroom and the teacher and student behaviors that you observed.

Directives for professional development activities are not necessarily requirements in a specific incident memorandum. However, you may sometimes want to include them in order to demonstrate your commitment to support the teacher. When you write directives for changes in teacher behavior we recommend using the language of your teacher appraisal system. This may remove some of the possible negative emotion and minimize potential accusations of personal bias. *You are, after all, simply directing the teacher to do what the district has defined as the behavior of a proficient teacher.*

From the nine judgments marked NO on the focused observation instrument, we have selected/combined four to discuss in the conference with the teacher and to include in the memorandum. These four were selected, in part, because they were the focus of the observation and the data indicate there are problems on all four areas.

- Managing Student Behavior
- Routines/Procedures
- Classroom Culture/ Environment
- Engagement of all Students in Relevant, Meaningful Learning

As we have noted previously, your professional judgment may lead you to a different prioritization of the problems. Using the data from the focused observation instrument, our specific incident memorandum might look like the following. Note that for illustrative purposes, we have included on the left side of the memorandum the essential elements of a specific incident memorandum. You would not include these in the actual memorandum you send to the teacher.

ESSENTIAL ELEMENTS	
Letterhead Stationery	**BESTEVER ISD** **1234 Sunny Lane** **Bestever, TX 70000**

Date	TO: Mr. Benson Burner FROM: Dr. Great Principal DATE: November 10, 2023 SUBJECT: Classroom Observation on November 8 and Conference on November 10
Allegations and Investigation	This memorandum will formally communicate information gathered during my observation in your classroom on November 8, 2023 and discussed with you in our conference on November 10, 2023. I observed from 8:30 to 8:55. You were conducting a lesson on comparing and contrasting potential and kinetic energy using lecture, question/answer, the textbook, a handout, and a hammer with a group of 26 sixth graders.
Findings of Fact	The observation revealed the following information in the context of T-TESS, our district's teacher assessment system.

<u>Managing Student Behavior</u>
<u>Routines/Procedures</u>

- Most students did not open their textbooks when directed
- Twenty students never took notes as directed
- Seven students were talking or sorting papers while you were lecturing and asking questions
- Five students were talking while you were lecturing and asking questions
- You did not intervene to stop or redirect the behavior
- You spent six minutes passing the handout to each individual student

<u>Classroom Culture/ Environment</u>
<u>Engagement of all Students in Relevant, Meaningful Learning</u>

- When students were not successful, you responded
  - (to Jacob): "Oh my gosh. You are completely missing the point, as usual."
  - (to Aaron): "Not hardly, Aaron; you completely missed the point"; Aaron closed his book and puts down his pen.
  - (to whole class when no one volunteered): "You duds are going to have to start reading the assignment if you ever expect to pass my class."
- Six of the 26 students were actively engaged with the learning.

Conclusions

Based on these data, I have concluded that you are not meeting the district's expectations of a proficient teacher as set forth in the Domains and Dimensions of T-TESS. These include:

- Procedures and routines were not efficient (Domain 3, Dimension 1).

ESSENTIAL ELEMENTS
- Most of the students were not engaged in relevant, meaningful learning (Domain 2, Dimension 4; Domain 3, Dimension 3).
- Most students did meet expected classroom behavior standards (e.g., are on task, behave appropriately, follow classroom rules/procedures). You did not stop/redirect the behavior (Domain 3, Dimension 2).
- When you responded to students who had become confused or disengaged you did not interact with them in respectful ways (Teacher Standard 4: Learning Environment).

Directives

In all future lessons you will plan and implement all lessons in such a way that:

1. You design and use procedures and routines so that students actively manage supplies/routines and consume very little time.
2. Most of the students are actively engaged in relevant, meaning learning.
3. Most students meet expected classroom behavior standards (e.g., are on task, behave appropriately, follow classroom rules/procedures). If they do not, stop/redirect the behavior in ways that are courteous and respectful and so that the behavior stops.
4. All of your interactions with students are respectful at all times.

Opportunity to Respond

I have received a copy of this memorandum. I understand that my signature does not necessarily indicate that I agree with its content. I further understand that I have a right to respond in writing within 10 days.

Dated Employee Signature

/s/ Mr. Benson Burner   Date

NOTE: This memorandum contains comprehensive directives for changes in behavior. The directives are written in the form described in Chapter 6 and in Appendix C. While such comprehensive directives are not essential in a specific incident memorandum, you may choose to include them for the reasons previously expressed. This memorandum does not include directives for professional growth activities; they are optional in a specific incident memorandum.

How to Adjust Classroom Data Collection When the Lesson Includes Students Working in Groups or Working Independently

These three observation instruments are designed primarily for gathering data is the classroom of a marginally effective teacher whose lessons may typically be teacher-centered, whole group instruction. If the lesson design is small groups working together or involved in individual learning tasks, you may design your own focused observation instrument that reflects:

- The physical arrangement of the classroom
- The task in which students are engaged
- No more than 2-3 specific issues on which you want to focus your data collection

The figure below is an example.

- The classroom is physically organized in quads.
- In the second box, you would record the learning objective and describe the learning task.
- Your desired focus is active student participation, student success, monitoring, and feedback to students.

For small group and individual learning tasks, record in the white boxes at the bottom the names (descriptions, seat assignment) of students who participated in ways other than passive listening. Make notes about what the students were asked to do. Place + inside the box of students whose participation was successful. Place - inside the box of students whose participation was not successful. Place a ? inside the box if you cannot determine student success. In the shad- owed boxes at the bottom, record the teacher's response to the student's response/ performance/ demonstration. Periodically put a T at the location of the teacher and note the time.

FIGURE 4-1
Key:
✓ + student participated successfully
✓ – student participated unsuccessfully
✓ ? student participated; success unknown/unclear
T location of the teacher + time

Record the Learning Objective Here
Objectively describe below the task that students were asked to do. Include enough information below for you to later determine the academic content they were using and what they were being asked to do with the content.

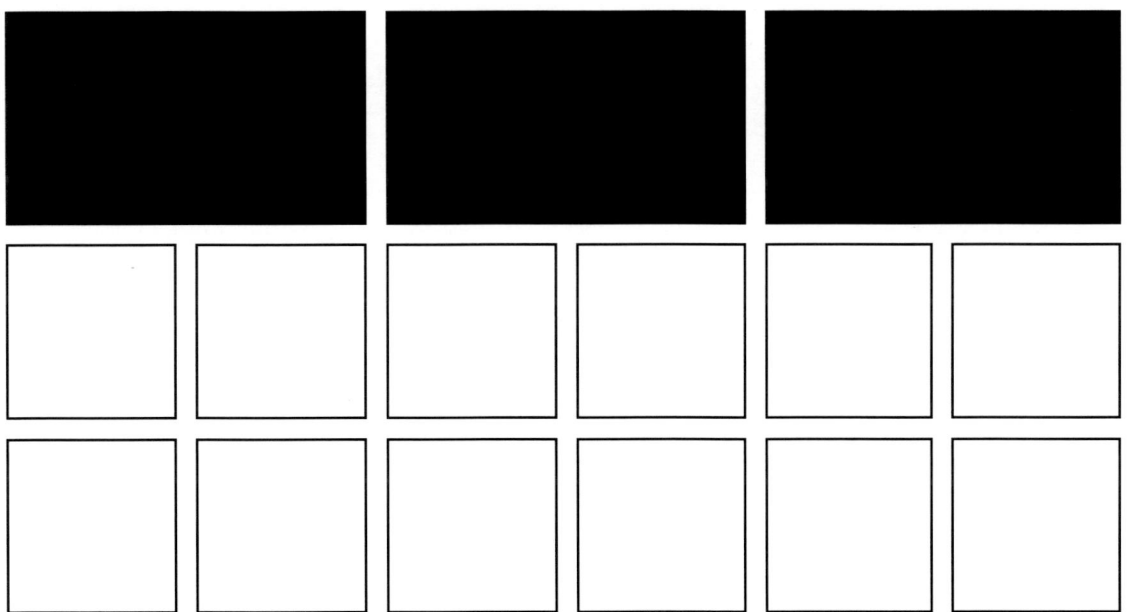

A WORD ABOUT SUBJECT-MATTER KNOWLEDGE AND COMMUNICATION SKILLS

Our discussion has thus far highlighted meeting the proficient standard for planning, instruction, and learning environment. However, we do not want to ignore two other serious matters related to the presentation of subject matter: (1) knowledge of subject matter itself and (2) accurate communication skills (literacy in oral or written language). Obviously, both are prerequisites to effective teaching. During an observation it is not necessary to use a separate focused observation instrument for documenting in either area. Indeed, you are likely to notice subject matter or communication problems at any time during routine observations. Earlier in this chapter we raised the possibility of taking a content expert with you for a classroom observation, especially if you have concerns about accurate knowledge.

> **Teachers are expected to have mastery of the academic content that they are teaching and to use accurate written and verbal language.**

When the teacher exhibits weak knowledge of the teaching field or communicates poorly, it is appropriate to write a specific incident memorandum to alert the teacher to the problem and to the need for remediation. This issue is specifically referenced in T-TESS Doman II (Instruction), Dimension 2 (Content Knowledge and Expertise). Suppose that Mr. Ziebarth is a physics teacher in your school. Some of his students and some of their parents, as well as other science teachers, have complained that Mr. Ziebarth is giving students inaccurate information in his physics class. Your concern is to follow up the complaints by gathering data to determine whether a problem exists. In order to do so, there are several sources of information that you can use:

- Ask for copies of written materials he has used in class.

- Check what is written on the board, anchor charts, word walls, bulletin board, and media.

- Conduct classroom observations and focus on the academic content presented orally. If there are errors in content, record what the teacher says as an exact quotation whenever possible.

- If you are not expert in the teacher's academic area, find someone who is and have that person conduct classroom observations focusing on the accuracy of academic content. The person should provide findings to you and you will write the specific incident memorandum.

Let us assume that you have used these strategies and have noted several inaccuracies in Mr. Ziebarth's presentation. First, you read the following on a handout that he provided to his students.

> "A machine's efficiency is restricted only by gravity. If it weren't for gravity, a machine could work at 100 percent efficiency. One of the reasons we do experiments in space is to show that a machine in a weightless environment can be 100 percent efficient."

On another occasion you watched Mr. Ziebarth conduct a demonstration of a pulley lifting a weight and heard him explain to his students:

> "The pulley in this instance has a mechanical advantage of '2.' That means that I only had to do half as much work to move the object. That's the chief advantage of simple machines."

During the same visit, after pushing against his desk, Mr. Ziebarth said, "The desk did not move. The more energy I expended in the effort, the more work was done. This is true even though the desk did not move."

The complaints about Mr. Ziebarth's accuracy have now been corroborated by data you have gathered. It is time to write a specific incident memorandum. This time, we have chosen to include a remediation directive, rather than develop a separate intervention plan (IP). Note that for illustrative purposes, we have included on the left side of the memorandum the essential elements of a specific incident memorandum related to instruction. You would not include these in the actual memorandum you send to the teacher.

ESSENTIAL ELEMENTS	
Letterhead Stationery	**BESTEVER ISD** **1234 Sunny Lane** **Bestever, TX 70000**
Date	`TO:` Mr. Ziebarth `FROM:` Dr. Great Principal `DATE:` November 10, 2023 `SUBJECT:` Errors on Presentation of Subject Matter
Allegation and Investigation	I have attached a copy of a handout that you constructed and gave to students on November 8, 2023. The handout contains the following physics information that is inaccurate: "A machine's efficiency is restricted only by gravity. If it weren't for gravity, a machine could work at 100 percent efficiency. One of the reasons we do experiments in space is to show that a machine in a weightless environment can be 100 percent efficient."
Findings of Fact	When I observed in your classroom on November 8, 2023, you conducted a demonstration of a pulley lifting a weight and gave the following explanation: "The pulley in this instance has a mechanical advantage of '2.' That means that I only had to do half as much work to move the object. That's the chief advantage of simple machines." During that same observation, you pushed against your desk and then stated: "The desk did not move. The more energy I expended in the effort, the more work was done. This is true even though the desk did not move." All these statements are inaccurate generalizations about the physics of simple machines.
Conclusion	One of the school district's basic expectations of all teachers is a thorough and accurate knowledge of subject matter. The three quotations above indicate that you are not meeting that expectation. You must begin immediately and at all times to teach only accurate content-related information in your classroom. Both Ms. Jones, your science department chairperson, and I agree that you should attend the workshop "Science AIMS Training" at the Regional Education Service Center

ESSENTIAL ELEMENTS	
Directives	on Thursday and Friday, December 7-8. Accordingly, I have made arrangements for you to attend. The district will provide a substitute for your classes on these two days and will pay the workshop registration fee. You will schedule a meeting with Ms. Jones during the week following the workshop to discuss how to prevent errors of the kind described above in future classes.
Expectations/Basis of Authority	
Opportunity to Respond	My signature indicates that I have received a copy of this memorandum. It does not necessarily indicate that I agree with its content. I understand that I have a right to present a written response within 10 working days.
Dated Employee Signature	/s/ Mr. Ziebarth Date

Note that the memorandum quotes the teacher and cites exactly the words on the handout and in the classroom presentation. Your message comes through clearly that there are errors in academic content and that they are not acceptable. But you make your point without castigating the teacher or using adjectives or adverbs that might be provocative or misleading.

The same approach is appropriate for a teacher who appears to have communication problems. Collect samples of notes to parents, observe the written language displayed in the classroom, obtain copies of student handouts, and/or write down samples of oral language to enable you to determine whether or not a problem exists. But proceed with caution. You will be best served by dealing only with grammar, punctuation, and spelling. Avoid addressing regional or ethnic dialects and other-language accents. These should become supervision issues only if the dialect or accent interferes with students' ability to understand instruction.

A memorandum that addresses problems with communication skills will look very similar to the one directed to Mr. Ziebarth but will include statements such as:

> During my observation in your classroom on December 14, 2023, you made the following errors in grammar: (1) "The primary reason they come to this country in 1939 was to continue their research" and (2) "Einstein and von Braun was typical of German scientists." I also noticed that you misspelled "a lot" and "occurring" on the whiteboard ("alot" and "occuring").
>
> This school district expects all faculty members to be role models for students in the use of correct grammar and spelling. The errors cited above indicate that you are not meeting that expectation.

Depending upon the seriousness of the matter, it may be appropriate to have someone edit the teacher's written communication to students and parents and to review the results with the teacher. More comprehensive remediation can be addressed through a formal intervention plan (IP) (see Chapter 6).

SUMMARY

Gathering classroom documentation data need not be an arduous task. The focused observation instruments presented in this chapter allow you to concentrate on particular aspects of instruction in which the teacher is having trouble. By focusing your attention, the instruments can help you document the ways in which a teacher is ineffective or marginally effective, plan improvement plan activities to improve the teacher's performance, and write clear and complete memoranda.

The use of focused observation instruments has a number of values:

- You are not burdened with non-stop note-taking.
- You are free to observe more and to detect non-verbal behaviors.
- You can concentrate your attention and data collection on the one or two areas in which a marginally effective teacher is having difficulty.

You are more likely to collect in-depth data on a narrow set of deficiencies that will aid you in writing and justifying directives for changes in behavior. School districts that use the Texas Teacher Evaluation and Support System (T-TESS) will find that the focused observation instruments are tailored to the domains and dimensions of that system. Some districts may elect to continue with the Professional Development and Assessment System (PDAS) or will have developed their own teacher evaluation systems using different evaluation instruments, peer coaching, portfolio assessment, teacher action research, student work products, and a host of other options. Regardless of the instrument or process used in a locally adopted teacher appraisal system, that system in all likelihood shares the same body of research on effective teaching. Criteria for teacher evaluation will always include the generic teaching issues targeted by each of our focused observation instruments.

Finally, your data collection in Domain 4 of T-TESS (Professional Practices and Responsibilities) primarily will consist of observation outside the classroom, examination of documents and records, and/or conferences with the teacher and with other stakeholders in the school. After you have gathered your data, you will write the kinds of memoranda illustrated in this chapter and in Chapter 2 and Chapter 6. This will document and communicate to the teacher notice of your concerns related to the requirements of the job, an opportunity to improve, and directives and a time line to change the teacher's behavior.

For schools transitioning from PDAS to T-TESS, the chart below may provide a more detailed understanding of how the common criteria and accompanying descriptive language of PDAS and T-TESS correlate with each other as well as with research-based accepted best practices.

Correlation Chart Professional Development and Appraisal System (PDAS) Texas Teacher Evaluation and Support System (T-TESS)	
Professional Development and Appraisal System (PDAS)	Texas Teacher Evaluation and Support System (T-TESS)
Domain I: Active, Successful Student Participation in the Learning Process I-1. Students are actively engaged in learning. I-2. Students are successful in learning. I-3. Student behaviors indicate learning is at a high cognitive level (e.g., critical thinking, creative thinking, problem solving, etc.). I-4. Students are self-directed/self-initiated as appropriate to the lesson objectives. I-5. Students connect learning to work and life applications, both within the discipline, and with other disciplines.	**Planning Dimension 1.1: Standards and Alignment** The teacher designs clear, well-organized, sequential lessons that reflect best practice, align with standards and are appropriate for diverse learners. **Planning Dimension 1.3: Knowledge of Students** Through knowledge of students and proven practices, the teacher ensures high levels of learning, social emotional development and achievement for all students. **Planning Dimension 1.4: Activities** The teacher plans engaging, flexible lessons that encourage higher-order thinking, persistence, and achievement. **Internalization Alternate Dimension 1.1: Standards and Alignment** The teacher internalizes the unit/lesson to deepen their understanding of content, research-based instructional strategies and identifies the vocabulary to ensure lessons reflect best practice, align with standards and are appropriate for diverse learners. **Internalization Alternate Dimension 1.3: Knowledge of Students** Through knowledge of students and proven practices, the teacher ensures high levels of learning, social- emotional development and achievement for all students while maintaining the integrity of the instructional resources. **Internalization Alternate Dimension 1.4: Activities** The teacher understands the lesson objectives and the level of rigor from a student perspective to ensure engaging, flexible lessons that encourage higher- order thinking, persistence, and achievement. **Instructional Dimension 2.1: Achieving Expectations** The teacher supports all learners in their pursuit of high levels of academic and social-emotional success. **Learning Environment Dimension 3.2: Managing Student Behavior** The teacher establishes, communicates and maintains clear expectations for student behavior. **Learning Environment Dimension 3.3: Classroom Culture** The teacher leads a mutually respectful and collaborative class of actively engaged learners

Professional Development and Appraisal System (PDAS)	Texas Teacher Evaluation and Support System (T-TESS)
Domain II: Learner-Centered Instruction II-1. Objectives and goals include basic knowledge/ skills and central themes/ concepts of the discipline. II-2. Instructional content is learner-centered (e.g., relates to the interests and varied characteristics of students). II-3. Instructional strategies promote critical thinking and problem solving. II-4. Instructional strategies include motivational techniques to successfully and actively engage students in the learning process. II-5. Instructional strategies are aligned with the objectives, activities, student characteristics, prior learning, and work and life applications, both within the discipline and with other disciplines. II-6. The teacher varies activities appropriately and maintains appropriate pacing and sequencing of instruction. II-8. The teacher uses appropriate questioning and inquiry techniques to challenge students. II-9. The teacher makes appropriate and effective use of available technology as a part of the instructional process.	**Planning Dimension 1.1: Standards and Alignment** The teacher designs clear, well-organized, sequential lessons that reflect best practice, align with standards and are appropriate for diverse learners. **Planning Dimension 1.3: Knowledge of Students** Through knowledge of students and proven practices, the teacher ensures high levels of learning, social emotional development and achievement for all students. **Planning Dimension 1.4: Activities** The teacher plans engaging, flexible lessons that encourage higher-order thinking, persistence, and achievement. **Internalization Alternate Dimension 1.1: Standards and Alignment** The teacher internalizes the unit/lesson to deepen their understanding of content, research-based instructional strategies and identifies the vocabulary to ensure lessons reflect best practice, align with standards and are appropriate for diverse learners. **Internalization Alternate Dimension 1.3: Knowledge of Students** Through knowledge of students and proven practices, the teacher ensures high levels of learning, social- emotional development and achievement for all students while maintaining the integrity of the instructional resources. **Internalization Alternate Dimension 1.4: Activities** The teacher understands the lesson objectives and the level of rigor from a student perspective to ensure engaging, flexible lessons that encourage higher- order thinking, persistence, and achievement. **Instructional Dimension 2.2: Content Knowledge and Expertise** The teacher uses content and pedagogical expertise to design and execute lessons aligned with state standards, related content and student needs.
Domain III: Evaluation and Feedback on Student Progress III-1. Academic progress of students is monitored and assessed. III-2. Assessment and feedback are aligned with goals and objectives and instructional strategies. III-3. Assessment strategies are appropriate to the varied characteristics of students. III-4. Student learning is reinforced. III-5. Students receive specific, constructive feedback. III-6. The teacher provides opportunities for relearning and re-evaluation of material.	**Planning Dimension 1.2 Data and Assessment** The teacher uses formal and informal methods to measure student progress, then manages and analyzes student data to inform instruction. **Internalization Alternate Dimension 1.2 Data and Assessment** The teacher uses formal and informal methods to measure student progress, then manages and analyzes student data to inform instruction. **Instructional Dimension 2.5 Monitor and Adjust** The teacher formally and informally collects, analyzes and uses student progress data and makes needed lesson adjustments.

Domain IV: Management of Student Discipline, Instructional Strategies, Time, and Materials	Learning Environment Dimension 3.1: Classroom
IV-7. The instructional materials selected by the teacher are equitable and acknowledge the varied characteristics of all students.	**Environment** The teacher organizes a safe, accessible and efficient classroom.
IV-2. The teacher establishes a classroom environment that promotes and encourages self-discipline and self-directed learning.	Learning Environment Dimension 3.2: Managing Student Behavior
IV-3. The teacher interacts with students in an equitable manner, including fair application of rules.	The teacher establishes, communicates and maintains clear expectations for student behavior.
IV-4. The teacher specifies expectations for desired behavior.	
IV-5. The teacher intervenes and re-directs off-task, inappropriate, or disruptive behavior.	
IV-6. The teacher reinforces desired behavior when appropriate.	
IV-8. The teacher effectively and efficiently manages time and materials.	
Domain V: Professional Communication	**Instructional Dimension 2.3: Communication**
V-1. The teacher uses appropriate and accurate written communication with students.	The teacher clearly and accurately communicates to support persistence, deeper learning and effective effort.
V-2. The teacher uses appropriate and accurate verbal and non-verbal communication with students.	**Instructional Dimension 2.4: Differentiation**
V-3. The teacher encourages and supports students who are reluctant and having difficulty.	The teacher differentiates instruction, aligning methods and techniques to diverse student needs.
V-4. The teacher uses appropriate and accurate written communication with parents, staff, community members, and other professionals.	**Professional Practices and Responsibilities Dimension 4.1** The teacher meets district expectations for attendance, professional appearance, decorum, procedural, ethical, legal, and statutory responsibilities.
V-5. The teacher uses appropriate and accurate verbal and non-verbal communication with parents, staff, community members, and other professionals.	**Professional Practices and Responsibilities Dimension 4.3** The teacher enhances the professional community.
V-6. The teacher's interactions are supportive, courteous, and respectful with students, parents, staff, community members, and other professionals.	**Professional Practices and Responsibilities Dimension 4.4** The teacher demonstrates leadership with students, colleagues, and community members in the school, district and community through effective communication and outreach.

REFERENCE

Powers v. Sonora I.S.D., Dkt. No. 112-R10-0812 (Comm'r Educ. 2015).

CHAPTER FIVE: PROFESSIONAL COMMUNICATION

Effective professional communication is increasingly important as teachers and administrators work together to improve school performance. Adhering to professional communication standards is even more important today as a result of the growing use of digital devices and the harm that can result from misuse.

The importance of effective communication and collaboration is clearly reflected in current Texas teacher appraisal law. Standard 6 in the Texas Commissioner of Education's standards that are to be incorporated in the training, appraisal, and professional development of teachers focuses on teachers holding themselves to a high standard for collaboration with other educational professionals.* Encompassed within this standard is communicating consistently, clearly, and respectfully with all members of the campus community including students, parents and families, colleagues, administrators, and staff. Domain 4 of the Texas Teacher Evaluation and Support System (T-TESS) references this standard in Dimension 4.1 on professional demeanor and ethics and in Dimension 4.4 on school community involvement. Both the commissioner standards and T-TESS also reference the Code of Ethics and Standard Practices for Texas Educators, Section II of which sets forth standards for ethical conduct toward professional colleagues. The Code is included in Appendix A of this handbook and in board policy DH of school districts that utilize the Texas Association of School Boards model policies.

In this chapter, we begin by briefly discussing developing law in the context of professional communication and then provide illustrations of how to address through careful documentation unprofessional teacher communication with colleagues and social networking with students.

THE LEGAL FRAMEWORK

As we noted in Chapter 1, public employees including those in both traditional public and charter schools have a constitutional right to free speech. To review, we know that school employees have a right to speak out as citizens on matters of public concern so long as they don't undermine their effectiveness as employees. However, this right does not extend to complaints about working conditions. Thus, a teacher who complains constantly about such matters as noise in the hallway outside her room, too many parental complaints, and too frequent walk-through classroom visits by school administrators is unlikely to be successful in asserting that these comments are constitutionally protected and cannot be used to support a contract nonrenewal or termination recommendation. The teacher should be directed to follow school policy and procedures to vent complaints (e.g., by discussing the matter with the principal in private or by following the district's grievance procedure) or to cease making them altogether.

Based on a 2006 U.S. Supreme Court ruling involving a deputy district attorney who suffered retaliation when he wrote an internal office memorandum to his supervisors noting serious deficiencies in a governmental affidavit used to obtain a search warrant, public employees

---

* Locating the standards contained in the rules set forth by the commissioner of education on teacher appraisal is relatively easy. Go to the Texas Education Agency website at http://tea.texas.gov/ and click on "About TEA" then go to "Laws and Rules" on the right side of the page and click on "Commissioner Rules." This will take you to Title 19 of the Texas Administrative Code. Click on <u>Texas Administrative Code - Currently in Effect</u> and scroll down to Chapter 149. Then click on <u>Subchapter AA. Teacher Standards</u>. Section 6 is contained in subsection (b) a ways down.

who speak out on matters of public concern when acting within the scope of their employment appear to enjoy little constitutional protection.[1] Thus, a teacher who is assigned to a meeting of parents whose children will be enrolling in the school next year and opts to speak out about the lack of effective discipline procedures at the school is unlikely to find the remarks constitutionally protected. Of course, if the teacher is invited by school administrators to address this matter or if the teacher does so outside the scope of employment — for example, by writing a comment on a blog or calling into a late-night radio talk show — the speech is more likely to be constitutionally protected.[2]

Also, recall from Chapter 1 that teachers in Texas have a constitutional right to lead classroom discussion on controversial matters and can't be penalized for doing so unless there is documented evidence that the teacher's ability to teach has been undermined. Of course the discussion has to be germane to the school curriculum for that subject and grade level. Thus, an algebra teacher who facilitates a discussion on the propriety of having American troops in Syria would be unlikely to assert successfully a constitutional right to do so. And even if germane to the school curriculum, the discussion has to be age-appropriate and unbiased for the teacher to have a viable free speech claim.

While these are legal distinctions regarding constitutionally protected versus unprotected speech, it is important to note that governing board members who hear employee grievances and conduct contract nonrenewal hearings often are less concerned with nuances in the law and more concerned that employees are treated fairly. Thus, if there are other reasons related to job performance to rely upon in making a negative employment recommendation, you are best advised to use them rather than cite what a teacher says or writes. Sometimes, however, the major concerns do relate to how employees communicate with others, and you have no choice but to focus on the manner in which they do so. Just remember that much employee speech on the job is not constitutionally protected and make sure that you point this out in your documentation so that those not familiar with the law will understand that you have acted within legal boundaries. If you are uncertain about what is and is not constitutionally protected, check with the human resources department or the school attorney.

Finally, we need to note that teachers and administrators increasingly are using digital devices on and off campus to interact with colleagues and students. Quite often, this is part of the school's instructional program. Teachers engage with students online through the school's internet connection system for assignments, projects, and the like. Such communication facilitates learning in that it extends face-to-face time with teachers beyond the classroom and capitalizes on student expertise in using digital devices. Clearly, the future of teaching and learning will incorporate utilization of these devices in the instructional program. But in accord with T-TESS or the school's alternative assessment system, it is important to assure that communication between school employees and students is professional and collaborative at all times whether on or off campus. School officials now are beginning to educate teachers and students about appropriate conduct when engaging in communication via digital devices. In addition, most school districts and charter schools hold teachers and students accountable when using the school-hosted internet connection system and school-owned digital devices by having them (and the parents of students) sign Acceptable Use Policies (AUPs) – sometimes called Responsible Use Policies (RUPs) – that set forth the conditions and rules for doing so. Violation of the rules can result in disciplinary action against both students and school employees, with the added penalty of contract nonrenewal or termination for the latter.[3]

Controlling what teachers, other school employees, and students do with their personal electronic communication devices on their own time away from school is more difficult, because as private citizens they have the right of free speech and association. Yet reports repeatedly surface of teachers and administrators who have crossed the line between what is professional and what is not in social networking. Some teachers, for example, use Facebook to comment with their fellow teachers about matters at school. This isn't a problem unless the comments go too far. For example, a teacher who makes critical comments about the teacher's students or about fellow employees may learn that the communication has been forwarded to others including the school principal and parents. Imagine the turmoil that would result if a teacher's statement on Facebook that "I doubt our principal could even make it through kindergarten" surfaces at school! The fact that the comment was forwarded by others to persons at the school is unlikely to prevent sanctions against the teacher.[4]

What is important about applying sanctions against the teacher is to document how the electronic communication undermines the teacher's effectiveness. An example is a widely publicized 2019 decision of the Fort Worth I.S.D. to terminate the employment of a continuing contract teacher who on her own time sent a number of tweets to Donald Trump urging him to take action against the large number of illegal students from Mexico enrolled in the Fort Worth district. The district asserted that when the teacher signed her continuing contract, she waived her First Amendment rights. The Texas Commissioner of Education rejected this claim, noting that teachers retain free speech rights when employed in a public school district and that bringing concerns to an elected official who has authority over those claims "has a very high First Amendment interest." In this case, the commissioner side-stepped the free speech claim, noting that the district's decision to reject most of the independent hearing officer's conclusions of law and not add any job-related deficiency basis for termination left the district's decision arbitrary.[5] The decision was later affirmed by a state district court.

Litigation is now emerging in the social networking context. A good illustration is a case involving a Connecticut high school teacher who opened a MySpace account after students asked him to view their MySpace pages. The teacher, Jeffrey Spanierman, called one of the profiles on this account "Mr. Spiderman." He used his MySpace account to communicate with students about homework, to learn more about the students so he could relate to them better, and to conduct casual non-school related discussions. In social media parlance, he sought to "friend" his MySpace students electronically by including them on this profile. The matter came to attention of school personnel who viewed the profile page. There they found a picture of Spanierman taken some 10 years earlier when he was about the same age as the students he was friending. Also appearing were pictures of his students along with several pictures of naked men with inappropriate comments underneath them. Spanierman removed the Spiderman profile but then started another that was similar. His teaching contract was not renewed.

Spanierman sued in federal court, contending that the nonrenewal violated his right to free speech and association. The federal district court judge noted that his MySpace statements were made outside the scope of his employment and thus were not restricted by the 2006 U.S. Supreme Court decision referenced above. He noted as well that a poem Spanierman had posted on the MySpace profile expressing opposition to the Iraq war was constitutionally protected free speech. However, the judge agreed with school officials regarding the inappropriate manner in which Spanierman was communicating with students. The judge cited this exchange with a student who used the profile name "Repko."

Spanierman: "Repko and Ashley sittin in a tree.KISSING.1st comes love then marriage. HA HA HA HA HA HA HA!!!!!!!!!!!!!!!!!!!LOL [can mean 'laughing out loud']"

Repko: "don't be jealous cuase you cant get any lol :)"

Spanierman: "What makes you think I want any? I'm not jealous. I just like to have fun and goof on you guys. If you don't like it. Kiss my brass! LMAO [can mean 'laughing my ass off']."

The judge pointed out in his decision denying Spanierman's challenge to his contract nonrenewal that it is reasonable to expect a teacher with supervisory authority over students to maintain a professional, respectful association with them. "This does not mean that the [Spanierman] could not be friendly or humorous," wrote the judge. "However, upon review of the record, it appears that the [Spanierman] would communicate with students as if he were their peer, not their teacher." Such conduct could very well disrupt the learning atmosphere of a school, the judge observed. In short, the communication between the teacher and his students had ceased being professional. Indeed, some students maintained that they were uncomfortable with what Spanierman was saying.[6]

Most school districts and charter schools now have policies and regulations setting forth the conditions for appropriate use of electronic media at all times and the consequences for misuse. For example, Policy DH (Local) in most school district policies states that "All employees shall be held to the same professional standards in their use of electronic devices as for any other public conduct. If an employee's use of electronic communication violates state or federal law or District policy, or interferes with the employee's ability to effectively perform his or her duties, the employee is subject to disciplinary action, up to and including termination of employment." Given the potential for harm through electronic communication, giving employees guidelines for how to use their own digital devices appropriately would be wise. Points to make include:

- Reminding teachers that what they say on the internet could be disseminated in seconds and that they need to read carefully the privacy protections available on social communication networks.
- Pointing out that privacy protections of social communication networks do not prevent persons on the networks from forwarding pictures and messages to others. For example, the critical comments about the school principal described earlier could easily become widely known in the school community and undermine a teacher's effectiveness.
- Advising teachers that engaging in social communication with students and colleagues outside district internet access routes and not related to academic matters could easily undermine a teacher's effectiveness.
- Advising teachers to contact the school principal for advice if in doubt.

The Code of Ethics and Standards Practices for Texas Educators contains a section specifically directed to social networking with students via cell phones, text messaging, email, instant messaging, blogging, and the like. As noted in Appendix A of this handbook, Standard 3.9 sets forth factors to be considered in determining whether such networking is inappropriate. These include:

- The nature, purpose, timing, and amount of communication
- The subject matter addressed
- Whether the communication was open or secretive
- Whether a romantic relationship could be inferred

- Whether the communication was sexually explicit
- Whether the communication involves discussion of the physical or sexual attractiveness or sexual history, activities, preferences, or fantasies of either the educator or the student

School board policies usually incorporate the Code of Ethics. Thus, a teacher who engages in misuse of his or her own digital device in the ways indicated in this standard is violating school board policies as well.

DOCUMENTING UNPROFESSIONAL TEACHER COMMUNICATION

Inappropriate Written and Verbal Communication with Colleagues

One of the most frequent personnel issues that we encounter when we work with school administrators involves staff members who are discourteous and/or confrontational in their communication with students, other staff, and parents. They do not work and play well with others! With the increased importance of Professional Learning Communities (PLC) and collegial planning in schools, it is more important than ever for teachers to learn and to work together as a team for the best learning experiences for students. Unfortunately, a common scenario is the teacher who does not work professionally and cooperatively with other staff members.

A second facet of the issue is the teacher who is (or is perceived to be) rude, discourteous, or confrontational in the teacher's communication. Sometimes you may personally hear such communication; typically, the problem is brought to you by third parties.

Several problems emerge:

1. When a teacher is uncooperative with other staff or parents or when communication is rude or discourteous, you may not have had the opportunity to observe the uncooperative behavior or hear the rude/discourteous conversation personally. You may be relying on information from third parties, probably from other staff members or parents. Therefore, you may have to consider whether they are willing to complete and sign a complaint or witness statement form (templates for both are set forth in Appendix D) and/or testify in a hearing as to what they have seen or heard.

2. The teacher may completely deny having been rude or discourteous. He may assert that the complaining party is overreacting or misinterpreting his behavior. You may need to meet with the teacher to point out that regardless of his intent, others are receiving his messages as rude/discourteous and that he must change his behavior. You will be the arbiter of what is or is not rude or discourteous.

3. The teacher may assert that she is merely exercising her right of free speech. As we pointed out in this chapter and in Chapter 1, not all speech is protected. Still, absent clear abuse of free speech, it is better to focus on the time, place, and manner of expression rather than the content of what is being communicated.

For example, let's assume that Nick Negative is an eighth grade science teacher with many years of experience. You have an expectation that Nick participate with other teachers in designing and implementing quality lessons in all eighth grade science classes. All of the other eighth grade teachers have, at one time or another, complained to you that Nick is very difficult and unpleasant to work with. Comments from his co-workers include:

- "He's so negative about the kids—he calls them 'stupid,' says they are not capable of doing high level academic work, and says 'they just don't care and neither do their parents.'"
- "He gets angry when we try to discuss new ways of teaching. He insists that his traditional way of teaching is the best and that our 'newfangled methods' just do not work."
- "He argues and yells at us when we do not agree with him. If we argue back, he gets very rude and sarcastic."

Although you have not personally observed this behavior/language in planning meetings, you have confidence in the teachers who reported it. Two teachers agreed to complete a complaint form following a particularly confrontational meeting with Nick. Another who observed the fiery exchange completed a witness statement form. Your own experience with Nick suggests that he is entirely capable of the behavior that his co-workers have reported. You schedule a conference to talk with him about your concerns.

At the conference, he first wants to know who is doing the complaining. You explain that who is complaining is not the issue; the issue is having a productive, professional eighth grade PLC. He responds in a very loud voice, "They are just a bunch of young inexperienced teachers. I've been at this for more than 20 years, and I know what I am doing. I am not rude or sarcastic when I talk to them. I have very strong convictions and I want them to know that." At another point he says, "What do you expect me to do? Just cave in and do the Mickey Mouse lessons they come up with?" You point out that in your judgment, both the tone and content of his statement are unprofessional and sarcastic. He replies, "I'm just being honest, and I don't like being told what to do." You explain that you expect all members of the team to work together harmoniously and reach consensus on lesson planning and delivery of lessons. You also explain that you expect all team members to communicate with each other courteously and respectfully, even when they disagree with each other. You tell him that whether or not it his intention, his co-workers interpret his behavior as rude and confrontational. Finally, you tell him that his behavior is impeding his own job performance and that of his co-workers. The next day you write him a memorandum that follows the essential elements of a specific incident memorandum as set forth in Chapter 2 and in Chapter 4. The numbers in parentheses correspond with the observations in the commentary section following the memorandum. (You would, of course, not include these in the memorandum you send.)

ESSENTIAL ELEMENTS	
Letterhead Stationery	**PRAIRIE HIGH SCHOOL** *Home of the Prairie Howlers* Coyote I.S.D. 1000 High Road Coyote, TX 70000
Date	October 13, 2023
	TO: Nick Negative FROM: Sterling Leader, Principal RE: Planning, Working, and Communicating With Team Members
Allegation and Investigation	This memorandum addresses concerns that I expressed to you in our meeting yesterday about your work with other members of your team **(1)** in cooperatively planning lessons and reports that you use loud, unprofessional language in the planning meetings. My concerns are

ESSENTIAL ELEMENTS	
	based on my conversations I have had with you and with several members of your team.
Findings of Fact	As I explained to you at our meeting on October 13, several members of your team have reported to me that you are uncooperative in your planning meetings. They have also reported that when you disagree with the team that you yell at them and are rude and sarcastic. You **(2)** indicated that you believed that your teaching methodologies were better than the team's ideas. You also said to me in a very loud voice, "I am not rude or sarcastic when I talk to them. I have very strong convictions and I want them to know that."
	When I advised you that I expect all members of the team to work together harmoniously and reach consensus on lesson planning and delivery of lessons, you replied, "What do you expect me to do? Just cave in and do the Mickey Mouse lessons they come up with?" I told you that both the tone and content of your statement were unprofessional and sarcastic. You replied, "I'm just being honest, and I don't like being told what to do." I advised you that I expect all team members to communicate with each other courteously and respectfully, even when you disagree with each other.
Conclusions	T-TESS Domain 4, Dimension 2 encompasses leading colleagues collaboratively in and beyond the school, while Dimension 4 encompasses joining colleagues in collaborative efforts that enhance student learning and welfare. The latter is based on Standard 6 of the Texas Commissioner of Education's teacher standard rules that **(3)** there is an expectation that "teachers communicate consistently, clearly, and respectively." I have concluded that these expectations are not being met. I also should point out to you that one of the grounds for nonrenewal of a teacher contract in this district under Board Policy DFBB (Local) is "Failure to maintain an effective working relationship, or maintain good report, with parents, the community, or colleagues."
Directives	Beginning immediately, I will expect you to:
	1. Interact with other staff members in a manner that is supportive, **(4)** courteous, and respectful in such a way that complaints about your communication from other professionals decrease significantly and stop by the end of the semester.
	2. Stop all rudeness and sarcasm in such a way that complaints from other professionals decrease significantly and stop by the end of the semester.
	3. Work collaboratively with all staff and community, particularly in your professional learning community and eighth grade science team. We will incorporate this goal in future iterations of your Goal-Setting and Professional Development plan.
Opportunity to Respond	I have received a copy of this memorandum. I understand that my signature does not necessarily indicate that I agree with its contents. I further understand that I have a right to respond within 10 working days.
Dated Employee Signature	/s/ Nick Negative Date

Commentary

(1) The concern/allegation is that Nick does not work cooperatively with his team and that he is rude and sarcastic in the planning meetings.

(2) You summarized your concerns about cooperative planning and professional communication and accurately reflect what he said in response to these allegations. When he wanted to know who had complained, you focused instead on your concern. You cited both the complaints from co-workers as well as your own experience in the conference. Should a contract nonrenewal or termination hearing occur over this matter, you have the complaint and witness statement forms to back up your assertions.

(3) You chose language from two dimensions in T-TESS Domain 4 and Standard 6 from Chapter 149 of the Texas Administrative Code as the source of your expectations. This is important because it will be the anchor/basis of authority for the directives that you write in the next section of the memorandum. Citing the contract nonrenewal provision for failure to maintain a good working relationship and rapport with colleagues will certainly catch Nick's attention, as it relates directly to his current behavior.

(4) Your directives are specific regarding what you expect Nick to do in the future with regard to working courteously and cooperatively with colleagues. Note that these directives follow the formula discussed in Chapter 6: teacher behavior + linking language + outcome. Models of these directives also can be found in the sample memoranda in Chapter 4 and in Appendix C. The teacher behaviors are anchored in the expectations from section 3 of the memorandum. The outcomes are "complaints from other professionals decrease significantly and stop by the end of the semester." This is the evidence that you will use determine whether he has complied with the directives. In addition for failure to follow directives, "failure to maintain an effective working relationship or maintain good rapport with parents, the community, or colleagues" is a cause for contract nonrenewal or termination in most district policies [see DFBB (Local) from TASB Policy Services].

Social Networking with Students Through Digital Devices

Let us assume that Sterling Leader, principal of Prairie High School in Coyote I.S.D., is concerned about one of his English teachers, 24-year-old Sarah Novice. She is a good teacher, but Sterling has observed her at various school events texting a lot on her cell phone. He notes that when she finishes a text message, she often glances toward several students who also seem to be texting. Their smiles and laughter in her direction while the messaging is ongoing suggest to him that Sarah and the students are texting each other. Sterling spoke with Sarah about this after a home football game where he observed her texting on her cell phone and waving to several of her students elsewhere in the stands. They waved in response and also were busy texting. When Sterling talked with Sarah about this the following Monday, she said that she indeed was texting with her students. She said they were discussing matters related to the football game. She showed Sterling the message threads on her cell phone. He noted text exchanges over such matters as the prowess of the cheerleaders and the tripping of one of the high school band's tuba players on the field during half-time. Sterling advised Sarah to be careful about texting students, noting that what might seem innocuous communication can easily become less so. Sterling felt some unease when Sarah responded, "I just want to be friendly with my students. If they like me, they will do well in my classes." But he decided not to pursue the matter further at the time

Several weeks later, Sarah's cell phone dropped out of her purse when she was searching for a notepad as she was walking down the hall toward the school cafeteria. With the rush of students to the cafeteria and the surrounding noise, she was unaware of the incident. Several students some distance behind her found the cell phone but didn't know to whom it belonged. They checked the email, text messages, and photographs. Sarah's identity surfaced immediately. So did some other messages and images. Among the photographs was Sarah holding a glass of wine at a post-football game party attended by some of her students. The game was hosted by the parents of several football players. The students were clustered around Sarah, holding soft drinks. One student in the background was flipping his middle finger toward the camera. One of the two text messages on the phone was from a senior student who asked her if they could meet for lunch on Saturday at a nearby McDonalds to talk about his college plans. The students were laughing and hooting as they came across the photo and the message. Before they could do more searching, Sterling, who was walking down the hall, came upon them. The students told him that they had found the phone on the floor and had checked some of its contents to see whose it was. They couldn't help laughing as they pointed out the photo at the football game party. Sterling thanked them for finding the phone and told them to head on to the cafeteria.

Later that day, Sterling asked Sarah to come by the office. He handed her the phone, noting that the students had seen the photographs and read the text messages. Sarah was delighted that her cell phone was found and returned to her, but a little upset about what the students had seen. Sterling talked with her about the potential pitfalls of communicating electronically with students and then directed her to lock her cell phone and restrict her communication with students. Two days later, he sent her a follow-up memorandum. The numbers in parentheses correspond with the observations in the commentary section following the memorandum.

ESSENTIAL ELEMENTS	
Letterhead Stationery	**PRAIRIE HIGH SCHOOL** *Home of the Prairie Howlers* Coyote I.S.D. 1000 High Road Coyote, TX 70000

Date	`November 16, 2023`
	
	`TO:   Sarah Novice`
	`FROM: Sterling Leader, Principal`
	`RE:   Cell Phone Use`

Allegation and Investigation	`This memorandum addresses concerns that I have expressed to you over use of your personal cell phone with students at this high school. My concerns are based on my own observations and well as conversations I have had with you and with several of your students.` **(1)**
Findings of Fact	`On Friday, October 13, I observed you at the home football game texting students in the stands with your cell phone. I spoke with you the following Monday before classes began regarding what I had observed. You acknowledged that you were texting with students. You showed me several of the text messages. I advised you to be careful in social interaction with students either by electronic or non-electronic means both on and off campus, given the potential for misuse. You responded by noting that you would be careful, adding that "I just want to be friendly with my students."` **(2)**

ESSENTIAL ELEMENTS	

On Monday, November 13, your cell phone dropped out of your purse as you headed to the cafeteria for lunch. Four students some distance behind you found the cell phone and were able to access its contents. They told me they did so to discover the owner. They also said they had come across a text message from another student asking you to have lunch with him at McDonalds on a Saturday. They showed me the message and also a photograph of you holding a wine glass at an after-hours post-football game party hosted by several parents. You were surrounding by smiling students, one of whom displayed an obscene hand gesture to the camera.

As I explained to you at our meeting after school that day, there was nothing I could do to prevent the students who found your cell phone from accessing this material. I also advised you on how to use your cell phone appropriately at school and elsewhere. I am sending you this follow-up memorandum to make sure my directives are clear and to explain why I have made them.

Conclusions

At this time, I don't believe you have violated our district policy on communication with students via electronic means. **(3)**

However, as I explained to you, it is important to note that School Board Policy DH (Local) incorporates the Code of Ethics and Standard Practices for Texas Educators. Standard 3.8 states that the educator "shall maintain appropriate professional educator-student relationships and boundaries based on a reasonably prudent educator standard." Standard 3.9 goes on to address inappropriate use of electronic communication devices in social interactions with students. I am attaching both the policy provision and the Code of Ethics to this memorandum. Please pay particular attention to the components of Standard 3.9 of the Code that address conditions under which educators violate the standard in engaging in electronic communication with students. I also ask that you read our Teacher Handbook, pages 15-20 of which address use of electronic media with students.

I am not including this matter in your appraisal for this year. I would like us to put it behind us.

Directives

At our meeting, I requested that you set a password so that you can lock your cell phone at school. That way, no one can access its contents should it not be in your possession. Second, I directed you to limit your electronic communication with students at school and school-related activities only to matters related to your professional responsibilities. These include class work, homework, and tests. I also strongly advised you to limit your communication with students off campus in a similar manner, because any misuse that undermines your effectiveness as a teacher can be grounds for disciplinary action including contract nonrenewal or termination. Both you and I agreed that you would not have any social contact with the student who requested you join him for lunch. The same is true for any other student. **(4)**

If you have any questions about communicating electronically with students, please let me know. In your first two years at Prairie High School, you have proven yourself to be a good teacher. I don't want you to do anything to jeopardize your career. The matter of communicating with students in this electronic age can be tricky. If you have any questions about this in the future, don't hesitate to contact me.

Att.

Opportunity to Respond

I have received a copy of this memorandum. I understand that my signature does not necessarily indicate that I agree with its contents. I further understand that I have a right to respond within 10 working days.

Dated Employee Signature

/s/ Sarah Novice   Date

Commentary

(1) This is less an allegation than a statement of fact, because much of what Sterling addresses is based on his own observation. However, he did talk with students and obtained information from them which he relies on in part in writing the memorandum.

(2) It probably would have been better if Sterling had directed Sarah not to text message students at all or only related to her work as a teacher when they spoke after the football game. It could be that he opted to be less directive because of Sarah's reactions and his desire not to damage their working relationship. Note that Sterling is specific as to dates, times, and substance in his findings of fact. These are based on his notes to the file. As we point out in Chapter 2, making notes to the file is essential to effective documentation where prior events are incorporated in the findings of fact. It may be that Sterling sought to have each of the students he spoke with in the hallway complete a witness statement form (see Appendix D) describing in factual terms how they found Sarah's cell phone, what they accessed on the cell phone, and what they came across. This is a judgment call.

(3) While Sterling does not find that Sarah has violated Coyote I.S.D. policy, he takes advantage of the situation to make her fully aware of district policy and related legal sources pertaining to social communication with students via electronic means. It is extremely important for both administrators and teachers to be fully aware of the policies, rules, and procedures of the district within which they are employed. Here, the principal even broadens the scope of his discussion to include both nonelectronic social interaction and interacting with students off campus. Note that he attaches both the district policy and the Code of Ethics and Standard Practices for Texas Educators to his memorandum. He also references the teacher handbook.

(4) Sterling's directives are specific regarding what he expects her to do in the future with regard to using her cell phone at school. Clearly, Sarah knows exactly what she needs to do to avoid problems in this area in the future. She also undoubtedly will be cautious in engaging in social interaction with students off campus on her own time. And the principal has left the door open should she have future concerns over the use of digital devices in interacting with students. Some districts and charter schools have provisions in faculty handbooks restricting text messaging with students during school or at school-related activities. Others require teachers to use a professional social network page for communicating with students rather than through a personal social network page. Whether time, place, and manner rules like these can apply to teacher communication using their own devices off campus during non-school hours is less certain, given the lack of definitive law. Thus, it is important for school administrators to check board policies and employee handbooks and to consult with human resources officials and the district's attorney when crafting directives that encompass non-school time.

SUMMARY

Here is a summary of main points discussed in this chapter.

- Professional communication expectations between and among employees are encompassed in Domain 4 of T-TESS as well as in Standard 6 of the Texas Commissioner of Education's appraisal rules found in Section 1001(b) of Chapter 149 in Title 19 of the Texas Administrative Code. With an emphasis on professional learning communities and team planning, cooperative and professional communication is an increasingly important aspect of job responsibilities.

- Addressing communication between and among professional employees and with the larger school community may raise the question of First Amendment free speech rights. Communication may also be a somewhat subjective issue because the problem may be rooted in judgments about volume, tone, or inflection that are interpreted as being sarcastic, rude, or discourteous.

- If employees are not communicating courteously and respectfully, direct them to meet the expectations of the district or charter school policies in their communication with students, staff, and the larger school community.

- The law dealing with communication using digital devices is a new and still emerging field. If you are unsure how to proceed when you believe misuse has occurred, contact human resources personnel or the school attorney.

- If you know or suspect that an employee is using digital devices and social networking sites inappropriately, direct the employee to follow school policy and/or the Code of Ethics and Standard Practices for Texas Educators.

REFERENCES

1. *Garcetti v. Ceballos,* 547 U.S. 410 (2006).
2. A school employee who posts a message on a personal blog about suspected violation of law by school officials and then asserts that the Texas Whistleblower Act provides protection from an adverse employment action would not likely be successful because the Act requires reporting of suspected violation of law to appropriate law enforcement personnel or to someone in the district that the employee believes is responsible for enforcing the law. Posting a message on a blog doesn't fulfill these criteria. However, the employee also would likely assert that any adverse employment action violates the employee's free speech exercised away from school and not within the scope of employment.
3. The U.S. Supreme Court weighed in on the matter when it ruled that police department officials could search the text messages on an officer's cell phone in compliance with an acceptable use agreement. The officer had signed the agreement. The search was conducted to determine why the officer was using the cell phone excessively while on the job. The search was judged not to be a violation of the officer's constitutional right to be free from unreasonable search and seizure because of the agreement and because there were reasonable grounds for the officials to conduct the search. Nor was the search excessively intrusive. *Ontario v. Ouon,* 130 S.Ct. 2519 (2010).
4. *Esparza v. Edinburg Consolidated I.S.D.*, Dkt. No. 017-R2-01-2017 (Comm'r Educ. 2017). A middle school principal used her cell phone to take a nude picture of herself and then email it to her husband. Someone gained access to the picture and forwarded it to students at the school. The matter surfaced in the press. Disagreeing with the hearing examiner, the commissioner held that the school board could consider whether the dissemination of the photo undermined the principal's effectiveness to justify contract termination even though done by a third party. The commissioner noted that "There is good cause to terminate a contract when the employee cannot perform essential job functions. This is so whether or not the reason the employee cannot perform essential job functions is, in part, caused by a third party." Thus the school board had good cause to terminate the contract based on its findings of fact. The commissioner's decision and the reasoning behind it were upheld by a Texas appellate court in 2020. *Edinburg Consolidated I.S.D. v. Esparza*, 603 S.W.3d 468 (Tex. App. Corpus Christi-Edinburg 2020).
5. *Clark v. Fort Worth I.S.D.,* Dkt. No. 006-R2-10-2019 (Comm'r Educ. 2019).
6. *Spanierman v. Hughes,* 576 F.Supp.2d 292 (D. Conn. 2008). The judge also rejected Spanierman's claim that his right to association was violated by the nonrenewal, questioning whether that right encompasses a medium like MySpace. MySpace, wrote the judge, doesn't express itself about anything but is merely a means to set up a private community. Even if a right of association did exist, the school had sufficient justification for its nonrenewal action in light of what Spanierman was doing with his MySpace profile.

CHAPTER SIX: WRITING AND MONITORING INTERVENTION PLANS

Sometimes employee deficiencies are serious enough that informal conferences and follow- up memoranda won't work. What is called for is the development of a written document that sets forth deficiencies in detail and expectations for improved performance within a specific time frame. In this chapter, we discuss this process.

It is important to note at the start that whatever formal teacher appraisal system a school district or charter school uses has its own professional growth component. For those using the Texas Teacher Evaluation and Support System (T-TESS), for example, this is called the Goal-Setting Professional Development (GSPD) plan that is completed at the beginning of the academic year and reviewed at its end. This goal-setting is not necessarily focused on teacher deficiencies. The system assumes that even a master teacher will have goals for becoming even better and has ideas about what professional development will support those efforts. The belief of the T-TESS system is that everyone wants to and has the ability to get better.

This belief is in sharp contrast with the growth plans in previous teacher appraisal systems. Those plans were generally developed only for teachers with deficiencies. A prime example is the Teacher in Need of Assistance (TINA) plan that was part of the former Professional Development and Assessment System (PDAS). While GSPD can address deficiencies, that is not its primary purpose. The GSPD is in no way punitive.

Sometimes there is an immediate need to alert the employee to serious deficiencies and set forth a time line from correction. If correction does not occur, then the supervisor may have no choice but to recommend contract nonrenewal or even termination. We will use the term intervention plan (IP) in this chapter to refer to this type of document. A template for an IP is included in Appendix D. While this document is developed outside of the formal appraisal system with a professional or auxiliary employee, it does not replace it. Nor does it replace the Goal-Setting Professional Development (GSPD) plan embedded in T-TESS or a similar plan embedded in a locally developed appraisal system. Rather, it provides a means of gathering information about employment deficiencies, expected changes of behavior, a time line for changes, and evidence to determine whether improvement has occured—all of which will then be incorporated in future T-TESS appraisals and revisions of the GSPD plan or their counterparts. Thus, IPs need to be linked to the formal appraisal system that the school district, campus, or charter school uses as will be explained in this chapter.

THE LEGAL DIMENSION

An intervention plan (IP) is important not only as a remedial tool for an ineffective teacher or other employee, but also as documentation in the event that you as the supervisor decide to recommend nonrenewal or termination of the employee's contract. While the law reflects a number of reasons for a negative employment decision, your strongest and most objective rationale probably will be "failure to comply with school board policies and administrative directives," a reason cited frequently by the Texas Commissioner of Education and the courts in upholding a school district's decision to nonrenew or terminate an employment contract.[1] In the classroom context, administrative directives can best be communicated through a written IP. Proving that the employee failed to follow an IP is much easier and less inflammatory than proving that the employee is incompetent or ineffective. The two case summaries that follow illustrate the value of an intervention plan in defending negative employment decisions.

In 1990 the Texas Commissioner of Education was confronted with an appeal by a continuing contract teacher who was returned to probationary status. The teacher had a long history of marginal performance. Although district administrators had prepared several growth plans for the teacher and noted some improvement, deficiencies still remained. Therefore, the school board voted to place the teacher back on a probationary contract on the ground of incompetence. (As noted in Chapter 1, employment law provisions now require the employee's consent before the employee can be placed back on a probationary contract.)

The commissioner overturned the local board's action, noting that the teacher had shown some improvement and that the school district was unable to refute the teacher's claim that she was capable of performing her duties. The board could have shown that the teacher had failed to comply with the elements of her growth plan, yet the board opted instead to list incompetence as the only basis for its action. The school board argued that the teacher had in fact not improved and that the improvement noted on her improvement plan was not genuine but rather was intended as a motivational technique. Nevertheless, the commissioner rejected the board's assertion and ruled in favor of the teacher.[2] In addition to avoid focusing on "incompetency" as the basis for a negative employment decision, the lesson here is not to say positive things that are not justified in association with a nonrenewal or termination action. Of course, if such comments are justified, then why move forward with a contract nonrenewal or termination?

A termination case that arose several years later was decided quite differently. This time the commissioner rejected the appeal of a continuing contract teacher whose contract was terminated for failing to meet the requirements of his improvement plan. The teacher's 1990-91 appraisal scores had decreased significantly from the previous year. The teacher's supervisor had written an improvement plan specifying six areas in which the teacher needed to improve his classroom performance. The man failed to implement the requirements set forth in the plan. In supporting the local board's decision to terminate the contract, the commissioner found that the teacher had failed to "comply with the reasonable requirements of the board of trustees for achieving professional growth and improvement."[3] The teacher did not meet the specific directives regarding his classroom performance and rapport with students, even after the district had issued the plan and provided warnings.

Two important lessons can be learned from these decisions. First, use "failure to comply with directives in an intervention plan" rather than "incompetence" as the basis for nonrenewal or termination. Second, be honest in employee evaluation. Trying to motivate employees by inflating their performance scores works to everyone's disadvantage. This is especially true when the supervisor's goal is to move toward a recommendation of contract nonrenewal or termination. It is important to understand the circumstances in which giving employees the opportunity to improve their job performance may be a legal as well as an ethical consideration. The commissioner of education has issued a number of decisions over the years where remediation has come up. In a 2002 decision, he noted that the thrust of these decisions is that there is no automatic right to remediation if a teacher's conduct constitutes good cause for termination. Rather, remediation is only required if a teacher's conduct "does not rise to the level of good cause."[4] For example, the commissioner observed that errors concerning lesson plans and grade books normally will require remediation. But serious grading infractions such as manufacturing grades will not, absent extenuating circumstances. Other behavior that does not require remediation includes violent conduct or conduct that involves significant or potentially significant emotional or physical harm to students. In the 2002 decision, the commissioner upheld the termination of the teacher's contract after the teacher had been given ample warning that his lesson plans and grade books were unacceptable and had failed to change his behavior. The teacher also had taken excessive absences.

Basically, remediation requires advising employees of deficiencies and consequences, developing an intervention plan, assisting employees to meet the plan, and giving them a reasonable time to comply. An intervention plan also should include an assessment component so that it can be determined whether the employee has completed the components of the plan and whether improvement in performance has occurred. And, as we will note later in this chapter, it is important whenever possible to link expected changes in teacher behavior to improved student performance/behavior. Most districts have as one reason for contract nonrenewal a significant lack of student progress attributable to the educator. In a 2008 decision, the commissioner cited this reason in rejecting a high school math teacher's appeal of her contract nonrenewal. The teacher taught at a school in the Dallas I.S.D. that had been reconstituted after being rated unacceptable for two consecutive years. The teacher claimed that the Classroom Effectiveness Index used by the Campus Intervention Team was inappropriate and should not have been used. The commissioner rejected the assertion, noting that the teacher had not taken advantage of opportunities to make these assertions during the time of the reconstitution. She could have filed a grievance when given notice that she would not be retained as a teacher at the campus. The commissioner supported the decision of the Campus Intervention Team that she should not be retained because her students were not passing or showing significant improvement on the Texas Assessment of Knowledge and Skills (TAKS) tests.[5]

In another decision involving a teacher in a reconstituted school in the Dallas district, the commissioner ruled in favor of a teacher who maintained that her contract termination for poor performance of her students on TAKS was unwarranted. The findings of fact demonstrated that the reason for poor student performance was the school environment, including the lack of discipline, and not the teacher's performance.[6]

The lesson from these decisions is to make sure that there is significant linkage between teaching behavior and student performance after taking into account intervening factors such as a high student classroom migration rate, the negative influence of a peer group, or a breakdown in campus discipline.

Developing an intervention plan offers several definite dividends. First, the school board in a nonrenewal case or hearing officer in a termination case may expect that, as a matter of basic fairness, the employee should be told of his or her deficiencies and be given an opportunity to correct them. Second, the intervention plan puts the employee on notice that future employment is conditioned on complying with its components. To this extent, noncompliance later in the employment relationship will provide the groundwork for a negative employment decision. In a 1998 decision, the commissioner noted that, while performance in a previous year cannot be used to terminate a present year contract, a previous year evaluation that includes an expectation for changes in future years is different. As the commissioner observed, "A failing is particularly damaging to a teacher when the error was pointed out and was not corrected."[7]

As we noted in the 1990 commissioner's decision above, it is easier to establish failure to comply with the reasonable terms of a remediation plan than incompetence as a ground for contract nonrenewal or termination—especially when the problems are related to instruction.

In Chapter 3, we discussed in detail the circumstances under which you choose the appropriate style of supervision for a particular teacher. The goal setting in T-TESS in most circumstances will be nondirective or collaborative. After all, the focus is on continuous improvement, and the teacher must at least share in the decision-making process. We also discussed the small percentage of time that you may need to consider a more directive style. During the school year, if your goal shifts to a serious consideration of recommending contract termination or nonrenewal, you may want to consider stepping outside the T-TESS process and developing an intervention plan (IP) well before the end of year review of the teacher goals from the fall. If so, the Goal-Setting and Professional Development (GSPD) plan needs to be modified following completion of the IP so that it incorporates your concerns. This is necessary because the GSPD plan is viewed as a "live plan" that is central to guiding teacher behavior. When you change the plan either following completion of the IP and/or at the end of the year and when you and the teacher revisit the goals set in the fall, you may need to take a directive supervisory role to reflect the concerns, expectations, and time lines contained in the IP. This certainly would be the case for a teacher who has one or more T-TESS dimension ratings in the "improvement needed" category. Beginning in 2017-2018, the same is true for a teacher rated as "improvement needed or well-below expectations" in the student performance category under commissioner rules (19 TAC § 150.1002(f)).

When additional paperwork is required from the teacher, the IP needs to be linked to the GSPD plan because Education Code Section 11.164, commonly known as the Paperwork Reduction Act, limits the types of paperwork teachers are required to produce.[8] One exception in this statute is "any information specifically required by law, rule, or regulation." Since a teacher evaluation system is mandated by law, the IP should be linked to the domains and dimensions of T-TESS for districts and charter schools that use it. As you will later see, the best place to do that is in the first section of the IP where you identify areas related to the evaluation instrument that are in need of improvement. To establish clearly the linkage between the evaluation instrument and the IP, use the T-TESS domain and dimension language. For districts, campuses, and charter schools using an alternative teacher appraisal system under Chapter 150.1007 of Title 19 of the Texas Administrative Code, the IP should be similarly linked to the alternative system. And as noted above, the administrator needs to be cautious in directing teachers to produce more paperwork to comply with the IP. If there are questions about this, you are best advised to contact human resources personnel.

WHY WRITE AN INTERVENTION PLAN IF ONE IS NOT REQUIRED?

Remember that your primary goal is to help the employee be the best that he/she can be. The employee may be a classroom teacher, an administrator, or an at-will employee. Often, an intervention plan (IP) is viewed as punitive (especially by the person receiving it), but punishment should not be the motivation to create one. There are many reasons that you may need to write an IP, and not all of these reasons reflect the employee's lack of ability.

When Job Performance Does Not Meet Expectations and More Extrinsic Motivation May Be Needed

Recall the Quadrant I and Quadrant III employees from Chapter 3. These employees share one common characteristic: low level of motivation. When formal and informal conversations fail to cause the employee to change behavior, it may be time for the supervisor to provide some more significant extrinsic motivation. Writing an IP may have the triple effect of communicating to the employee:

- Job behavior does not meet expectations,
- Descriptions of what behavior is expected, and
- An indication that the deficiencies are significant — significant enough to warrant an intervention plan.

The most common purpose for an IP is to formally communicate that the employee's job performance does not meet expectations. In one scenario, the employee has exhibited a pattern of behavior that does not meet job expectations. While the failures may not rise to the level of "serious job deficiencies," the supervisor has met with the employee on more than one occasion. There may be notes to the file for some of the early conversations and specific incident memoranda to document the later conversations. Specific incident memoranda are discussed in Chapter 2. The specific incident memoranda may or may not have included directives for specific changes in behavior. Despite the conversations and memoranda, the employee's behavior has not changed. It may be time to write an IP.

In a second scenario, there is not a history of conversations and memoranda, but the employee's failure to meet job expectations is considered serious, yet remediable. [Note: If the behavior is serious and irremediable, no notice of deficiency and no opportunity for remediation may be needed.] Even without a pattern of behavior, the employee's behavior is sufficiently serious to warrant writing an IP.

When Job Expectations May Not Be Clear

You should not necessarily assume that an employee is not meeting the expectations of the job because of laxness or indifference. The employee may not be meeting job expectations because the organization has not effectively communicated them. Unfortunately, some employees in public education are hired without a job description, particularly for middle management and educational support positions. Even when job descriptions do exist, they may be "boiler-plates" that come from a personnel manual or professional organization and are not customized to the district's specific expectations for the position. This may be especially true for administrative personnel such as assistant principals, central office support personnel, people who work in instructional support positions (e.g., educational technology, special education supervisors and diagnosticians, and other federally funded programs), and other personnel (e.g., counselors, librarians, and auxiliary personnel). While customizing job descriptions to the specific expectations of the district is probably the best way to communicate these expectations, writing an intervention plan also serves as a vehicle to inform the employee what specific job behaviors the district expects.

When the Supervisor Needs to Begin Laying Groundwork for Nonrenewal or Termination of Employment

You may have made a determination that the employee cannot or will not change job-related behavior. You have had conversations, provided assistance to the employee, and documented your actions through specific incident memoranda to the employee. You want to both formalize and document your efforts and the seriousness of the job-related deficiencies. Once you have determined that the employee will not or cannot change behavior, your goal is no longer growth and improvement — it is to begin laying the groundwork for a recommendation of nonrenewal or termination.

HOW TO WRITE AN INTERVENTION PLAN

An intervention plan should consist of these four components, each of which is explained in this section:

1. Notice of areas of job performance in which improvement or change is needed.
2. Offer of (or directives for) assistance and support through growth activities.
3. Time lines and evidence that will be used to determine if growth activities have been completed.
4. Time lines and evidence of changes in behavior that will be used to determine if the requirements of the intervention plan have been met.

Step 1: Notice of Areas of Job Performance in Which Improvement or Change is Needed

The first step in creating an IP is to give the employee notice of areas of job performance which need improvement or in which change is needed. In the case of teachers, you are required both ethically and legally to alert the teacher to any conduct or performance that does not meet the expectations of the school district. The improvement or change you direct the teacher to make may involve problems with instruction and classroom management and/or problems that lie outside the classroom. There are four categories of employee behavior that may require an IP.

Classroom Instructional Issues and Student Performance

When supervising classroom teachers, the most common reason to create an IP will most likely be performance in the classroom. This category includes both classroom instructional behavior and behaviors related to instruction such as written lesson plans, assignments for campus supervision, grading and reporting of student grades, timely arrival and departure. As we will discuss in more depth later in this chapter, language in the plan should be anchored in the language of T-TESS or the locally adopted teacher appraisal system.

We are in an era of increasing student accountability within both the state and federal (Every Student Succeeds Act) systems. An analysis of data may indicate that a teacher's students perform less well on accountability tests than other teachers who teach similar students.

Your documentation of classroom observations is very important in establishing that observed behaviors do not meet district expectations. In Chapter 4, you gathered this kind of information by observing in Mr. Burner's classroom. You might, therefore, include a section similar to the following in Mr. Burner's IP.

The following areas are in need of improvement:

- Engagement of all students in relevant, meaningful learning
- Student mastery of the objective
- Responding to students who become confused or disengaged
- Teacher interaction with students

You will note that these statements are broadly worded and reflect the dimension level language of T-TESS. Your comments will become more specific when you write the directives for improvement in the fourth section of the IP. We will demonstrate this later in this chapter in developing an intervention plan for a marginally effective teacher known as Susie Dud.

If the performance of a teacher's students on the State of Texas Assessment of Academic Readiness (STAAR) test was significantly lower than the students in similarly constituted classes, the area in need of improvement might be worded:

- Increase the percentage of students who meet minimum expectations on the 8th grade STAAR social studies test.

Compliance With Laws/Policies/Procedures

Sometimes, the job deficiency may lie in the employee's failure to comply with state or federal law or with local operating policies and procedures. The employee may be a classroom teacher, campus administrator, central office administrator, or someone who works in an instructional support program. As we will discuss later in this chapter, language in the plan should be anchored in the language of the law, policy, or procedure. If an employee you supervise is deficient in one of these areas, a statement like the following will let him know what kind of change or improvement is needed:

- Following district/campus policies in reporting student grades to the office and to parents.
- Writing lesson plans according to the campus format.
- Being present at your assigned duty station.
- Following the state inspection requirements before the school bus is moved from the bus barn parking lot.
- Following federal law in implementing all of the provisions of the Individualized Education Program (IEP) for all special education students in your classroom.
- Following district grievance policies for complaints regarding conditions of employment.

Recall that directives similar to these were included in the specific incident memoranda illustrated in Chapters 2 and 4.

Other Job-Related Behaviors

For classroom teachers, the job deficiency may include such issues as assignments for campus supervision and timely arrival and departure. For employees who are not classroom teachers, job-related deficiencies may involve issues such as planning, producing products, meeting deadlines, and timely arrival and departure. For administrators and support personnel, the deficiencies for that position should be anchored in the language of the employee's job description and/or the appraisal instrument. For classroom teachers, the deficiencies should be anchored in the language of the district's teacher appraisal instrument or in law/district policy. Statements like the following will let the employee know what kind of change or improvement is needed:

- Administering diagnostic tests and completing the educational diagnostician's portion of the written assessment based on state and local guidelines and the specific needs of the students *(for an educational diagnostician)*.

- Preparing and implementing long- and short-range plans for district instructional technology *(for a director of technology)*.

- Submitting campus PEIMS data to the central office before the district deadline *(for a PEIMS clerk)*

- Meeting deadlines for reports and documents for the agenda for local board of trustees meetings.

"Affective Issues"

The most difficult job-related issues to address in an improvement plan are what we will call "affective issues." Effective communication with stakeholders, "team work," cooperation, and negative/critical comments are all behaviors in that category. These issues were discussed more fully in Chapter 5. Statements like the following will let the employee know what kind of change or improvement is needed:

- Communicating courteously and professionally with students, staff, and parents.

- Meeting on a weekly basis and working collaboratively with grade-level team members for instructional planning.

- Following district grievance policies for complaints regarding conditions of employment.

- Communicating effectively with staff *(for administrative and support personnel)*.

While these behaviors can significantly affect the quality of job performance, they are more difficult to include in the intervention plan for three reasons: (1) because of the nature of the desired behavior, it may be impossible to provide growth activities related to the deficiency if you desire to do so; (2) it may not be easy to gather and objectively document the behaviors that will indicate that improvement has or has not occurred; and (3) free speech issues may arise.

When identifying areas in which improvement is needed, it may be important to use language that lays a foundation for your authority to issue the directive. This may help avoid accusations that your directives are merely your subjective opinion about how things should be done or are arbitrary and capricious. When possible, use language from the following:

- The Texas Teacher Evaluation and Support System
- Teacher standards set forth in the Texas Administrative Code (19 TAC § 149.1001)
- Locally adopted district appraisal system
- Campus plan
- The essential knowledge and skills in the state curriculum
- District, campus, charter school policy
- Job description (especially for administrators, support staff, and at-will employees)
- Code of Ethics and Standard Practices for Texas Educators
  (see Appendix A)

Examples of "basis of authority" language can be found in Appendix C.

Step 2: Offer of (or Directive for) Assistance and Support Through Growth Activities.

The second part of the IP encompasses a listing of requirements (or suggestions) designed to assist the employee in meeting the specific directives you give for improvement. From an ethical and professional perspective, your concern lies in helping the employee meet the district's expectations for effectiveness. From a legal perspective, you probably will be required to demonstrate that you have attempted to help the employee improve and that you have not simply tried to get rid of him/her. Should you decide to pursue nonrenewal or termination of employment, including this second set of administrative directives will establish a stronger basis for your decision.

Directed activities that offer support for the teacher in her efforts to improve may include training sessions, observing other teachers, submitting written lesson plans, or reading journal articles (see Appendix C). Any directive should be aimed at providing information or assistance for the employee in meeting the behavioral expectations that you outlined in the first section of the plan. Examples:

1. Attend the training on TEKS-based mathematics instruction at the educational service center on November 14.

2. Schedule a meeting with me within one week of that training to discuss how you plan to implement the strategies learned in the workshop.

3. Read the book, What Great Coaches Do Differently. Provide a written summary and identify three to four elements discussed in the book. Submit the summary to your supervisor no later than September 15.

4. Prepare and submit to me your detailed, written lesson plans to specifically include:
   a. Texas Essential Knowledge and Skills that will be learned in each class
   b. Time allocations for activities
   c. Activities that maximize student participation and success

5. Schedule meetings and meet with me every two weeks to discuss your lesson plans and modifications/accommodations for special education students.

Note that training is not the only option in directing professional development activities for teachers. Developing plans or reports, meeting with a supervisor or team leader, and visiting/observing other teachers may be more appropriate activities. Remember that if you clearly linked areas in need of improvement to T-TESS and its GSPD plan or the school's alternative teacher appraisal system language in the first section of the IP, you will be able to require written reports from the teacher without violating the Reduction in Paperwork Act. One improvement activity that you may wish seriously to consider is to assign a mentor to a marginally effective teacher. As noted in the first chapter, the legislature has enacted the optional mentor program. Many districts may see the mentor program as a cost-effective way of improving teacher performance. The mentor could observe in the teacher's classroom, conduct model demonstration lessons for the teacher to observe, and assist with planning instructional and discipline management strategies. A more complete listing of other possible growth activities is found in Appendix C.

Step 3: Time Lines and Evidence That Will be Used to Determine if Growth Activities Have Been Completed.

For each growth activity in Step 2, you will need to write a corresponding statement of evidence that you will use to determine whether or not the activity has been completed and give a time line for completion of each activity. For example:

1. Submit a certificate of your attendance for the November 14 training session within five working days of the workshop.

2. Schedule a meeting with me to discuss how you plan to implement the strategies learned in the workshop within five working days of the workshop.

3. Submit lesson plans with the specifications included in #2 above by 8:00 a.m. on the first instructional day of each week.

4. Schedule meetings and meet with me every two weeks during the school year.

Step 4: Directives for Changes in Behavior Plus Time Lines and Evidence That Will Be Used to Determine if Improvement Has Occurred or Is Occurring

If it seems likely that you will decide to recommend nonrenewal or termination of an employee's contract based on "failure to comply with administrative directives," you will want to consider carefully the specific set of directives you give. Because these directives form the basis for your employment decision, they should consist of behaviors that are objectively observable and should include changes in specific job-related behavior. Imagine that a hypothetical Ms. Dud is one of your teachers in the following example, which is, unfortunately, very typical.

You have just completed the third observation in Ms. Dud's classroom. In the appraisal process so far you have collected data and written memoranda documenting that Ms. Dud spends most of her time sitting at her desk while students complete workbook pages and low level work sheets. In post-observation conferences you have suggested that she use more direct instruction, engage the students in question-and-answer sessions as she presents information, and actively monitor and interact with students by walking around when they are doing paper and pencil work. You conduct a fourth classroom observation and find that nothing has changed. You write an intervention plan that directs Ms. Dud to do the following within a six-week time frame:

1. Submit and implement lesson plans that include at least 50 percent interactive instruction.
2. Observe another teacher who is an expert in conducting question-and-answer sessions and schedule an appointment with me to discuss your observation.
3. Attend a district training session on monitoring and giving feedback to students as they engage in learning activities.

Within the designated six-week time frame, Ms. Dud provides you with documentation that she has complied with all three directives. You return to visit her classroom. You observe Ms. Dud seated at her desk for thirty minutes while students complete three workbook pages. Absolutely nothing in her classroom has changed, yet Ms. Dud *did* comply with all your administrative directives and *has* fulfilled the requirements of the intervention plan.

While there was nothing *wrong* with the directives you gave, they were *incomplete*. What you did was to direct the teacher to complete a series of professional growth activities but did not direct that her *teaching behavior* change. Whether your goal is to help Ms. Dud improve her teaching or, failing that, to recommend nonrenewal or termination of her contract, the IP should contain directives for both professional growth and changes in behavior.

In the case of classroom teachers, those could be either teacher or student behaviors, or both. Directives can be written using a cause-and-effect formula. The expected outcome or effect is the evidence which would be used to determine if improvement has occurred or is occurring:

INSTRUCTIONAL INDICATOR		EXPECTED OUTCOME
Teacher behaves in a certain way	**so that**	**students behave in a certain way.**
(Teacher Behavior)	**+ (Linking Words)** ⟶	**(Student Behavior)**

Examples:

Teacher solicits student participation	in such a way that	most students are participating and most are successful.
Teacher redirects inappropriate behavior	so that	the behavior stops.
Adapt all lessons to address individual needs of students	in such a way that	most (all) students master the objective
Implement the campus behavior system	so that	you meet expected standards for classroom behavior
Comply with requirements of all Individual Education Plans (IEP)		(no student behavior)
Interact courteously and respectfully with all students at all times		(no student behavior)

Note that it will not be possible to write all directives to include student behavior. This is particularly true with behaviors related to learning environment. For example, research indicates that students who receive appropriate, specific positive reinforcement are more engaged, more willing to take risks, and more motivated to participate. These student behaviors tend, however, to emerge over a longer period of time. It would not be reasonable to expect <u>immediate</u> changes in student behavior simply because a teacher begins to use positive reinforcement. When these kinds of instructional behaviors are the directed teacher behavior, you probably will not see an immediate student response.

In the case of writing directives for administrators, instructional support employees, and at-will employees, the same basic principles apply. Instead of "student behaviors," the directives will sometimes specify the effect that the changes on employee behavior should have. Sometimes there may not be an outcome/effect.

Employee Behavior	**+ Linking Language —>**	**Expected Outcome**
Communicate with staff	in such a way that	complaints about rude/discourteous communication from staff are reduced and stop by the end of the semester.
Develop and implement a plan for integration of instructional technology	in such a way that	all/almost all classrooms integrate technology into core curriculum at least two times a month.
Plan and deliver training in balanced literacy reading strategies	in such a way that	all K-5 teachers are trained before the beginning of the next school year.
Always conduct the state and local required walk-around system check before leaving the bus lot.		(no outcome/effect)

Why Write in Terms of Teacher/Employee Behavior?
Ms. Dud's problem in her classroom is not that she has failed to submit lesson plans, observe other teachers, or attend workshops. Instead, her teaching behavior generally is at the heart of the problem that you have observed: the passive, non-interactive format and the failure to monitor students. Therefore, when you write administrative directives for her (using a cause-and-effect formula), you need to describe specific changes she must make in her teaching behavior. *These directives now form the standard against which you will conduct future classroom observations.* If Ms. Dud's teaching behavior changes, you have been effective in helping her to improve. If not, your observations and subsequent documentation build your case for a recommendation for contract nonrenewal or termination based on her failure to comply with administrative directives.

In the directives for administrative/support personnel, including the expected outcome is critical. For example, "developing and implementing a plan for integration of instructional technology" is all well and good. The real purpose, however, is to make certain that technology is integrated into on-going classroom instruction; therefore, it is important to include the outcome "all/ almost all classrooms integrate technology into core curriculum at least two times a month."

Benefits of Using Instructional Indicators

In a hearing, you may be asked to prove that the behaviors you required were reasonable, legitimate, and job-related. Ms. Dud may allege that you are substituting "your way of doing things" for her exercise of her own unique teaching style. If you use instructional indicators as the directed teacher behavior, you will be able to defend yourself against any of these accusations for the following reasons:

1. Descriptions of teacher and student behavior like those in the Texas Teacher Evaluation and Support System (T-TESS) were developed by the Texas Education Agency and published as the commissioner of education's recommended teacher appraisal system. In a sense, you are simply directing the teacher to meet the standards of "proficiency" as defined by the State of Texas.

2. Generic criteria such as those in T-TESS assure a strong, research-based body of teaching behaviors.

3. Many states, school districts, and professional associations have conducted validation research on a variety of instructional programs and practices. For example, you may direct a teacher to use a balanced literacy approach, including phonemic awareness and good literature, large groups, small groups, and centers for teaching reading. Likewise, you could direct a teacher to utilize manipulatives to introduce mathematics concepts since their use is included in the Texas Essential Knowledge and Skills (TEKS) and recommended by the National Council of Teachers of Mathematics.

Why Include Student Behavior in the Directives?

Your judgment on the effectiveness of Ms. Dud's teaching practices goes beyond conformity to appraisal criteria. You are interested in the quality and effectiveness of her teaching. "Quality" and "effectiveness" are concepts, however, that are sometimes difficult to assess. From your perspective, they are best measured by a sole criterion: the impact of her teaching on her students. As we noted in Chapter 4, "…you can watch two teachers teach the exact same lesson the exact same way, and one lesson can rate Developing and one can rate Accomplished because what really matters is how the students respond to the learning" *(TEA Evaluation Refinement Year Newsletter*; Texas Education Agency, September, 2015.)

You want to change her classroom behaviors because they are not effective, that is, they are not having the desired impact on student learning and behavior. By including student behavior as part of your administrative directive, you help Ms. Dud to improve as a teacher, or failing that, you help yourself build an effective case for a recommendation for nonrenewing or terminating her contract. The commissioner of education underscored this very point in a 2008 decision upholding the contract nonrenewal of a teacher who complied with all the remediation directives set forth in the intervention plan but was unable to meet an additional directive that she change her teach- ing behavior in the areas of classroom management and instruction so that student academic success would improve (see endnote 9 for a brief discussion).

There are other specific advantages to including student behavior in your administrative directives:

1. Student behavior has for many years been part of the state-adopted teacher appraisal system. Furthermore, the Texas Legislature mandates that appraisal criteria include a teacher's implementation of discipline management procedures and the performance of the teacher's students (TEC § 21.351(a)(1) and (2)). You are not being arbitrary or capricious when you reference student behavior and performance; you are simply directing the teacher to meet a standard of proficiency as defined by the commissioner of education and the Texas Education Agency. If you are using a locally developed teacher evaluation system that includes student behavior as now required, you are directing the teacher to meet the district's expectations.

2. Including student behavior reduces the likelihood of a "dog and pony show" lesson. Ms. Dud may be able to change *her* behavior when you are in the classroom, but it is less likely that she can change her *students'* behavior while you are there.

3. As we have pointed out, directives for administrative and support personnel will probably not include student behaviors. They will, however, include the anticipated outcome of the employee's behavior changes. You do not want the employee to merely create a plan. You want the plan implemented, and you want the plan to have an effect.

> **Student Performance Component**
>
> **With T-TESS**
>
> ▶ *If scores for the 16 dimensions are aggregated to compute a single summative evaluation score: student performance must count at least 20%.*
>
> ▶ *If the scores in the 16 dimensions are not aggregated to compute a single summative evaluation score: the student performance score is simply the 17th score*
>
> **With a Locally Developed System**
>
> ▶ *The performance of the teacher's students must be evaluated. The 20% rule does not apply.*

With classroom teachers, focus on the student behaviors that might tell you whether or not the teacher is effective. For administrative and support personnel, focus on the expected outcome of the change in behavior. We have provided numerous examples of *general* directives for teacher behavior, as well as more *specific* directives and expected outcomes, in Appendix C.

Writing Directives Related to Student Performance

Teacher appraisal under both T-TESS and a district or campus locally developed appraisal system are to include (1) the implementation of pedagogical practices as a form of discipline management that produces student engagement and establishes the learning environment and (2) the performance of a teacher's students in response to the teacher's pedagogical practices (19 TAC §§ 150.1001(f) and 150.1007). Pursuant to a court settlement in May 2017 between teacher associations and the Texas Education Agency, the academic growth measures of a teacher's students under T-TESS are no longer spelled out. Effective on or before October 12, 2017, districts can choose one or more measures they prefer including student value-added data based on STAAR or other assessments. They also can include how students progress as a group.

Under T-TESS, the performance of a teacher's students must count for at least 20 percent of a teacher's score in a single overall summative appraisal score. For teachers in non-tested grades or subjects or for teachers where value-added scores cannot be calculated, districts and campuses have the flexibility of using the other listed above. The 20 percent rule does not apply to a locally developed appraisal system and only applies under the T-TESS system if there is a single overall summative score. Given the controversy over value-added methodology, administrators need to keep abreast of future developments in this area. Already litigation has begun in Texas challenging the validity of using student test scores to justify the nonrenewal and termination of teacher contracts (see endnote 10 for a discussion of a recent judicial decision).

Success of Students During an Observation

The first way of looking at student performance is during a single classroom observation. In this case, the observer notes the objectives or lesson outcomes and gathers evidence of student success or lack of success *during that class period*. The focused observation instruments we have provided in Appendix B provide a means of gathering these kinds of student performance data.

Most of the directives for changes in behavior in this chapter and in Appendix C are linked to student performance as observed in the classroom. For example:

Teacher Behavior	**+**	**Linking Language** —>	**Student Behavior/ Performance**
Monitor student behavior and responses		so that	(most) students are engaged and successful

Success of Students Over Time

A second way of looking at student performance is to look at student performance over time. Some schools require teachers to maintain portfolios of student work products that reflect student learning over an extended period of time. The success (performance) of students is then evaluated by examining the work products in the portfolio. More than half the school districts in Texas use the curriculum product TEKS Resource System (TRS), designed by a consortium of 19 of the regional educational service centers. One of the assessment components of TRS is a set of Performance Indicators. These indicators are typically student-designed products, performances, or demonstrations that answer the question "Have the students learned the content of the curriculum at the cognitive level of the performance standard?" The evaluator would examine these student work products and ask such questions as:

- Do the products reflect student success in learning that has depth and complexity?
- Do the products reflect student success in connecting learning to other disciplines, the world of work, and/or issues in the world beyond the classroom?
- Do the products reflect student success in critical thinking and problem solving?
- Do the products reflect improved student performance over time?

If the answer to these kinds of questions is "no," the evaluator then would write the same kinds of instructional directives contained in this chapter and in Appendix C. The only substantial difference from looking at student success/performance during a single classroom observation is the evidence of student success — in this case the student work products in the portfolio and/or the products, performances, and demonstrations contained in the TEKS Resource System.

Success of Students on a Criterion-Referenced Test

A third way of looking at student performance is evaluating the results of student performance on a criterion-referenced test. The State of Texas Assessment of Academic Readiness (STAAR) is one such criterion-referenced measure of student performance. The commissioner of education some time ago upheld the nonrenewal of a term contract based, in part, on the performance of teacher's students on the TAAS mathematics test (the predecessor of the TAKS and STAAR test) and on a district practice test modeled on the TAAS test specifications.[11] As a finding of fact, the commissioner indicated that "Over a two-year period . . ., there is substantial evidence to support that not only was there a significant lack of student progress under Ms. Wood's tutelage, there was a significant decrease in student progress. There is substantial evidence to support that Ms. Wood's eighth grade students were not progressing satisfactorily as they only had a pass rate of thirty-one percent (31%) in 1992-93 and on the practice test of twenty-six percent (26%)."

In this case it is significant to note that student performance on these tests was one of the reasons cited by the board of trustees in making its nonrenewal decision. In supporting the board's decision, the commissioner found that, "The TAAS test is specifically designed to indicate student progress on a statewide basis and should be considered one of the criteria upon which a teacher's performance is evaluated (emphasis added)." The commissioner has apparently opened the door for using performance data from the state student assessment system as one element of teacher evaluation and/or negative employment decisions.

STAAR results are released in the summer following the end of the academic year. A Texas appellate court has ruled that summer results may not be retroactively used to determine a teacher's prior year appraisal score.[12] The results may be used, however, in creating the Goal Setting and Professional Development (GSPD) and/or as an issue in future contracts. Student performance on STAAR examinations, therefore, could be used as the "student behavior" in writing directives for change. These directives might follow the following three formants:

Teacher Behavior +	**Linking Language** —>	**Student Behavior/Performance**
Use models and manipulatives for teaching mathematical concepts	in such a way that	most students demonstrate progress/improvement on the STAAR mathematics test.
Use the district's balanced literacy program (phonics, authentic text, large group, small group, centers)	in such a way that	most students demonstrate progress/improvement on the STAAR reading test.
Design and deliver instruction on a weekly basis that is aligned with the Texas Essential Knowledge and Skills and the district science curriculum	in such a way that	most students demonstrate progress/improvement on the STAAR science test.

The use of student performance on a criterion-referenced test as a major element of teacher evaluation has not been fully tested. Until it has been, we urge the following cautions.

1. Make student performance on STAAR *one* of the directives in an intervention plan. Include other directives related to the teacher's classroom behavior. Rely on those teaching indicators that are a part of the state-adopted teacher appraisal system or the locally adopted system.

2. Be cautious about setting specific levels of increase of the value added/ measure (e.g., "so that 80% of students demonstrate progress/improvement . . ."). Keep the expected student performance more general, as we have indicated in the examples cited above.

3. Finally, recall that we recommend as part of writing a specific incident memorandum that you include the "basis of authority" for issuing directives for changes in behavior. In this instance, the "basis for authority" cited in a memorandum might be any of the following types:
   - The STAAR reading has an expectation that students identify the best summary of written texts.
   - The district English language arts curriculum includes an expectation that you use a balanced literacy approach in the teaching of reading.
   - The Texas Essential Knowledge and Skills (TEKS) has an expectation that you use models and other manipulatives in teaching algebra.
   - The National Council of Teachers of Mathematics curriculum and assessment standards include the use of mathematics manipulatives in teaching mathematics concepts.

Writing Directives for Nonclassroom-Based Intervention Plans

Classroom instruction will be only one of the reasons for writing an intervention plan. The second of the four steps was *Compliance with Laws/Policies/Procedures* (see p. 7). The areas in which improvement was needed included:

1. Following district/campus policies in reporting student grades to the office and to parents.
2. Writing lesson plans according to the campus format.
3. Being present at your assigned duty station.
4. Following federal law in implementing all of the provisions of the Individualized Education Program (IEP) for all special education students in your classroom.
5. Following district grievance policies for complaints regarding conditions of employment.

You will need to specify the evidence that you will use to determine if growth has occurred or is occurring in each of the areas listed. That evidence could be:

1. Submit all student progress reports and grade reports on the date/ time specified in the district calendar (progress reports: 4:00 p.m. on the third Friday of each grading period; report cards: 4:00 p.m. on the last instructional day of each grading period).

2. Submit written lesson plans to the principal's office in the district format by 8:00 a.m. on the first instructional day of each week.

3. Be present at your assigned duty station 15 minutes before and 15 minutes after school.

4. You must comply with federal law in implementing all of the provisions of the Individualized Education Program (IEP) for all special education students in your classroom.

5. You must follow district grievance policies for complaints regarding your conditions of employment. You will immediately stop all complaining about your conditions of employment to staff, students, and members of the community.

In Chapters 1 and 5, we distinguished between the difference in speaking out about matters of public policy and speaking out about conditions of employment. The last directive ("stop all complaining about your conditions of employment to staff, students, and members of the community") may raise concerns about First Amendment free speech protection. When this is the only issue related to the employee's job performance, you should exercise caution and consult with the school district's human resources director and/or the school district's attorney for guidance. See the discussion about free speech in Chapter 5 for more information.

The third reason for writing an improvement plan was *Other Job-Related Behaviors* (see p. 8).

The areas in which growth was needed were:

1. Administration of diagnostic tests and completion of the educational diagnostician's portion of the written assessment based on state and local guidelines and the specific needs of the students *(for an educational diagnostician)*.

2. Preparation and implementation of long- and short-range plans for district instructional technology *(for a director of technology)*.

3. Meeting deadlines for reports and documents for local board of trustees agenda.

Once again, you will need to specify the evidence that you will use to determine if growth has occurred or is occurring in each of the areas listed. That evidence could be:

1. 1. Complete all assessments and assessment reports and submit them to the Director of Special Education at least *48 hour*s prior to scheduled SST, PARD, and/or ARD meetings.

2. Write a long- and short-range plan for district instructional technology using the district planning format and submit it to the superintendent no later than December 10. The plan will include detailed implementation components.

3. Submit all reports and documents for the agenda of the board of trustees meeting no later than 12:00 noon on the Friday preceding each board of trustees meeting.

The fourth reason for writing an improvement plan was *"Affective Issues."* The areas in which professional growth was needed were:

1. Courteous, professional communication with students, staff, and parents.

2. Meeting and working collaboratively with grade-level team members for instructional planning.

3. Following district grievance policies for complaints regarding conditions of employment.

4. Communicating effectively with staff *(for administrative and support personnel)*.

Consider the following evidence for the areas of concern noted above:

1. Beginning immediately, all of your communication with students, staff, and stakeholders will be courteous, respectful, and professional; complaints about discourteous or rude communication will decrease significantly and cease altogether by the end of the semester.

2. Beginning immediately, you will meet with your grade level team each instructional day during your team planning period. All work and communication will be courteous and respectful. You will abide by the decisions made by the team and implement them in your classroom. Complaints from team members about rude/discourteous behavior from you will decrease significantly and cease altogether by the end of the semester.

3. You will follow district grievance policies for complaints regarding your conditions of employment. You will immediately stop all complaining about your conditions of employment to staff, students, and members of the community.

4. Beginning immediately, you will speak courteously and respectfully with staff members so that complaints about your treating them in a rude/discourteous manner including the use of profanity cease.

As we noted In Chapter 5, these behaviors can significantly affect the quality of job performance. They are, however, the most difficult issues to address in an intervention plan. The greatest challenge is to identify objective evidence that can be used to document whether or not the behaviors have changed and the extent to which professional growth has occurred. Decisions in this area should be made in consultation with the district director of human resources and/or the school district's attorney, particularly because free speech issues oftentimes are likely to arise.

Providing a Reasonable Time Line for Growth and Improvement

Failure to allow the teacher or other employee a fair and reasonable amount of time to correct deficiencies may lead to reinstatement of the dismissed employee.[13] In the absence of a Texas statute spelling out remediation procedures, interpretations of what constitutes "adequate time" vary. As the Texas Commissioner of Education indicated in a 1995 decision, there are no set rules on how much remediation is necessary in a particular case. Rather, each case must be judged individually.[14] In one case involving a teacher of mentally handicapped students, an Illinois court found a period of 45 days between the notice of deficiency and the final evaluation to be unreasonable since the teacher was making some improvement.[15] In another case, the same court found a 64-day remedial period a reasonable length of time for a teacher to improve instruction and classroom management.[16] However, in a contrasting Minnesota case, an eight-week time span was viewed as unreasonable when a supervisor first identified as deficient the classroom practices of a veteran teacher in the seventeenth year of the teacher's career.[17] A Louisiana court concluded in 1995 that there is no injustice in requiring a one-year probationary teacher to remediate performance sometime prior to the completion of the contract.[18]

While there is no magic number for the amount of time allowed for improvement and for complying with directives, here are some factors that administrators should consider in making this determination:

1. Complexity of Change
   - Time lines for simple changes such as developing and submitting a discipline management plan may be short.
   - Complex changes in behavior such as implementing cooperative learning will take longer.
   - Developing a district plan for a new instructional delivery system for bilingual and ESL students will take longer.

2. Previous Evaluations
   - The existence of previous negative evaluations may allow a short time line.
   - The existence of previous positive evaluations may require a longer time line.

3. Type of Contract/Length of Service
   - At-will employees may require short time lines.
   - Probationary contract teachers and administrators may require short time lines.
   - Continuing contract teachers or term contract teachers/administrators with long experience may require longer time lines, especially if their previous evaluations have been positive.

4. Whether or Not Employee's Behavior is Remediable (see the first section of this chapter)
   - If behavior is remediable, a longer time line may be required.
   - If behavior is irremediable, no time line for improvement is required.

5. Local District Politics
   - Whether the person is a long-time employee.
   - Whether the person is a beloved employee.
   - Whether the person has deep roots in the community.

Supervisors also need to remember to update directives for improvement if the teacher or other employee complies with earlier directives but remains deficient in certain areas..

Sample Intervention Plan for Teachers

The following sample intervention plan for Ms. Dud is based on what you already have learned about her. The numbers in parentheses correspond with the observations in the commentary that follows this improvement plan. The template for this memorandum is contained in Appendix D.

INTERVENTION PLAN

Employee: __Susie Dud__   Position: __4th Grade__

Supervisor/Appraiser: __Dr. Great Principal__   School: __Fine I.S.D.__

1. Area/s related to the job description, evaluation instrument and/or campus/district policy in which improvement is needed. Establish priorities if two or more areas are listed. **(1)**

    Dimension 1.4: Activities

    Dimension 2.5: Monitor and Adjust

2. Specify growth activities and dates for completion if warranted. **(2)**

    a. Attend a district training session on February 2-3 on monitoring and giving feedback to students as they are engaged in learning. The district will provide a substitute teacher.

    b. Observe in Mrs. Cathy Coop's class within the next two weeks and focus on her strategies for soliciting student participation and for providing feedback to students. Schedule an appointment with me within a week of your observation to discuss what you saw.

    c. Following the workshop and your conference with me, submit all lesson plans that include a variety or strategies for monitoring and providing feedback to students as they are engaged in learning. Lesson plans will be due in my office by 7:45 a.m. on the first instructional day of each week. **(3)**

3. Specify evidence that will be used to determine whether growth activities specified in Section 2 have been completed.

    a. Provide certificate of completion of district workshop on monitoring and giving feedback to students (due in supervisor's by February 10th).

    b. Hold conference with supervisor to discuss observation in Mrs. Coop's class (no later than February 15th).

    c. All future lesson plans will include a variety of strategies for monitoring and providing feedback to students as they are engaged in learning.

4. Directives and time lines for changes in employee behavior in the future and evidence that will be used to determine if employee behavior has changed.

    a. Dimension 1.4: Activites: Plan and implement all instruction so that students are interacting with each other at least 50 percent of the instructional time starting the first week of February, 2023.

    b. Dimension 2.5: Monitor and Adjust: Monitor students by moving around the classroom and by interacting with them starting the first week of February, 2023 in such a way that:

- **Students who are successful receive positive reinforcement/ acknowledgement of the learning.**
- **Unsuccessful students receive corrective feedback in such a way that they are successful.**

As we agreed, these expectations will be incorporated in future classroom appraisals and in modifications to your Goal-Setting and Professional Development Plan. **(4)**

I was consulted in the development of this plan. I understand that I have a right to file a grievance or appeal within 10 days consistent with school policies if I disagree with its contents.

	December 8, 2023
Employee Signature	Date
	December 8, 2023
Supervisor Signature	Date
Other Appraiser Signature *(if applicable)*	Date

Commentary

(1) Areas for improvement are addressed at the general *domain* level rather than at the dimension level of the rubric which identified more *specific* teacher and student behavior. More specific concerns are addressed in the directives in Sections (3) and (4). The areas of concern are the level of active student participation in the learning process and the teacher's failure to verbally or physically monitor and assess a reasonable number of students.

(2) This is the section of the plan for directing professional growth activities. These directives have nothing to do with directing changes in classroom behavior. They represent the supervisor's good faith effort to assist the teacher to improve.

(3) This section stipulates the evidence and dates for completion of the growth activities. If the plan stopped here, the teacher could simply attend the workshop, observe in Mrs. Coop's classroom, and submit a written lesson plan. Ms. Dud could successfully complete the entire growth plan and never address the real problem of her instructional shortcomings.

(4) These are the directives for changes in classroom behavior and the evidence that will be used to determine if Ms. Dud has complied with the directives. Failure to follow these directives may be the basis for a future recommendation to nonrenew or terminate employment. Notice that the directives use the formula that we have recommended:

Teacher Behavior   **+ Linking Language —>**   **Student Behavior/ Performance**

Note that at the end of the IP we have included language that links the IP back to the Goal-Setting and Professional Development (GSPD) component of T-TESS.

Sample Intervention Plan For Non-Teaching Employees

The following sample illustrates an intervention plan for Fred Fieldhouse, an assistant athletic director who is employed on a one-year term contract as a certificated employee. From your own observations and from interactions with district staff, you have reached the following conclusions: Mr. Fieldhouse is not meeting the expectations of his job description: e.g., he does not meet deadlines for producing UIL and other reports; on at least three occasions he has not been present at contests to make sure that officials are greeted and directed; he sits in the coaches' office when events are taking place and does not actively supervise students at the contest; and he has been absent or left early from events he was responsible for supervising. In addition, you have received frequent complaints from game officials and other coaches about his "rude" and "intimidating" behavior and language. You have had two conferences with him about these issues, but his behaviors and the frequency of complaints have continued.

The following IP for Mr. Fieldhouse is based on what you already have learned about him. The numbers in parentheses correspond with the observations in the commentary that follows the plan. As noted in the case of Susie Dud, the IP template is contained in Appendix D.

INTERVENTION PLAN

School District: <u>Fine ISD</u>   Campus: <u>District-Wide</u>

Employee: <u>Fred Fieldhouse</u>   Assignment/Grade: <u>Assistant Athletic Director</u>

1. Areas related to the job description, evaluation instrument and/or campus/district policy in which improvement is needed. Establish priorities if two or more areas are listed. **(1)**

   - Professional communications and professional relationships
   - Fulfillment of duties of assistant athletic director (as specified in the district job description)

2. Specify growth activities and dates for completion if warranted. **(2)**

   - Read the book, <u>How to be a Successful Athletic Administrator</u>. Provide a written summary of the book (no more than four pages) by September 1, 2023. As part of the summary, identify three to four lessons discussed in the book that are the most significant in your position. Schedule a conference to discuss your summary and findings with your supervisor (no later than September 8, 2023).

   - Prepare a set of questions and interview two athletic directors and two assistant athletic directors in other districts identified by your supervisor. Determine (1) the major job responsibilities for their positions, (2) what skills and/or work habits they believe are the most valuable to their position, (3) what they do to make certain that are working professionally and courteously with others, and (4) significant mistakes that they have learned to avoid. Submit the list of questions to your supervisor prior to conducting the interviews. After conducting the interviews, provide a written summary of your findings to your supervisor no later than September 8, 2023. Schedule a conference to discuss your findings with your supervisor (no later than September 14, 2023).

3. Specify evidence that will be used to determine whether growth activities in Section 2 have been completed. **(3)**

   - The book, <u>How to be a Successful Athletic Administrator</u>: A written summary of the book is submitted to your supervisor by September 1, 2023. A conference to discuss the summary and conclusions is held no later than September 8, 2023.

   - Survey: A list of questions is submitted to the supervisor and approved prior to conducting the interviews. Interviews are conducted and the summary and findings are submitted to the supervisor no later than September 9, 2021. A meeting to discuss your findings with the supervisor is held no later than September 14, 2023.

4. Directives and time lines for changes in employee behavior in the future. **(4)**

   - All schedules, reports, supervision assignments, and all other administrative tasks will be accurately completed by their due dates.

- Perform all of the duties in your job description at all athletic events assigned by your supervisor in such a way that you have (1) introduced and made yourself available to the officials for the games, (2) moved around during the event in order to identify and assist with potential problems, and (3) act to stop or redirect problems in such a way that problems are courteously and effectively resolved.
- Report to each assigned duty on time and remain on duty until all work at each event is completed.
- Maintain positive relationships with your co-workers in such a way that complaints about your behavior are reduced and stop by the end of the semester.
- Communicate (orally and in writing) with internal district staff and external communities in a courteous, non-threatening, and respectful manner in such a way that complaints about your communication are reduced and stop by the end of the semester.
- Personally notify your supervisor no later than 7:00 a.m. in the event that you must be absent or late. Immediately and personally notify your supervisor prior to leaving an event for which you have responsibility.

I was consulted in the development of this plan. I understand that I have a right to file a grievance or appeal within 10 days consistent with school policies if I disagree with its contents.

	August 1, 2023
Employee Signature	Date

	August 1, 2023
Supervisor Signature	Date

Other Appraiser Signature *(if applicable)*	Date

Commentary

(1) Areas for improvement are identified from Mr. Fieldhouse's job description and from a general district expectation for professional communication. These areas for improvement could have come from any one or a combination of job description, evaluation instrument, district policies/handbooks, law, or general expectations for a district employee.

(2) This is the section of the plan for directing growth activities. These directives have nothing to do with directing changes in job behavior. They represent the supervisor's good faith effort to assist Mr. Fieldhouse to improve.

(3) This section stipulates the evidence and dates for completion of the growth

activities. If the plan stopped here, Mr. Fieldhouse could simply read the book, conduct the survey, and produce the reports. He could successfully complete the entire growth plan and never address the real problem — his failure to meet the expectations in his job description and to communicate courteously and respectfully with others.

(4) This section contains a combination of directives and changes in Mr. Fieldhouse's job-related behavior and the evidence that will be used to determine whether his behavior has changed. Failure to follow directives for changes in behavior may be the basis for a future recommendation to nonrenew or terminate his employment. Notice that some of the directives in the intervention plan follow the formula we have recommended:

Employee Behavior   **+ Linking Words**   —>   **Outcome**

ROLE OF THE EMPLOYEE IN DEVELOPING AN INTERVENTION PLAN

As noted earlier in this chapter, while an intervention plan (IP) is outside the components of T-TESS and very likely a district or charter school alternative formal teacher appraisal system as well, it should be linked to the issues and language embedded in the state-recommended Texas Teacher Evaluation and Support (T-TESS) system and its GSPD plan or something similar in the alternative appraisal system. However, teachers do not have veto power over the contents of an intervention plan.

For districts using T-PESS to evaluate principals and, in modified form, other administrators, an intervention plan should be linked to it, given the focus on collaboration in developing annual appraisals. For districts and charter schools using an alternative appraisal system for administrators, the same is true.

While you are in ultimate control of the contents of the intervention plan, basic fairness suggests that you want to include the employee in developing the IP to the extent possible. For example, Ms. Dud comes to your office to develop an intervention plan. You have a blank form of the plan on your desk. You reach some early agreement that the plan will contain behavioral changes in monitoring students and in providing more interactive instruction. When you propose that she attend a no-cost workshop on cooperative learning (on a regular instructional day, with the district providing a substitute for her class), she refuses, saying "I don't believe in cooperative learning and these outlaws I have would never do it. I don't want that in the plan."

You explain that cooperative learning is a part of the general campus improvement plan and that you have an expectation that this approach at least be given a fair try. She still refuses to attend the training. You then tell her, "I'm sorry that you don't agree, but this is an important part of this school's plan for improvement, and I believe that the workshop would teach you how to conduct lessons that would maximize student involvement in the learning process. Even though you don't agree, I'm still going to include this professional development activity in your intervention plan."

While one might argue the wisdom of requiring Ms. Dud to attend the training against her will, there is no question that you as supervisor have every right to require that she do so and to include that requirement in the IP. You are not being arbitrary in requiring this training since it is part of the campus improvement plan and is a major instructional focus in the school district. Furthermore, you are sending her on school district time, the district is providing a substitute teacher, and there is no financial cost to her.

MONITORING INTERVENTION PLAN ACHIEVEMENT

After the intervention plan (IP) is developed, you will need to monitor whether or not the employee complies with its provisions. Your monitoring may result in a series of specific incident memoranda and one or more last chance memoranda. Both are discussed in Chapter 2. Let us take Susie Dud's IP presented earlier in the chapter and see what the process might look like. We will assume that, in the case of the second and third memoranda, you used the focused observation instruments presented in Chapter 4 to guide your documentation of classroom activities.

Writing Specific Incident Memoranda

Specific Incident Memorandum #1

Fine Independent School District
101 Wonderful Way
Fine, Texas 70000

```
TO:        Susie Dud
FROM:      Dr. Great Principal
DATE:      February 22, 2023
SUBJECT:   Intervention Plan Compliance
```

As of this date I have not received your certificate of completion for the workshop on monitoring and giving feedback to students as they engage in learning activities (due February 7th) and you have not met the deadlines for observing in Mrs. Coop's class and for scheduling a follow-up conference with me (deadline of February 15th). In addition, you have not turned in your lesson plans showing 50 percent student-to-student interaction in your classroom. All three were requirements of your intervention plan that we completed on December 8, 2023. This memorandum is to inform you that you have not complied with these directives.

> I have received a copy of this memorandum. I understand that my signature does not necessarily indicate that I agree with its contents. I further understand that I have a right to respond within 10 working days.

/s/ Susie Dud   Date

Specific Incident Memorandum #2

Fine Independent School District
101 Wonderful Way
Fine, Texas 70000

TO: Susie Dud
FROM: Dr. Great Principal
DATE: February 28, 2023
SUBJECT: Intervention Plan Compliance

I observed in your classroom from 9:20-10:00 on February 24, 2023. You lectured from the front of the classroom for the entire time. Three of 22 students participated in ways other than passive listening and taking notes. You have not complied with the provisions in your intervention plan that directed you to "plan and implement all instruction so that it is focused on at least 50 percent student-to-student interaction." This memorandum is to inform you that you have not complied with these directives.

> I have received a copy of this memorandum. I understand that my signature does not necessarily indicate that I agree with its contents. I further understand that I have a right to respond within 10 working days.

_____

/s/ Susie Dud   Date

Specific Incident Memorandum #3

Fine Independent School District
101 Wonderful Way
Fine, Texas 70000

TO: Susie Dud
FROM: Dr. Great Principal
DATE: March 9, 2023
SUBJECT: Intervention Plan Compliance

I observed in your classroom from 1:30-2:10 on March 6, 2023. In your lesson, you introduced students to the skill of dividing common fractions. During the first 15 minutes of the observation, you told students the rules and process and then worked four problems at the board. You then assigned students to work 15 division problems. For the remaining 25 minutes you sat behind your desk and graded papers while students did written work at their desks.

During that time, I walked around the room. Seven students spent the entire time sitting and staring at the work. When I asked all seven why they were not working the problems, they told me that they did not understand how to do the assignment. I examined the work of 12 students, all of whom had worked the problems incorrectly.

> Your intervention plan (IP) directed you to (1) "plan and implement all instruction so that students are interacting with each other at least 50 percent of the instructional time starting the first week of February" and (2) "monitor students by moving around the classroom and by interacting with them starting the first week of February, 2023."
>
> This memorandum is to inform you that you have not complied with these intervention plan directives.
>
> > I have received a copy of this memorandum. I understand that my signature does not necessarily indicate that I agree with its contents. I further understand that I have a right to respond within 10 working days.
>
> _____
>
> /s/ Susie Dud   Date

Note the common elements in all three memoranda:

- Written on school letterhead stationery.
- Written within a few days of noncompliance.
- Short and specific.
- Information presented in an objective manner: what happened and what did not happen (findings of fact).
- Teacher is informed that requirements of the intervention plan have not been met (conclusions/judgments).
- Teacher signature to acknowledge receipt of memorandum.

NOTE: In Memorandum #3, the appraiser focused both on student active participation and on student success in learning that day's objective. In order to make a determination about student success, the appraiser walked around the room, examined student work, and interacted with students. You may need to do the same to determine if students are on task and are learning. Use common sense and good professional judgment as to when to move around. If the teacher needs all student attention focused on him or her, you should remain seated and unobtrusive. Sit so that you can see the students. At the side of the room near the front is a good position. It is best to move around the room when the teacher is not involved in delivering direct instruction.

Writing a Last Chance Memorandum

Following these three memoranda, you held a conference with Ms. Dud. It is reasonably apparent that she either cannot or will not do the things that she was directed to do. This is an appropriate time to write a last chance memorandum. The numbers in parentheses correspond with the comments that follow the memorandum.

Fine Independent School District
101 Wonderful Way
Fine, Texas 70000

TO: Susie Dud
FROM: Dr. Great Principal
DATE: March 22, 2023
SUBJECT: Follow-Up to Our Conference of March 20, 2023

This memorandum is a follow-up to our March 20, 2023 meeting during which I expressed my concerns regarding your failure to comply with the directives contained in your intervention plan. **(1)**

As you will recall, we first discussed my memorandum of February 28th informing you of your failure to document attendance at the district workshop on student monitoring and feedback, to turn in your lesson plans, and to observe interactive instructional strategies in Mrs. Cathy Coop's classroom. I told you that your explanation that "I simply was too busy and did not have time" is not acceptable. **(2)**

I explained to you that my observations in your classroom on February 24th and March 6th revealed the same pattern of instruction that led to our creating the intervention plan (IP). I expressed my continuing concern that students still were not actively and successfully interacting with each other in the learning process and that you were not monitoring student learning and providing them with feedback. I told you that your stated reasons for not complying — "My students are not sufficiently motivated" and "Six-weeks grades were due that week" — are not acceptable. I reminded you that student-to-student interaction, together with teacher monitoring and feedback, are expectations in all Fine I.S.D. classrooms. I further reminded you that both issues were addressed as specific directives in your IP. **(3)**

Failure to follow the directives in your IP constitutes failure to follow administrative directives and will result in my recommendation that your contract not be renewed. If I do not see immediate efforts to comply with the terms of your IP and consequent change in student behavior, I will have no alternative but to take this action **(4)**

If you disagree with the content of this memorandum, please respond to me in writing within 10 working days. I will be pleased to talk with you further about this matter if you wish. **(5)**

Copy: Personnel File

Dr. Ima Humane, Director of Personnel

I have received a copy of this memorandum. I understand that my signature does not necessarily indicate that I agree with its contents. I further understand that I have a right to respond within 10 working days. **(6)**

_____

/s/ Susie Dud   Date

Commentary

(1) Notice how promptly Dr. Principal acted on these incidents. Following each incident (February 24th, February 28th, and March 6th), he wrote a specific incident memorandum. Immediately following the third incident, he held a conference with Ms. Dud. It is clear that he considers this a serious matter.

(2) He first deals with the failures (1) to document attendance at the staff development session, (2) to observe in Mrs. Coop's classroom, and (3) to submit the lesson plan. He also includes Ms. Dud's explanation of these failures.

(3) He spends considerable time spelling out exactly what was observed in the two classroom observations. He presents this information in an objective and non-judgmental manner. He then explains that the behaviors observed did not meet the expectations for the school district and did not comply with the directives of the intervention plan.

(4) He unambiguously informs Ms. Dud (1) that she has not followed the directives in the intervention plan, (2) that failure to do so constitutes a failure to follow an administrative directive, and (3) that failure to follow administrative directives will lead to a recommendation of contract nonrenewal.

(5) He reminds Ms. Dud that she may respond in writing if she disagrees with the content of the memorandum. It is important that Dr. Principal set a reasonable deadline to respond, rather than leave the response date open-ended.

(6) Ms. Dud does not have to agree with the content of the memorandum; she just has to acknowledge that she received it.

SUMMARY

In writing intervention plans and their directives for improvement, remember the following:

1. Give written notice that improvement or change is needed.

2. Provide specific written directives for improvement. For teachers, make certain that these directives include teacher behavior linked with student behavior when appropriate.

3. Provide assistance and support to demonstrate a good-faith effort to help the employee improve.

4. Establish reasonable time lines for growth and improvement to occur. Consider the complexity of the changes directed, previous evaluations, years of experience, seriousness of the problem, and type of employment contract in determining a standard for what is reasonable.

5. Link the IP to T-TESS and its GSPD plan or the school's alternative appraisal system.

6. Periodically monitor the employee's progress toward complying with the terms of the intervention plan. In the case of teachers, use the focused observation instruments discussed in Chapter 4 during classroom observations. Follow-up with written memoranda indicating areas of deficiency. If improvement does not occur, send the employee a last chance memorandum delineating the continuing problems and stating that a recommendation of contract nonrenewal or termination is likely if improvement is not forthcoming.

REFERENCES

1. See, for example, *Roberts v. San Benito C.I.S.D.*, Dkt. No. 102-R1-598 (Comm'r Educ. 1998); *Foley v. Houston I.S.D.*, Dkt. No. 034-R2-1097 (Comm'r Educ. 1997); *Hernandez v. Asherton I.S.D.*, Dkt. No. 028(2)-R2-1079 (Comm'r Educ. 1983); *Lopez v. Edinburg C.I.S.D.*, Dkt. No. 122-R2-481 (Comm'r Educ. 1982); *Phillips v. Houston I.S.D.*, Dkt. No. 026-R2-1081 (Comm'r Educ. 1983); *McConnell v. Alamo Heights I.S.D.*, 576 S.W.2d 470 (Tex. App. — San Antonio 1978, writ ref'd n.r.e.).
2. *Brandhorst v. Northside I.S.D.*, Dkt. No. 034-R3-1088 (Comm'r Educ. 1990).
3. *Fetchin v. Lewisville I.S.D.*, Dkt. No. 384-R2-691 (Comm'r Educ. 1993). See also *McGrath v. Webb C.I.S.D.*, Dkt. No. 171-R 2-294 (Comm'r Educ. 1997).
4. *Johnson v. Houston I.S.D.*, Dkt. No. 074-R2-402 (Comm'r Educ. 2002).
5. *Strickland v. Dallas* I.S.D., Dkt. No. 075-R1-0808 (Comm'r Educ. 2008).
6. *Toussaint v. Dallas I.S.D.*, Dkt.No.071 R2-0708 (Comm'r Educ. 2008).
7. *Wooten v. Dallas I.S.D.*, Dkt. No. 018-R2-997 (Comm'r Educ. 1998).
8. In *Ysleta I.S.D. v. Porter*, 2015 WL 1735542 (Tex. App. – Corpus Christi-Edinburg 2015) (not reported), the appellate court faced questions about what could be included in a teacher's lesson plan. Education Code Section 11.164(a)(6) states that a teacher can be required to prepare "a unit or weekly lesson plan that outlines, in a brief and general manner, the information to be presented during each period at the secondary level or in each subject or topic at the elementary level." The appellate court agreed with the trial court that the lesson plan cannot include assessments and cognitive levels embedded in Bloom's Taxonomy because neither is taught in the classroom. The same is true for including differentiated activities and modifications for special student populations. While this decision was not reported, it does provide insight into this area of law.
9. *Lyman v. Blooming Grove I.S.D.*, Dkt. No. 046-R1-0508 (Comm'r Educ. 2008). In his findings of fact, the commissioner stated that the teacher complied with her intervention plan directives to attend a workshop, observe one teacher per week for the first 12 weeks of school and complete an observation form on each, and meet with her principal bi-weekly for critique and discussion about the improvement plan. But he went on to note that her intervention plan also contained directives for changes in teacher behavior, including improving classroom management and altering instructional strategies so that students would be on task and their academic success would increase. These directives were not complied with. The evidence established that after the intervention plan was in place, students continued to wander freely about the classroom and were off-task. Students shoved each other and threw paper clips, coins, and paper wads at each other. Throughout the year, less than 70 percent of the teacher's students were on task during instructional time. Students had "zero response" to teacher's re-direction attempts, and the students demonstrated that it was routine to ignore the teacher. In addition, the teacher was observed at least twice a week throughout the school year yelling at students in an effort to maintain discipline. The teacher excessively referred students to lunch detention. Based on the inability of the teacher to change her classroom behavior in such a way that students were on task and improving academically, the commissioner upheld the teacher's contract nonrenewal.
10. *Houston Federation of Teachers v. Houston I.S.D.*, 251 F.Supp.3d 1168 (S.D. Tex. 2017). The Houston Houston Federation of Teachers challenged the district's use of a value-added student performance appraisal system to justify ending teacher employment contracts. Called the Educational Value-Added Assessment System (EVAAS), the system was developed by a private software company to track teacher impact on student test scores over time. A teacher's EVAAS score is based on comparing the average test score growth of students taught by the teacher compared to the statewide average for students in that grade or course. In denying the district's effort to dismiss the case, the U.S magistrate judge noted that because a teacher's employment could be ended based on low value-added scores and both the district and the teacher were denied access to the computer algorithms and data to verify the accuracy of scores, EVAAS violated a teacher's right to procedural due process. Access was denied because the third party vendor treated the algorithms and related software as trade secrets. The magistrate also noted that shortly after adopting the EVAAS model for determining teacher effectiveness, the district amended its contract nonrenewal policy to include insufficient student academic growth as reflected by value-added data and planned on exiting 85

percent of teachers with ineffective EVAAS ratings. The magistrate concluded that "teachers have no meaningful way to ensure correct calculation of their EVAAS scores, and as a result are unfairly subject to mistaken deprivation of constitutionally protected property interest in their jobs." The case was allowed to proceed.

11. *Wood v. Post I.S.D.,* Dkt. No. 335-R1-794 (Comm'r Educ. 1996).
12. *Davis v. Morath,* 590 S.W.3d 80 (Tex. App. – Austin 2019). The appellate court held that Dallas I.S.D. had not followed the requirement of TEC Section 21.352(c) that all appraisal data must be included in an annual appraisal when it delayed informing teachers employed during the 2014-2015 school year of student performance data for that year until September of the following year.
13. *Trimboli v. Board of Education of Wayne Cnty.,* 280 S.E.2d 686 (W. Va. 1981).
14. *Baker v. Rice C.I.S.D.,* Dkt. No. 227-R2-493 (Comm'r Educ. 1995).
15. *Board of Education of School District No. 131 v. Illinois State Board of Education,* 403 N.E.2d 277 (Ill. App. 2d 1980).
16. *Community School District No. 60 v. Maclin,* 435 N.E.2d 845 (Ill. App. 2d 1982).
17. *Ganyo v. Independent School District No. 832,* 311 N.W.2d 497 (Minn. 1981).
18. *McKenzie v. Webster Parish School Board,* 653 S.2d 215 (La. App. 2 Cir., 1995).

APPENDIX A

Code of Ethics and Standard Practices for Texas Educators[1]

STATEMENT OF PURPOSE

The Texas educator shall comply with standard practices and ethical conduct toward students, professional colleagues, school officials, parents, and members of the community and shall safeguard academic freedom. The Texas educator, in maintaining the dignity of the profession, shall respect and obey the law, demonstrate personal integrity, and exemplify honesty and good moral character. The Texas educator, in exemplifying ethical relations with colleagues, shall extend just and equitable treatment to all members of the profession. The Texas educator, in accepting a position of public trust, shall measure success by the progress of each student toward realization of his or her potential as an effective citizen. The Texas educator, in fulfilling responsibilities in the community, shall cooperate with parents and others to improve the public schools of the community. This chapter shall apply to educators and candidates for certification.

The State Board for Educator Certification (SBEC) is solely responsible for enforcing the Educators' Code of Ethics for purposes related to certification disciplinary proceedings.

ENFORCEABLE STANDARDS.

I. **Professional Ethical Conduct, Practices and Performance.**

Standard 1.1. The educator shall not intentionally, knowingly, or recklessly engage in deceptive practices regarding official policies of the school district, educational institution, educator preparation program, the Texas Education Agency, or the State Board for Educator Certification (SBEC) and its certification process.

Standard 1.2. The educator shall not knowingly misappropriate, divert, or use monies, personnel, property, or equipment committed to his or her charge for personal gain or advantage.

Standard 1.3. The educator shall not submit fraudulent requests for reimbursement, expenses, or pay.

Standard 1.4. The educator shall not use institutional or professional privileges for personal or partisan advantage.

---

1. Texas Education Code § 21.041(b)(8) requires the State Board for Educator Certification (SBEC) to set forth an educators' code of ethics. The Code of Ethics and Standard Practices is used by SBEC for educator certification and discipline (19 TAC §§ 247.1 – 247.2). Most school districts incorporate the Code through one or more policies relating to employee standards of conduct (e.g., Policy DH-Legal, Policy DH-Local, and Policy DH-Exhibit), thus making them part of the district's conditions of employment. Here we include a key paragraph from the "Purpose and Definitions" of the Code and then its entire "Enforceable Standards" as of the start of 2021.

Standard 1.5. The educator shall neither accept nor offer gratuities, gifts, or favors that impair professional judgment or to obtain special advantage. This standard shall not restrict the acceptance of gifts or tokens offered and accepted openly from students, parents of students, or other persons or organizations in recognition or appreciation of service.

Standard 1.6. The educator shall not falsify records, or direct or coerce others to do so.

Standard 1.7. The educator shall comply with state regulations, written local school board policies, and other state and federal laws.

Standard 1.8. The educator shall apply for, accept, offer, or assign a position or a responsibility on the basis of professional qualifications.

Standard 1.9. The educator shall not make threats of violence against school district employees, school board members, students, or parents of students.

Standard 1.10. The educator shall be of good moral character and be worthy to instruct or supervise the youth of this state.

Standard 1.11. The educator shall not intentionally, knowingly, or recklessly misrepresent his or her employment history, criminal history, and/or disciplinary record when applying for subsequent employment.

Standard 1.12. The educator shall refrain from the illegal use, abuse, or distribution of controlled substances and/or abuse of prescription drugs and toxic inhalants.

Standard 1.13. The educator shall not be under the influence of alcohol or consume alcoholic beverages on school property or during school activities when students are present.

II. Ethical Conduct Toward Professional Colleagues.

Standard 2.1. The educator shall not reveal confidential health or personnel information concerning colleagues unless disclosure serves lawful professional purposes or is required by law.

Standard 2.2. The educator shall not harm others by knowingly making false statements about a colleague or the school system.

Standard 2.3. The educator shall adhere to written local school board policies and state and federal laws regarding the hiring, evaluation, and dismissal of personnel.

Standard 2.4. The educator shall not interfere with a colleague's exercise of political, professional, or citizenship rights and responsibilities.

Standard 2.5. The educator shall not discriminate against or coerce a colleague on the basis of race, color, religion, national origin, age, gender, disability, family status, or sexual orientation.

Standard 2.6. The educator shall not use coercive means or promise of special treatment in order to influence professional decisions or colleagues.

Standard 2.7. The educator shall not retaliate against any individual who has filed a complaint with the SBEC or who provides information for a disciplinary investigation or proceeding under this chapter.

Standard 2.8. The educator shall not intentionally or knowingly subject a colleague to sexual harassment.

III. Ethical Conduct Toward Students.

Standard 3.1. The educator shall not reveal confidential information concerning students unless disclosure serves lawful professional purposes or is required by law.

Standard 3.2. The educator shall not intentionally, knowingly, or recklessly treat a student or minor in a manner that adversely affects or endangers the learning, physical health, mental health, or safety of the student or minor.

Standard 3.3. The educator shall not intentionally, knowingly, or recklessly misrepresent facts regarding a student.

Standard 3.4. The educator shall not exclude a student from participation in a program, deny benefits to a student, or grant an advantage to a student on the basis of race, color, gender, disability, national origin, religion, family status, or sexual orientation.

Standard 3.5. The educator shall not intentionally, knowingly, or recklessly engage in physical mistreatment, neglect, or abuse of a student or minor.

Standard 3.6. The educator shall not solicit or engage in sexual conduct or a romantic relationship with a student or minor.

Standard 3.7. The educator shall not furnish alcohol or illegal/unauthorized drugs to any person under 21 years of age unless the educator is a parent or guardian of that child or knowingly allow any person under 21 years of age unless the educator is a parent or guardian of that child to consume alcohol or illegal/unauthorized drugs in the presence of the educator.

Standard 3.8. The educator shall maintain appropriate professional educator-student relationships and boundaries based on a reasonably prudent educator standard.

Standard 3.9. The educator shall refrain from inappropriate communication with a student or minor, including, but not limited to, electronic communication such as cell phone, text messaging, email, instant messaging, blogging, or other social network communication. Factors that may be considered in assessing whether the communication is inappropriate include, but are not limited to:

(i) The nature, purpose, timing, and amount of the communication;

(ii) The subject matter of the communication;

(iii) Whether the communication was made openly or the educator attempted to conceal the communication;

(iv) Whether the communication could be reasonably interpreted as soliciting sexual contact or a romantic relationship;

(v) Whether the communication was sexually explicit; and

(vi) Whether the communication involved discussion(s) of the physical or sexual attractiveness or the sexual history, activities, preferences, or fantasies of either the educator or the student.

APPENDIX B

    Appendix B includes blank versions of the three focused observation instruments discussed and completed in Chapter 4. The copyright protection for this handbook has been modified to the extent that purchasers of the book may reproduce the forms in this section for their own use or use the digital link to download them at www.ed311.com/docbookforms6th/. We advise that you contact the school district's human resources director and/or school attorney before doing so to make sure that the forms are consistent with local policy and practice. Neither the authors nor the publisher assumes any responsibility for liability associated with their usage.

FOCUSED OBSERVATION INSTRUMENT #1: Planning /Internalization and Instruction

- ✔ Student Participation & Success
- ✔ Feedback to / Interacftion with Students
- ✔ Depth/Complexity/Creativity of Learning
- ✔ Alignment: Objective, Activities, Materials

Name of Teacher:

Subject/Grade Level:

Specific Content/Activity:

Date of Observation:

Time of Observation: Begin: _____

End: _____

Number of Students in Class: _____

For whole-group, teacher-centered instruction, record the names (descriptions, seat assignment) of students who participated in ways other than passive listening. Record the question/prompt from the teacher. Circle the + beside the name(s) of students whose participation was successful. Circle the – beside the name(s) of students whose participation was not successful. Circle a ? if you cannot determine student success. Record the teacher's response to the student's response/performance/demonstration.

STUDENT	QUESTION	SUCCESSFUL/ UNSUCCESSFUL	TEACHER RESPONSE TO STUDENT
1.		+ – ?	
2.		+ – ?	
3.		+ – ?	
4.		+ – ?	
5.		+ – ?	
6.		+ – ?	
7.		+ – ?	
8.		+ – ?	
9.		+ – ?	
10.		+ – ?	
11.		+ – ?	
12.		+ – ?	
13.		+ – ?	

Evidence of Activities Planned and Implemented to Promote Participation, Success, Complex/Creative Learning, and/or Connectivity

Check any techniques that the teacher used to promote active, successful student participation, complex learning, and/or connectivity of learning. Checking the technique does not necessarily mean that the technique was used effectively — it simply means that the technique was used. Make any specific notes that will help you remember what the teacher did/failed to do.

_____ Used strategies that provided for students to make connections of new learning (e.g., prior/future learning within the discipline, own interests/experiences, other disciplines, world beyond the classroom)

_____ Provided opportunities for students to interact with each other

_____ Provided opportunities for students to volunteer, offer feedback, make independent choices

_____ Asked questions/assigned tasks at the application level or higher (Bloom's Taxonomy)

_____ Instructional activities provided for students to produce products that represent complex learning

_____ Designed inductive learning for students to explore/research

_____ Used pair/share, elbow partners, quick-write, etc.

_____ Used group discussion

_____ Used random calling

_____ Sent students to board/chart/map

_____ Varied activities

_____ Provided activities/materials that made lesson relevant/interesting to students

_____ Provided application/lab activity

_____ Instructional activities allowed/encouraged students to interact with each other around the learning

_____ Positively reinforced student participation and/or success

_____ Recognized when students become confused or disengaged and responds to student learning or social/emotional needs

_____ Addresses student mistakes and follows through to ensure student mastery

_____ Other technique/strategy

_____ Other technique/strategy

_____ Other technique/strategy

Evidence of Student Engagement/No Engagement

Summary of Data and Preliminary Judgments on Planning /Internalization and Instruction

In the space below, summarize the data from the previous two pages and make judgments about the quality of instructional strategies.

Active, Successful Student Participation

▶ How many students participated? _____ of _____ participated.

(total # of students)

▶ How many students did not participate? _____

▶ How many students were successful? _____

▶ How many students were unsuccessful? _____

▶ What was the learning/curriculum objective? _____

_____

▶ What instructional activities, strategies, and materials/resources were used in teaching this lesson?

_____

Based on the data, circle YES if the statement describes what you say/heard. Circle NO if the statement does not describe what you saw/heard. If you have no data or insufficient data, do not circle anything. In making judgments, rely on the preponderance of the data/evidence.

All descriptions, unless otherwise noted, are based on the Proficient language of the Texas Teacher Evaluation and Support System (T-TESS). For corresponding language from the Professional Development and Appraisal System, see the correlation chart at the end of this chapter.

PLANNING & INSTRUCTION: Student Participation & Success	PLANNING AND INSTRUCTION: Depth and Complexity of Learning
• Most students demonstrate mastery of the objective **YES NO**	• Insured high levels of learning, social emotional development and achievement for all students **YES NO**
• Engaged all students in relevant, meaningful learning **YES NO**	• Lesson was flexible and encouraged higher-order thinking, persistence, and achievement **YES NO**
• Addressed student mistakes and followed through to ensure student mastery **YES NO**	• Asked questions that encouraged all students to engage in complex, higher-order thinking **YES NO**
• Led a mutually respectful and collaborative class of actively engaged learners **YES NO**	
• Recognized when students become confused or disengaged and responds to student learning or social/emotional needs **YES NO**	**PLANNING AND INSTRUCTION: Alignment**
• Established classroom practices that provided opportunities for most students to communicate effectively with the teacher and their peers **YES NO**	• All goals were aligned to state content standards. **YES NO**
• Used probes to clarify, elaborate thinking. **YES NO**	• Activities, resources, technology and instructional materials that are all aligned to instructional purposes (objectives) **YES NO**
• Asked remember, understand and apply level questions that focus on the objective of the lesson and provoke discussion **YES NO**	• All activities were sequenced and relevant to students **YES NO**
• Students worked respectfully individually and in groups **YES NO**	• The lesson integrated learning objectives with other disciplines **YES NO**
• Anticipates possible student misunderstandings. **YES NO**	• Lesson accurately reflected how the lesson fits within the structure of the discipline and state standards. **YES NO**
• Interacted with students in respectful ways at all times (Teacher Standard 4: Learning Environment) **YES NO**	• Provided opportunities for students to use different types of thinking (e. g., analytical, practical, creative and research-based) **YES NO**

FOCUSED OBSERVATION INSTRUMENT #2: Planning /Internalization and Instruction

- ✔ Student Mastery
- ✔ Monitoring
- ✔ Feedback to Students
- ✔ Instructional Adjustment
- ✔ Differentiation
- ✔ Re-teaching

Name of Teacher:　　　　　　　　　　　**Date of Observation:**

Subject/Grade Level:　　　　　　　　　**Time of Observation: Begin:** _____

Specific Content/Activity:　　　　　　　　　　　　　　　　　　**End:** _____

　　　　　　　　　　　　　　　　　　　Number of Students in Class: _____

For whole-group, teacher-centered instruction, record the names (descriptions, seat assignment) of students who participated in ways other than passive listening. Record the question/prompt from the teacher. Circle the + beside the name(s) of students whose participation was successful. Circle the – beside the name(s) of students whose participation was not successful. Circle a ? if you cannot determine student success. Record the teacher's response to the student's response/performance/demonstration.

STUDENT	QUESTION	SUCCESSFUL/ UNSUCCESSFUL	TEACHER RESPONSE TO STUDENT
1.		+ – ?	
2.		+ – ?	
3.		+ – ?	
4.		+ – ?	
5.		+ – ?	
6.		+ – ?	
7.		+ – ?	
8.		+ – ?	
9.		+ – ?	
10.		+ – ?	
11.		+ – ?	
12.		+ – ?	
13.		+ – ?	

Instructional Strategies Used to Monitor, Provide Feedback, and Differentiate/Reteach

Check any techniques that the teacher used. Checking the technique does not necessarily mean that the technique was used effectively — it simply means that the technique was used. Make any specific notes that will help you remember what the teacher did/ failed to do.

Monitoring

_____ Verbally monitoring/assessing *individual students* (random questioning, interacting during group/seat work)

_____ Physically monitoring *individual* students (walking around, examining work)

_____ Verbally monitoring/assessing *groups* of students (choral response, signal response)

_____ Physically monitoring *groups* of students

_____ Use dof formative assessments (paper/pencil, performances, demonstrations)

Feedback

_____ Used positive reinforcement of successful responses/ performances (verbal and/or non-verbal)

_____ Used specific corrective feedback to students who are unsuccessful

_____ Prompted/assisted students who are having difficulty responding

_____ Probed to clarify, elaborate thinking

_____ Clarified/extended learning in response to monitoring/ assessment

Differentiation/Corrective Teaching/Re-teaching

_____ Adjusted instruction and activities to maintain student engagement.

_____ Adjusted instruction/clarifies in response to monitoring/assessing

_____ Recognized when students become confused or disengaged and responded to student learning or social/emotional needs

_____ Provided differentiated instructional methods and content to ensure students have the opportunity to master what is being taught

_____ Adapted lessons to address individual needs of all, especially when they are not being successful

_____ Utilized instructional adjustments to address strengths and gaps in background knowledge, life experiences and skills of all students

_____ Invited input from students in order to monitor and adjust instruction

_____ Re-taught the lesson (some or all students)

Notes on Teacher/Student Behavior (impact on students)

_____ Other technique/strategy

_____ Other technique/strategy

_____ Other technique/strategy

Summary of Data and Judgments on Monitoring and Assessing

In the space below, summarize the data from the previous two pages and make judgments about the quality of instructional strategies.

▶ How many students participated? _____ of _____ participated. *(total # of students)*

▶ How many students did not participate? _____

▶ How many students were successful? _____

▶ How many students were unsuccessful? _____

▶ What was the learning/curriculum objective?

▶ What instructional activities, strategies, and materials/resources were used in teaching this lesson?

Based on the data, circle YES if the statement describes what you say/heard. Circle NO if the statement does not describe what you saw/heard. If you have no data or insufficient data, do not circle anything. In making judgments, rely on the preponderance of the data/evidence.

All descriptions, unless otherwise noted, are based on the Proficient language of the Texas Teacher Evaluation and Support System (T-TESS). For corresponding language from the Professional Development and Appraisal System, see the correlation chart at the end of this chapter.

PLANNING & INSTRUCTION: Monitoring/Feedback

- Used formal and informal assessments to monitor progress of all students **YES NO**
- Provided substantive, specific and timely feedback to students, families and other school personnel while maintaining confidentially. **YES NO**
- Used probes to clarify, elaborate thinking **YES NO**
- Monitored student behavior and responses for engagement and understanding **YES NO**

PLANNING AND INSTRUCTION: Achieving Expectations

- Addressed student mistakes and followed through to ensure mastery **YES NO**
- Recognized students misunderstanding and responded with an array of techniques to clarify concepts **YES NO**
- Used positive reinforcement of successful responses/performances (verbal and/or nonverbal **YES NO**
- Recognized when students became confused or disengaged and responded to student learning or social/emotional needs **YES NO**
- Interacted with students in respectful ways at all times (Teacher Standard 4: Learning Environment) **YES NO**

PLANNING AND INSTRUCTION: Differentiation & Communication

- Adjusted instruction to address strengths and gaps in background knowledge, life experiences and skills of all students **YES NO**
- Adjusted instruction and activities to maintain student engagement **YES NO**
- Implemented activities, resources, technology and instructional materials that were aligned to instructional purposes/objective **YES NO**O
- Persisted with the lesson until there was evidence that most students demonstrate mastery of the objective **YES NO**
- Provided opportunities for students to use different types of thinking (e.g., analytical, practical, creative and research-based) **YES NO**
- Provided differentiated instructional methods and content to ensure students had the opportunity to master what was being taught **YES NO**
- Recognized when students became confused or disengaged and responded to student learning or social/ emotional needs YES NO **YES NO**

Other Judgments

Evidence of Effective Practices for Classroom Environment, Routines and Procedures, Culture

Check any techniques that the teacher used to promote Effective Practices for Classroom Environment, Routines and Procedures, Culture. Checking the technique does not necessarily mean that the technique was used effectively — it simply means that the technique was used. Make any specific notes that will help you remember what the teacher did/failed to do.

_____ Implemented clear and efficient routines, procedures and transitions

_____ Created safe and accessible classroom

_____ Implemented campus/classroom behavior system

_____ Most students meet expected classroom behavior standards

_____ Successfully and respectfully intervenes to stop/ redirect off-task/inappropriate behavior

_____ Used best practices instructional strategies so that most students engaged in relevant, meaningful learning

_____ Students are worked respectfully in groups/individually

_____ Procedures were in place for students to manage supplies and equipment with very limited direction from teacher

_____ Materials are organized and managed in ways that consume very little instructional time

_____ All instructional time is used for learning

_____ Other techniques (specify _____)

_____ Other techniques (specify _____)

_____ Other techniques (specify _____)

FOCUSED OBSERVATION INSTRUMENT #3:
Classroom Environment, Routines and Procedures, Culture

- ✔ Environment
- ✔ Routines and Procedures
- ✔ Classroom Culture
- ✔ Managing Student Behavior
- ✔ Student Self-Directed Management
- ✔ Engagement of All Students In Relevant, Meaningful Learning

Name of Teacher:

Subject/Grade Level:

Specific Content/Activity:

Date of Observation:

Time of Observation: Begin: _____

End: _____

Number of Students in Class: _____

TIME	DESCRIPTION OF TEACHER/STUDENT BEHAVIOR	TEACHER RESPONSE/BEHAVIOR

Summary of Data and Judgments About
Classroom Environment, Routines and Procedures

Summary of Student Behavior

▶ _____ students were off-task/disengaged from the lesson
(*number*)
Describe:_____

▶ _____ students behaved inappropriately/disruptively
(*number*)
Describe:_____

▶ What was the learning/curriculum objective?

▶ What instructional materials, resources, and procedures were used in teaching this lesson? How were they managed?

Based on the data, circle YES if the statement describes what you say/heard. Circle NO if the statement does not describe what you saw/heard. If you have no data or insufficient data, do not circle anything. In making judgments, rely on the preponderance of the data/evidence.

All descriptions, unless otherwise noted, are based on the Proficient language of the Texas Teacher Evaluation and Support System (T-TESS). For corresponding language from the Professional Development and Appraisal System, see the correlation chart at the end of this chapter.

Classroom Environment, Routines and Procedures	Classroom Culture
• All procedures, routines and transactions were clear and efficient **YES NO**	• Teacher led a mutually respectful and collaborative class of actively engaged learners **YES NO**
• Students actively participated in groups, manage supplies and equipment with very limited teacher direction **YES NO**	• Engaged all students in relevant, meaningful learning **YES NO**
• The classroom was safe and organized to support learning objectives and is accessible to most students **YES N**	• Students worked respectfully individually/in groups **YES NO**
• Other conclusions/judgments	• Teacher interacted with students in respectful ways at all times (Standard 4: Learning Environment, Section 21.351 of the Education Code) **YES NO**
	• Other conclusions/judgments
	• Other conclusions/judgments
Managing Student Behavior	
• The teacher established, communicated and maintained clear expectations for student behavior **YES NO**	
• Consistently implemented the campus and/or classroom behavior system efficiently **YES NO**	
• Most students met expected classroom behavior standards (e.g., are on task, behave appropriately, follow classroom rules/procedures—PDAS) **YES NO**	
• Teacher successfully stopped/redirected off-task, inappropriate/disruptive behavior (PDAS) **YES NO**	
• Other conclusions/judgments	
• Other conclusions/judgments	

APPENDIX C

Appendix C contains a generic list of professional development/remediation activities and a list of sample directives for changes in teacher behavior, organized by T-TESS Domain and Dimension and linked to student outcomes. There is also a list of generic directives for non- instructional personnel.

I. A Generic List of Remediation Activities

THE TEACHER WILL . . .

- Attend professional development training on _____ at _____ and create a plan for incorporating the training into your classroom.
- Select a curriculum objective and outline methods/procedures, student activities, and evaluation strategies that are in alignment with the objective.
- Unpack a curriculum objective to show both the performance standard and content standard and describe what the instruction will look like when all the students are thinking/creating products at the level of the performance standard.
- Review selected list of instructional materials in the area of *(e.g., project-based learning)* and write a summary of how you will incorporate its elements in your classroom.
- Develop a questioning strategy at the application level or higher (based on Bloom's Taxonomy of Cognitive Learning).
- Schedule a time to observe in (another teacher's classroom) and summarize how you will incorporate what you observed into your classroom.
- Schedule a meeting with (a specialist) and develop *(e.g., methods of differentiation)* that you will use in your classroom.
- Attend an on-campus meeting with your team/department to brainstorm ways to (e.g., design more student-centered lessons).
- Invite a peer to visit your classroom and give you feedback on *(e.g., student engagement)*.
- Reflect on the lesson you just taught and determine the effectiveness.
- Write a self-critique or evaluation after the next lesson, emphasizing (whatever instructional issue you and the teacher are working on).
- Watch the U-Tube video on *(e.g., inductive, student-centered learning)* and develop a set of classroom strategies based on the video.
- Outline and give a rationale for the sequence of instruction for your next lesson.
- Develop a written strategy to . . .
- Develop a list of ways to . . .
- Review and summarize a list of possible techniques for . . .
- Provide a list of application activities for . . .

- Prepare a list of directions for . . .
- Develop and implement a lesson that . . .
- Outline a step-by-step plan for implementing/improving . . .
- Prepare a list of *(e.g., methods for constructive, corrective feedback/prompting).*
- Develop a system of *(e.g., scheduled feedback, rewards).*
- Create a sample list of questions that *(e.g., extend students' responses).*
- Develop a classroom management process in which *(e.g., students take responsibility for the management of materials).*
- Establish rules, procedures, and consequences with students.
- Post in the room *(e.g., expectation for classroom behavior)* and discuss them with your students.
- Develop and implement a questionnaire for students concerning *(e.g., their favorite music, television shows, movies, etc.).*
- Survey students' interests and strengths and group them for instruction.
- Discuss the students' needs with *(e.g., a resource teacher).*

II. Sample Directives for Changes in Teacher Behavior

In Chapter 6, we noted the desirability of using a formula that includes a teacher behavior linked to a student behavior/outcome.

Directives

Most of the descriptors of Proficient in T-TESS are teacher behaviors. This language will be your most likely source for the first part of the directive: one or more teacher behaviors.

Evidence of Compliance with Directives/Effectiveness

Within T-TESS, there is a compelling justification for looking at student behavior as the evidence of effective teaching.

1. T-TESS has a qualitative rating bias based on teacher-centered lessons on the low end of the rating scale to student-centered lessons on the high end of the rating scale.
2. The Goal-Setting template used at the beginning of the year asks: "How will you know your goal has been met? How will you know whether or not it has impacted instruction and student achievement?"
3. The Goal Reflection template used at the end of the year contains the following:
a. Identify the evidence of goal attainment/progress, *including the impact on student achievement* (emphasis added).
b. Describe how you used this goal and the professional development above to *impact instruction and student achievement* (emphasis added).
4. Texas Education Agency has pointed out, "…you can watch two teachers teach the exact same lesson the exact same way, and one lesson can rate Developing and one can rate Accomplished because what really matters is how the students respond to the learning" (*TEA Evaluation Refinement Year Newsletter*; Texas Education Agency, September, 2015.)

T-TESS Language Behavior	Linked to	Evidence that the Teacher Has Complied With the Directive
Teacher behaves in a certain way —>	**(Linking Words) (choice of options)** —>	**Outcome/Effectiveness (usually, student behavior)**
Design and implement instructional activities	in such a way that	students are engaged and successful in learning.

When choosing student behaviors related to participation/ success (e.g., students are engaged and successful in learning), you may precede the statement with reference to T-TESS or your adopted appraisal system. Here we have provided examples of directives for all four of domains of T-TESS plus a set of generic directives for non-teaching staff. There are more than 70 teacher behaviors and more than 90 student behaviors/ outcomes from which to choose.

When writing a directive, use or modify one of the teacher behaviors and then add linking language, followed by student outcomes. Notice that any one of the teacher behaviors on the left could potentially have more than one of the student behaviors/outcomes on the right. Choose the outcome that best reflects what you want to see happen in the teacher's classroom. Be certain that the teacher behavior on the left and the student behavior on the right logically match each other, i.e., that they are in a logical cause/effect relationship. For example, in Domain 1, you might choose the teacher behavior "Design clear, well-organized, sequential lessons that reflect best practice, align with standards, and are appropriate for diverse learners." You may then find more than one outcome on the right that you expect as the outcome. For language linking the two, you have a choice of options in the middle column. In our illustrations below for each of the four Domains, there are a number of ways to state linking words, thus the format of the sample directives on the left will not necessarily track across the column. Which linking phrase you choose is your decision.

Teacher behaves in a certain way —>	**(Linking Words) (choice of options)** —>	**Outcome/Effectiveness (usually, student behavior)**
Design clear, well-organized, sequential lessons that reflect best practice, align with standards and are appropriate for diverse learners	with the result that	most students are interacting with each other around relevant, meaningful learning and most students are actively engaged hight levels of academic success.

Sample Directives for Domain 1: Planning/Internalization
DIMENSION 1.1 Standards and Alignment

Teacher behaves in a certain way —>	**(Linking Words) (choice of options)** —>	**Outcome/Effectiveness (usually, student behavior)**
Design/analyze clear, well-organized. well-organized, sequential lessons that reflect best practice, align with standards and are appropriate for diverse learners	in such a way	most students are interacting with each other around relevant, meaningful learning.
		most students are successful in making connections to:
		O their life experiences,
All goals will be aligned to state content standards	so that	O the world beyond the classroom and/or
		O other disciplines.
All activities, materials and assessments must be:	with the result that	
O relevant to students	that results in	most students are engaged and successful in complex, higer-order thinking.
O provide appropriate time for lesson and lesson closure		
O fit into the broader unit and course objectives	to ensure that	most students are engaged and successful in different types of thinking:
O and appropriate for diverse learners	so that the outcome is	O analytical,
		O practical,
		O creative, and/or
		O researched-based.

All activities, materials and assessments must be:
○ relevant to students
○ provide appropriate time for lesson and lesson closure
○ fit into the broader unit and course objectives
○ and appropriate for diverse learners

All objectives must be aligned to the lesson's goal

Integrate technology into your instruction

| | as evidenced by | all students are actively engaged and successful in relevant meaningful learning. |

most students are actively engaged in high levels of academic success.

most students are interacting with each other around relevant, meaningful learning

most students are successfully participating in more than one activity.

most students are using technology to:
○ conduct research/inquiry
○ design/create products, and/or
○ that demostrate complex learning

most students work successfully individually and in groups

DIMENSION 1.2 Data and Assessment

Teacher behaves in a certain way —>	**(Linking Words) (choice of options)** —>	**Outcome/Effectiveness (usually, student behavior)**
Use formal and informal methods to measure student progress, then manage and analyze student data to inform instruction	in such a way that	classroom instructional design and strategies are aligned with the result of the data analysis.
Use formal and informal assessments to monitor progress of all students	so that	instructional time is allotted to align with the results of the data analysis.
Provide consistent feedback to students, families and other school personnel while maintaining confidentiality		other staff members are aware of individual/group strengths and weaknesses
	with the result that	parents of individual students are aware of the student's progress
		students are aware of their progress
Analyze student data connected to specific instructional strategies	that results in	differentiation in instructional grouping reflects the data.
		students are receiving consistent feedback.

DIMENSION 1.3 Knowledge of Students

Teacher behaves in a certain way →	(Linking Words) (choice of options) →	Outcome/Effectiveness (usually, student behavior)
Plan and deliver instruction to ensure high levels of learning, social-emotional development and achievement for all students	in such a way that	most students are consistently and successfully engaged in learning that has depth and complexity.
All lessons will connect to students' prior knowledge and experiences	so that	most students are consistently and successfully engaged in instructional activities that encourage and promote their social-emotional development.
Make adjustments to address strengths and gaps in background knowledge, life experiences and skills of all students, both prior to and during instruction	with the results that	most students are successfully making connections to their prior knowledge/experiences.
	that results in	instructional stratgies and activities align with unique needs and characteristics of the students.

DIMENSION 1.4 Activities

Teacher behaves in a certain way →	(Linking Words) (choice of options) →	Outcome/Effectiveness (usually, student behavior)
Plan and implement engaging, flexible lessons that encourage higher-order thinking, persistence and achievement	in such a way that	instructional strategies are aligned with the learning objectives.
Ask questions that encourage all students to engage in complex, higher-order thinking	in such a way that	students demonstrate persistence and do not give up, even when the task is challenging/difficult.
Organize instructional groups based on the needs of all students		most students are successful in connecting/applying learning within the discipline.
Provide clear direction/modeling of students' individual roles within instructional groups	so that	most students are successful in critical thinking and problem solving activities (i.e., application level or higher on Bloom's Taxonomy).
	with the results that	most students are successfully engaged in producing quality products which represent higher ordered thinking.
Plan and implement activities, resources, technology and instructional materials that are all aligned to instructional purposes	that results in	most students are successful in connecting the learning to work and life applications, both within the discipline and with other disciplines.

	to ensure that	most students correctly demonstrate their individual roles within instructional groups.
	so that the outcome is	most students are using all the activities, resouces, technolgy, and materials as tools in successfully achieving the instructional purpose of the lesson.

Sample Directives for Domain 2: Instruction

DIMENSION 2.1 Achieving Expectations

Teacher behaves in a certain way —>	**(Linking Words) (choice of options)** —>	**Outcome/Effectiveness (usually, student behavior)**
Support all learners in their pursuit of high levels of academic and social-emotional success		students demonstrate persistence and do not give up, even when the task is challenging/difficult.
Set academic expectations that challenge all students	in such a way that	most students take the initiative in their own learning by:
Persist with the lesson until there is evidence that most students demonstrate mastery of the objective		○ seeking out resources ○ using technology, ○ extending their own learning, ○ indentifying and correcting their own errors,
Support all learners in their pursuit of high levels of academic and social-emotional success		○ seeking assistance, and/or ○ providing theirown differentiation.
	so that	most students address their mistakes and are successful
Address student mistakes and follow through to ensure student mastery	with the results that	most students are successful in connecting/applying learning to work and life applications within the discipline and/or with other disciplines.
Provide students opportunities to take initiative of their own learning	that results in	most students are successful in critical thinking and problem solving activities (i.e., application level or higher on Bloom's Taxonomy).
	as evidenced by	most students are successfully engaged in producing quality products which represent higher ordered thinking.

DIMENSION 2.2 Content Knowledge and Expertise

Teacher behaves in a certain way →	**(Linking Words) (choice of options)** →	**Outcome/Effectiveness (usually, student behavior)**
Use content and pedagogical expertise to design and execute lessons aligned with state standards, related content and student needs	in such a way that	all lessons are aligned with both the content standard and performance of the state curriculum.
Convey accurate content knowledge in multiple contexts	so that	all lessons reflect a knowledge of student needs based on formative, summative, district, and or state assessment data.
Integrate learning objectives with other disciplines	with the result that	all academic content is accurate.
Anticipate possible student misunderstandings	that results in	potential student misunderstandings or misconception are addressed during the lesson.
Provide opportunities for students to use different types of thinking (e.g., analytical, practical, creative and research-based)	to ensure that	most students are using different types of thinking: ○ analytical, ○ practical, ○ creative, and/or ○ research based.
Accurately reflect how the lesson fits within the structure of the discipline and the state standards	as evidenced by	most students are successfully connecting learning objectives with other disciplines. most students produce responses, performances, or demonstrations that indicate they see how the lesson content fits within the structure of the discipline (e.g., how the lesson content relates to other concepts and big ideas within the discipline).

DIMENSION 2.3 Communication

Teacher behaves in a certain way →	(Linking Words) (choice of options) →	Outcome/Effectiveness (usually, student behavior)
Clearly and accurately communicate to support persistence, deeper learning and effective effort		most students are frequently interacting with the teacher and/or peers.
Establish classroom practices that provide opportunities for most students to communicate effectively with the teacher and their peers	in such a way that so that with the result that	there are no content errors or significant misunderstanding that students who are having difficulty are successful.
Recognize student misunderstandings and respond with an array of teaching techniques to clarify concept	that results in to ensure that	all communication (written and/or verbal) is supportive, courteous, and respectful.
Provide explanations that are clear and use verbal and written communication that is clear and correct	so that the outcome is	complaints from (students/parents/ staff/ community members/ professionals) stop (or decrease significantly or stop by the end of the semester).
Ask remember, understand and apply level questions that focus on the objective of the lesson and provoke discussion	as evidenced by	there are no errors (e.g., in grammar, pronunciation) or significant misunderstanding.
Use probing questions to clarify and elaborate learning		questioning and probing strategies result in: O discussion, O extension, O clarification, O greater depth of thinking, and/or O progress toward the learning objective.
All interactions with students will be courteous and respectful *(Note: This language is from Teacher Section 4: Learning Environment)*		

DIMENSION 2.4 Differentiation

Teacher behaves in a certain way →	(Linking Words) (choice of options) →	Outcome/Effectiveness (usually, student behavior)
Differentiate instruction, aligning methods and techniques to diverse student needs	in such a way that	assessment strategies produce evidence of student success and/or the need for differentiati Adapt lessons to address on.
Adapt lessons to address individual needs of all students	so that	students demonstrate persistence and do not give up, even when the task is challenging/ difficult.

Regularly monitor the quality of student participation and performance	with the result that	most students take the initiative in their own learning by:
Provide differentiated instructional methods and content to ensure students have the opportunity to master what is being taught	that results in to ensure that	○ providing their own differentiation, ○ seeking out resources, ○ using technology, ○ extending their own learning, ○ identifying and correcting their errors, and/or ○ seeking peer assistance.
Recognize when students become confused or disengaged and respond to student learning or social/emotional needs	so the outcome is as evidenced by	

most students address their mistakes and are successful.

most students are successful in connecting/applying learning to work and life applications within the discipline and/or with other disciplines.

most students are successful in critical thinking and problem solving activities (i.e., application level or higher on Bloom's Taxonomy).

most students are successfully engaged in producing quality products which represent higher ordered thinking.

DIMENSION 2.5 Monitor and Adjust

Teacher behaves in a certain way —>	**(Linking Words) (choice of options)** —>	**Outcome/Effectiveness (usually, student behavior)**
Formally and informally collect, analyze and use student progress data and make needed lesson adjustments	in such a way that	all students remain engaged (or reengage) in the learning. all students are verbally/physically monitored.
Consistently invite input from students in order to monitor and adjust instruction and activities	so that with the result that	students who are not being successful do not advance into activities/assessments for which they lack understanding.
Adjust instruction and activities to maintain student engagement	that results in to ensure that	the students who are having difficulty/not being successful are successful.

Monitor student behavior and responses for engagement and understanding	so that the outcome is as evidenced by	formative assessment tools are aligned with instructional goals, objectives, strategies and summative assessment. tools assess the extent to which students did/did not reach the goals/objectives. the assessment strategies produce evidence of student success and/or the need for differentiation. students demonstrate persistence and do not give up, even when the task is challenging/difficult. most students are successful in critical thinking and problem solving activities (i.e., application level or higher on Bloom's Taxonomy).

Sample Directives for Domain 3: Learning Environment
DIMENSION 3.1 Classroom Environment, Routines and Procedures

Teacher behaves in a certain way —>	**(Linking Words) (choice of options)** —>	**Outcome/Effectiveness (usually, student behavior)**
Organize a safe, accessible and efficient classroom		potential danger to student health/safety are eliminated.
Establish expectations for procedures and routines for students to actively participate in groups and manage supplies and equipment with very limited teacher direction	in such a way that so that with the result that	all areas of the classroom are accessible to most students. students are engaged in appropriate self-direction/ self-management of routines/ materials.
Create a classroom that is safe and organized to support learning objectives and is accessible to most students	that results in	students manage supplies, equipment, and transitions. routines and procedures consume very little time.
Design and implement clear and efficient procedures	to ensure that so that the outcome is	
All interactions with students will be courteous and respectful *(Note: This language is from Teacher Section 4: Learning Environment)*	as evidenced by	

DIMENSION 3.2 Managing Student Behavior

Teacher behaves in a certain way —>	(Linking Words) (choice of options) —>	Outcome/Effectiveness (usually, student behavior)
Establish, communicate and maintain clear expectations for student behavior	in such a way that	most students meet expected classroom behavior standards.
	so that	students are engaged in learning and behaving appropriately.
Consistently implement the campus and/or classroom behavior system proficiently	with the result that	there is a positive, supportive, respectful classroom environment.
Intervene to stop/redirect off-task or inappropriate behavior *(Note: This is not a T-TESS descriptor.)*	that results in	students are engaged in appropriate self-directed/ selfmanaged behavior.
	to ensure that	
	so that the outcome is	off-task/inappropriate behavior stops.
	as evidenced by	

DIMENSION 3.3 Classroom Culture

Teacher behaves in a certain way —>	(Linking Words) (choice of options) —>	Outcome/Effectiveness (usually, student behavior)
Lead a mutually respectful and collaborative class of actively engaged learners	in such a way that	students work respectfully individually and in groups.
Engage all students in relevant, meaningful learning	so that	all students are engaged in relevant, meaningful learning.
All interactions with students will be courteous and respectful	with the result that	there is a complete absence of disrespect, sarcasm, and negative criticism.
	that results in	
(Note: This language is adapted from Teacher Standard 4: Learning Environment).		

Sample Directives for Domain 4: Professional Practices and Responsibilities
DIMENSION 4.1 Professional Demeanor and Ethics

Since this dimension addresses the teacher's compliance with law and policy, directives in this area will typically consist only of a teacher behavior. There will typically not be linking language and an attached outcome.

Teacher behaves in a certain way

Meet all district expectations for attendance, professional appearance, decorum, procedural, ethical, legal, and statutory responsibilities, specifically, _____ (*identify the specific expectation that is not being met*).

Behave in accordance with the Code of Ethics and Standard Practices for Texas Educators, specifically _____ (*identify the specific part of the Code that is being violated*).

Meet all professional standards (e.g., attendance, professional appearance and behaviors), specifically _____ (*identify the specific standard that is being violated*).

Advocate for the needs of the students in the classroom.

Follow district grievance policies regarding conditions of employment.

Note: The following language may also prove helpful in crafting directives in Domain IV.

Selected Provisions (emphasis added) from the Commissioner's Rules Concerning Educator Standards [(Texas Administrative Code, Chapter 19, Subchapter AA (Rule 149.1001)]

Standard 4: Learning Environment. Teachers <u>interact with students in respectful ways at all times, maintaining a physically and emotionally safe, supportive learning environment</u> that is characterized by efficient and effective routines, clear expectations for student behavior, and organization that maximizes student learning. (A) Teachers <u>create a mutually respectful, collaborative, and safe community of learners</u> by using knowledge of students' development and backgrounds.
(ii) Teachers <u>maintain and facilitate respectful, supportive, positive, and productive interactions with and among students</u>.

Standard 6: Professional Practices and Responsibilities. Teachers ... <u>maintain professional relationships</u>, comply with all campus and school district policies, and <u>conduct themselves ethically and with integrity</u>.
(B) Teachers collaborate with their colleagues, are self-<u>aware in their interpersonal interactions, and are open to constructive feedback from peers and administrators</u>.
(D) Teachers model <u>ethical and respectful behavior and demonstrate integrity in all situations</u>.
ii. Teachers communicate <u>consistently, clearly, and respectfully with all members of the campus community, including students, parents and families, colleagues, administrators, and staff</u>.

DIMENSION DIMENSION 4.2 Goal Setting

Teacher behaves in a certain way	→ (Linking Words) (choice of options)	→ Outcome/Effectiveness (usually, student behavior)
Reflect on your practice	in such a way that	strengths and areas for refinement/improvement are accurately identified.
Set short- and long-term professional goals based on self-assessment, reflection and supervisor feedback	so that	goals are met.
	with the result that	student performance improves.
Meet all professional goals resulting in improvement in practice and student performance	that results in	areas of strength are maintained or improve.
Set short- and long-term professional goals based on self-assessment, reflection and supervisor feedback	to ensure that	practice improves in the area of ____ (*specify specific area(s) that are in need of improvement*).
Meet all professional goals resulting in improvement in practice and student performance	so that the outcome is	there is progress in areas identified for:
	as evidenced by	○ growth, ○ improvement, and/or ○ refinement.

DIMENSION 4.3 Professional Development

Teacher behaves in a certain way →	(Linking Words) (choice of options) →	Outcome/Effectiveness (usually, student behavior)
Collaboratively participate in all scheduled professional development activities, campus professional learning communities, grade- or subject-level team membership, committee membership or other opportunities	in such a way that so that with the result that that results in to ensure that so that the outcome is as evidenced by	the professional development activities align with the professional goals in the teacher self-assessment and goal-setting. activities align with the performance appraisal. activities align with the goals of the campus and/or district improvement plan. collaborative, respectful contributions to the team/committee are evident. classroom teaching and learning improve *(specify in some specific way)*. complaints about cooperation and collegiality from staff/ other professionals decrease significantly or stop by the end of the semester.

DIMENSION 4.4 School Community Involvement

Teacher behaves in a certain way →	(Linking Words) (choice of options) →	Outcome/Effectiveness (usually, student behavior)
Demonstrate leadership with students, colleagues, and community members in the school, district and community through effective communication and outreach	in such a way that so that with the result that that results in to ensure that so that the outcome is as evidenced by	parents/guardians receive regular communication regarding students' academic and social/ emotional growth you actively participate in all school outreach activities. you accurately communicate the mission, vision and goals of the school to students, colleagues, parents and families.

Sample Directives for Student Growth

The law requires that beginning in 2017-2018, each teacher appraisal, including T-TESS or a locally developed appraisal system, is to include the academic growth of the teacher's students at the individual teacher level.

The teacher behavior on the left could potentially have any of the desired outcomes on the right, depending on which measure(s) of student growth your district or charter school decides to use. Choose the outcome that best reflects what you want to see happen.

Be certain that the teacher behavior on the left and the student behavior on the right logically match each other, i.e., that they are in a logical cause/effect relationship. For linking language, you have a choice of options in the middle column. Remember that the format of the sample directives on the left do not necessarily track across the columns.

Growth of the Teacher's Students

Teacher behaves in a certain way —>	(Linking Words) (choice of options) —>	Outcome/Effectiveness (usually, student behavior)
Plan and implement all *(insert subject area)* lessons to align with the Texas Essential Knowledge and Skills (TEKS) and the district curriculum	in such a way that	student performance on *(specify TEKS/learning objective(s))* demonstrate ○ student growth. ○ significant student growth. ○ ___% student growth.
Analyze student performance data and plan instruction based on that data: • student learning objectives, student portfolios • pre- and post-test results on district-level assessment • value-added data based on student state assessment results	so that with the results that that results in to ensure that	student portfolios reflect ○ student growth. ○ significant student growth. ○ ___% student growth. pre- and post-test results on district-level assessments demonstrate ○ student growth. ○ significant student. growth ○ ___% student growth.
Plan and implement all instructional activities to include: • student to student interaction at least *(insert percentage)* of the time • student-centered, student-directed activities at least *(insert percentage)* of the time	so that the outcome is as evidenced by	Student performance on the STAAR *(insert specific STAAR test)* demonstrate ○ student growth. ○ significant student growth. ○ ___% student growth.

Plan and implement all instruction that includes student products, performances, or demonstrations that are aligned with both the content standard and the performance of the Texas Essential Knowledge and Skills and the district curriculum

Use concrete models and manipulatives (or any other research based practice)

Use the district's balanced literacy model for teaching reading, including phonics, authentic text, large groups, small groups, and centers (or any other research based practice)

NOTE: As a result of a May 2017 settlement agreement between the Texas Education Agency and various teacher organizations, school districts and public charter schools are not restricted to the four student growth measures in the original commissioner's rules (student learning objectives, student portfolios, pre- and post-test results on district level assessments, or value-added data based on student state assessment results). They are now free to choose their own student growth measures which may or may not include the four measures in the original rule. Should a district or charter school choose to use one or more of the original measures of student growth, the outcomes/effectiveness listed above are still potential measures of student performance.

Plan and implement the Texas Essential Knowledge and Skills (TEKS) and the district curriculum, including _____ *(insert percentage of laboratory instruction required at that grade level)* devoted to laboratory time

III. Other Kinds of Behaviors: General Directives, Including Directives to Non- Instructional Personnel

Plan for and engage in professional development (specify the professional development).

Comply with:

- (district or campus) policies *(specify policy)*
- (district or campus) operating procedures *(specify the operating procedures)*
- (district or campus) requirements *(specify requirements)*
- (state/district) law/requirements *(specify law/requirements)*

- Follow district grievance policies for complaints regarding conditions of employment.
- Meet all deadlines for submitting (e.g., reports, inspections, assessment results, surveys, etc.).
- Document (student progress/grades, curriculum or attendance records, reports, etc.) in conformity to campus/district policy.
- Design, communicate and implement a plan for (e.g., instructional technology, bilingual education, disaggregating and reporting student performance).
- Design a time line for communicating (e.g., district/campus expectations, reporting procedures, budgeting, purchasing) to all stakeholders.
- Conduct and write/deliver the report of all special education (504, ADA, dyslexia, ESL) assessments to the program director within (time frame) of receiving the referral.
- Schedule, notify all participants, and conduct all Admission, Review, and Dismissal (ARD) Committee meetings within the time frame required by law.
- Follow all provisions of the Individualized Education Program (IEP) for all special education students in your class (on your campus).
- Follow all provisions of the 504 Plan for all students in your class (on your campus).

APPENDIX D: SAMPLE FORMS

The following sample forms are included in this section. The copyright protection for this handbook has been modified to the extent that purchasers of the book may reproduce the forms in this section for their own use or use the digital link to download them at www.ed311.com/docbookforms6th/. We advise that you contact the school district's human resources director and/or school attorney before doing so to make sure that the forms are consistent with local policy and practice. Neither the authors nor the publisher assumes any responsibility for liability associated with their use.

Complaint Form. This form is to be completed by persons who have a complaint about a school employee. Its purpose is to provide detailed information in writing that will enable the administrator to conduct an effective investigation. For the reasons set forth in Chapter 2, no guarantee is made on the form or should be made orally that the contents of the complaint form will remain confidential, though every effort will be made to do so and at the same time to follow the requirements of the Texas Public Information Act and the Family Educational Rights and Privacy Act.

Witness Statement Form. This simple form formalizes the process of securing a statement from witnesses to incidents that are being investigated. For the reasons set forth in Chapter 2, no guarantee is made on the form or should be made orally that the contents of the witness form will remain confidential, though every effort will be made to do so and at the same time to follow the requirements of the Texas Public Information Act and the Family Educational Rights and Privacy Act.

Template for a Specific Incident Memorandum. This form is designed to guide you through the development of a specific incident memorandum by including both the essential elements and suggestions as to how each section should be written. Of course, when you write the memorandum, you will need to delete both the essential elements and the suggestions within each section of the memorandum..

Template for a Specific Incident Memorandum Related to Instruction. This form is designed to guide you through the development of a simple focused observation follow-up memorandum to a classroom observation. All you need to do is fill in the necessary information. The result is uniformity in writing this kind of instructional memorandum. Of course, when you write the memorandum, you will need to delete both the essential elements and the suggestions within each section of the memorandum.

Template for an Intervention Plan. This plan is designed to guide you through the development of an intervention plan outside the formal appraisal system for a professional or auxiliary employee that delineates employment deficiencies, expected changes in behavior, a time line for changes, and evidence to determine whether improvement has occurred. The plan needs to be linked wherever possible to the formal appraisal system that the district or charter school uses.

COMPLAINT FORM

Name of person filing this complaint: _____
Address: _____
Statement involves complaint against whom: _____

Please state your specific complaint or complaints. Please describe in detail the events surrounding the complaint against the above-named person. Please include dates, times, locations, persons present, substance of statements, and conversations, etc. Please be as factual as possible. If you must express an opinion, please make it clear that you are doing so. Attach additional pages if necessary. _____
_____
_____
_____
_____
_____
_____
_____
_____
_____

Please refer us to any persons having personal knowledge of the facts stated in this complaint.
_____
_____
_____

Please state the individual harm alleged and identify the person or persons alleged to be harmed, if other than yourself.
_____
_____

Please state what specific relief or resolution you are requesting.
_____
_____
_____

Please attach copies of any written documentation that may assist us in resolving this complaint.

Note: When you are finished, please reread your statement in its entirety. Make any necessary changes and initial those changes. Then initial each sheet in the bottom righthand corner. Sign and date below.

"I affirm that the above statement is the truth to the best of my knowledge."

_____ _____   _____ _____
Signature   Date   Signature   Date
Person making statement   Person receiving statement

WITNESS STATEMENT FORM

Please describe in your own words and handwriting what you observed. Be as factual and specific as you can. Try not to reach conclusions or make judgments.

___

Please provide the names of other witnesses if you know them, or descriptions if you do not.

___

Your Name (Please Print)

___

Signature   Date   Signature   Date
Person making statement   Person receiving statement

TEMPLATE FOR SPECIFIC INCIDENT MEMORANDUM

ESSENTIAL ELEMENTS

Letterhead Stationery

Date

TO:
FROM:
RE:
[State the subject of the memo above in neutral terms.]

Allegation and Investigation

This memorandum is a follow-up to our conference on at which we discussed
[Choose one: "my concern about" or "my observation of" or "reports to me that you" or "allegations that you" and complete the sentence in the space below. If your investigation is based on other than your own observation, describe briefly in a second sentence what it encompassed.]

Findings of Fact

As I noted at our conference, my concerns are based on the following: *[State below the findings of fact from your observation/investigation/conference in objective terms – follow the Sgt. Joe Friday Rule: "Just the Facts." Avoid judgmental terms like "unprofessional" and "inappropriate." These fit better in the conclusion section. If there are a number of findings, use bulleted sentences to set them apart.]*

Conclusions

Based on the above, I conclude that
[Complete this sentence below indicating whether or not there has been a violation of district policies, regulations, job description, handbook provisions, or previous directives. Cite them directly. Attach them if appropriate. If inconclusive with regard to whether there is a violation, so state and then use the opportunity to alert the employee to the importance of compliance.]

Directives

In the future, it is necessary that you
[Complete this sentence below by setting forth your directives and including remediation activities if you find the matter remediable and believe such activities would help the employee comply with the directives.]

Copy: Human Relations Department/Personnel File

Opportunity to Respond

I have received a copy of this memorandum. I understand that my signature does not necessarily indicate that I agree with its contents. I further understand that I have a right to respond in writing within 10 working days.

Dated Employee Signature

_____   _____

Signature of Employee   Date

TEMPLATE FOR SPECIFIC INCIDENT MEMORANDUM RELATED TO INSTRUCTION

ESSENTIAL ELEMENTS

Letterhead Stationery

Date

TO:
FROM:
RE:
[State the subject of the memo above in neutral terms, e.g., Classroom Observation on (date).]

Allegation and Investigation

This memorandum will formally communicate information gathered during my observation in your classroom on _____ [Date] and discussed with you in our conference on _____ [Date].
I observed from _____ [Beginning Time] to _____ [Ending Time]. You were conducting a lesson on _____ [Lesson Objective or Specific Content of Lesson] using _____ [Activities, Strategies, Resources] with a group of _____ [Number of Students] students.

Findings of Fact

The observation revealed the following information in the context of TTESS, our district's assessment system.
[State below the findings of fact from your observation / investigation / conference in objective terms – follow the Sgt. Joe Friday Rule: "Just the Facts." Avoid judgmental terms like "ineffective", "unprofessional", and "inappropriate." If there are a number of findings, use bulleted sentences to set them apart.]

Conclusions

Based on these data, I have concluded that you are not meeting the district's expectations of a proficient teacher as set forth in the Domains and Dimensions of T-TESS. These include:
[State below the conclusions / judgments you have drawn, using the language of T-TESS or your appraisal system. When possible, cite the domain / dimension from which you selected the language.]

Directives

In all future lessons you will plan and implement all lessons in such a way that:
[Complete this sentence below by setting forth your directives for changes in teacher behavior, utilizing the formula Teacher Behavior + Linking Language + Student Behavior / Outcome found in Appendix C. You may also include remediation activities if you find the matter

ESSENTIAL ELEMENTS

remediable, believe such activities would help the employee comply with the directives, and demonstrate your continuing support for the teacher.]

Opportunity to Respond

I have received a copy of this memorandum. I understand that my signature does not necessarily indicate that I agree with its content. I further understand that I have a right to respond in writing within 10 days.

Dated Signature of Employee

_____   _____
Signature of Teacher   Date

TEMPLATE FOR INTERVENTION PLAN

Employee _____   Position _____

Supervisor/Appraiser _____   School _____

1. **Area/s related to the job description, evaluation instrument and/or campus/district policy in which improvement is needed. Establish priorities if two or more areas are listed.**

2. **Specify growth activities and dates for completion if warranted.**

3. **Specify evidence that will be used to determine whether growth activities specified in Section 2 have been completed.**

4. **Directives and time lines for changes in employee behavior in the future and evidence that will be used to determine if employee behavior has changed.**

I was consulted in the development of this plan. I understand that I have a right to file a grievance or appeal within 10 days consistent with school policies if I disagree with its contents.

Employee Signature _____   Date _____

Supervisor Signature _____   Date _____

Other Appraiser Signature _____   Date _____
(if applicable)

ABOUT THE AUTHORS

Jennifer Childress is the Editorial Director for ED311 and has served in that role for more than 20 years. For more than ten years, she represented school districts in a wide variety of litigation matters for the Walsh Gallegos Law Firm. Jennifer currently serves as the Chief Deputy General Counsel for the Texas Department of Criminal Justice Office of General Counsel (OGC). Ms. Childress grew up in South Texas and attended Rice University in Houston, where she received a Bachelor of Arts Degree in English, with a minor in Sociology. She attended the University of Texas School of Law, receiving her Juris Doctorate degree in December 1993. During law school, Ms. Childress interned at the OAG's Law Enforcement Defense Division and, upon graduation, she clerked for the United States District Court, Southern District of Texas, Houston Division. She previously worked for TDCJ's OGC Division in 1995-1996 before transferring to the Law Enforcement Defense Division of the Office of the Attorney General (OAG) to represent TDCJ and other state agency clients in 1996-1998. Ms. Childress then transitioned to private practice with the Walsh Gallegos law firm where she represented school districts and district employees, as well as The GEO Group, Inc. in civil rights and employment litigation. Jennifer has four children who attended public school in Austin ISD.

Richard A. James is a 25-year veteran of Texas Public Schools and has worked at the district, regional, and state initiative levels. His primary concentration is in curriculum development and implementation with emphasis on instructional observation and feedback. Richard has worked as a secondary classroom teacher, instructional specialist, K-12 curriculum coordinator, and education service center regional consultant at Wylie Independent School District and Region 10 Education Service Center. He has led professional development workshops and presented at the state and national levels at professional organization conferences. Richard holds an Ed.D. in supervision, curriculum, and instruction from Texas A&M University-Commerce.

Frank R. Kemerer is Regents Professor-Emeritus at the University of North Texas where he taught education law and administration for thirty years until retiring in the spring of 2008. Frank founded the *Texas School Administrators' Legal Digest* in 1984 and continued as co-publisher until he and his wife Barbie sold their portion of the business to Park Place Publications in 2005. Frank has a Ph.D. in educational administration and policy analysis from Stanford University with a law minor from Stanford Law School.

John A. Crain is an independent educational consultant in DeKalb, Texas. John is well known to Texas educators for his training programs in teacher appraisal, effective teaching practices, curriculum development, and developmental supervision. In his more than forty years in education, John has worked as a secondary school and community college teacher, a principal at all three school levels (elementary, middle, and high school), and as assistant superintendent. John holds an Ed.D. in educational administration from the University of North Texas.